T0355592

# American Legal English

SECOND EDITION

*Using Language in Legal Contexts*

**Debra S. Lee, J.D.**
Language4Law, Inc.
Nashville, Tennessee

**Charles Hall**
The University of Memphis

**Susan M. Barone**
Vanderbilt University

MICHIGAN SERIES IN ENGLISH FOR
ACADEMIC & PROFESSIONAL PURPOSES

Series Editors: John M. Swales & Christine B. Feak

*Ann Arbor*
THE UNIVERSITY OF MICHIGAN PRESS

Published in the United States of America by
The University of Michigan Press
Printed and bound by CPI Group (UK) Ltd, Croydon, CR0 4YY

2010   2009   2008   2007     4   3   2   1

ISBN-13: 978-0-472-03206-8
ISBN-10: 0-472-03206-2

# *Acknowledgments*

We are grateful for the many students we have taught; without them and the feedback we received in our classes, this book would have been impossible. Special thanks go to the international team of attorneys, law professors, and language specialists working on the Language4Law project *(www.14law.org)* for their help, advice, and support.

We would all like to thank Kelly Sippell, our editor, for her patience and prompt replies to our email correspondence.

Source acknowledgments and thanks:

*Black's Law Dictionary, 5th ed.* (West Publishing Company)
*Restatement of the Law* (The American Law Institute)
*American Jurisprudence, 2d.* (The Lawyer's Co-Operative Publishing Company)
*Model Penal Code* (The American Law Institute)
West Group for headnote materials in Chapter 2

Our special thanks to Marsha Hurley, our friend and co-author, without whom the first edition of this book would not have been what it was. We thank her for all her hard work, her friendship, and her keen insights.

# *Contents*

# To the Student

*American Legal English: Using Language in Legal Contexts.* What does that mean? This book is designed to provide you with an introduction to basic legal information and to improve your ability to understand and communicate with your legal counterparts around the world. This is not a comprehensive introduction to the law of the United States; that would be impossible in a book this size. However, as you go through the materials, you will discover that the basic legal information given to you enhances your ability to use legal language.

*English proficiency needed:* To gain the most benefit from this book, your general English skills should be fairly well developed. In instructor terms, we would say you should be an intermediate to advanced student of English. As an intermediate student you will have to work a little harder to understand all the material that is presented. We have, however, not set you an impossible task.

*Topics:* We have chosen the topics in the book for three reasons: (1) to introduce you to the process of legal reasoning in the American legal system; (2) to give you a general introduction to American law; and (3) for general interest or usefulness in the workplace. Each chapter addresses a particular area of the law. Within each chapter are exercises designed to make you think about the legal topic in general, followed by a more detailed explanation of the law, incorporating materials from actual cases, treatises, and statutes.

*Organization:* The three levels in each chapter provide a smooth transition from simple concepts to more complex ones. **Discovering Connections** is a warm-up activity, focusing on law in your own country or non-legal concepts that lead into the law. **Legal Listening** and **Legally Speaking** give you the opportunity to practice new vocabulary terms before beginning to get into more depth in the chapter. The **Legal Thumbnail** provides a simplified summary of the law along with actual statutory and case materials.

For this second edition, we have moved to a system of appendixes for language, culture, writing, reading, and oral communication tasks. Depending on the language level of your class, your instructor will refer you to the appendixes as needed. Of course, you are free to review the appendixes on your own.

The theory behind this book is that you will already have an idea of how the law works in your own country; what we have done is provide a simplification of some aspects of American law and the vocabulary to discuss them along with opportunities for you to employ that vocabulary. Although you will learn many new words in this text, we have chosen to **boldface** only legal terminology. You should pay careful attention to all boldfaced terms and their definitions often placed in brackets. Though the legal exercises are less complicated than a practicing attorney might encounter, they nonetheless contain the same types of skills that the attorney must put to work for his or her clients.

Learning about an area such as law is hard work; the issues are complicated, the evidence not always clear cut, and the statutes frequently ambiguous. It is our hope that after having completed your study of this book you will not only find that American law is a bit more comprehensible to you but also that you have improved your understanding of how to decipher legal English and make that language work for you, your clients, and your colleagues.

# To the Teacher

This text represents a collaborative effort to put together an introduction to the basic concepts of law in the U.S. legal system, while at the same time providing communicative activities that allow students to put that newly acquired knowledge to use. Law is a profession that requires critical reading skills, the ability to write well, the ability to synthesize sources resulting from research, and the ability to speak clearly and concisely. In this respect, a legal English course is no different from any upper-intermediate to advanced English course that requires those same skills.

The text is not intended as a comprehensive introduction to U.S. law because that would be an impossible task to ask of one book. It does, however, address major areas of the law, giving students real cases and statutes to work with so that they can become familiar with both legal syntax and legal vocabulary. We have tried to choose topics and cases that will be of interest to the students and be of use in the workplace.

You do not have to be an attorney to use this book, even though at first glance you might think so. If you have been assigned a legal English course, you need to think of it as you would any other ESP (English for Specific Purposes) course. Approach the course with an interest in the subject matter, and use your students as resources. Your approach to the class may be different from that taken by an attorney/ESP instructor, but the final goal is the same. Your students should be able to communicate about legal matters in English by the time they finish the book.

Although the book is primarily intended for upper-intermediate to advanced students of English, with some adaptation a teacher of intermediate-level students should be able to make use of it. A good basic knowledge of general English on the part of the students is assumed, but there is no assumption that the students have any command of legal terminology or even a basic understanding of the U.S. legal system. Legal terminology is in boldface in the chapters. Brief definitions often follow in brackets. A knowledge of the basics of the legal system in their own country is extremely helpful, for then the student has a schema for some of the concepts that this book introduces.

## Organization

The chapters are ordered so that students are given important basic information about the U.S. legal system first, then move into specific areas of the law (criminal law, civil procedure, torts, etc.). The chapters can be reordered if the instructor so desires. However, Chapter 8, The Negotiation, requires students to use all the skills that they have learned in the text.

In this second edition, we have changed the format of the chapters. We now include three levels for each chapter with references to Part 2 for skills that are useful in all chapters. We believe that this format gives you, the instructor, more flexibility to tailor the course to the needs of your students.

The three sections of each chapter are:

I. **Discovering Connections:** A schema activator—an activity designed to stimulate the students' thoughts about the chapter content.

II. **Legal Discussion, Legal Listening, Legal Listening and Writing, or Legal Listening and Speaking:** A practical application of legal language— designed to put into practice some of the language used in a particular chapter.

III. **Legal Thumbnail:** This section is designed to provide some basic legal information, since this is, after all, a content-specific text. The information, however, is not intended to represent anything more than general knowledge, for as is pointed out repeatedly in the text, a statute may or may not exist in a jurisdiction, and if the statute does exist, it is most probably subject to different interpretations within different jurisdictions. The Legal Thumbnail also presents legal vocabulary. Law has its own language, and it is vital that one understands the precise meaning of a legal term since decisions in the United States may hinge on just such a point.

If you are an attorney, you will notice what might appear to be glaring holes in the law; but the purposes of the book are to provide a *basic* legal overview for students *and* to exercise language use. This is not intended to simulate even a **legal nutshell** [abbreviated overview of the law written by law professors for American law students], but it is intended to provide a framework for practicing use of legal language.

We have added Parts 2 and 3 for you to use as needed with your students because we believe this gives you more flexibility to adapt the text to the needs of your particular students.

Part 2, Further Language Development, includes:

1. Writing Activities
2. Reading Activities
3. Oral Communication Activities
4. Grammar Activities
5. Culture Activities

Part 3 includes Student Resources.

We have provided references throughout the text to appendixes that we have found useful at particular points in the book. However, as the instructor, you will know what is best for your particular group of students, so the final decision regarding what to include and where belongs to you.

This book is meant to help you engage students in collaborative activities and create an active classroom environment. Students actively engaged in the process of learning are students who succeed in the classroom. We wish you luck and hope that you enjoy using the text.

PART 1

# Introduction to Law and Its Language

# *Origins of the American Legal System*

## Discovering Connections

The history and development of a nation influence the shape, focus, and scope of its legal system. For example, the United States, Canada, and Great Britain once shared the same system, but since the American War of Independence that common system has split into three distinct systems.

    The United States has one relatively brief document that is known as the Constitution; all other laws in the United States, whether state or federal, must be consistent with it. In Canada, however, there are many documents that together form that country's constitution. The United Kingdom, on the other hand, has no such special documents, and Parliament may change the law at any time.

### ACTIVITY

A. Divide into groups of three. As a group, choose the five most significant events, documents, or even people that have shaped the growth of your legal system. Your answers might include items such as

- the Napoleonic Code
- World War I or II
- your constitution
- becoming an independent nation
- joining the European Union
- the Koran
- English common law
- Roman law

B. As a group, present your choices to the rest of the class. Be prepared to defend your choices.

---

## Legal Listening and Speaking

## Introductions

**CONVERSATION MODEL**

Listen to the conversation twice. The first time, listen for general understanding. The second time, try to answer the questions on a separate sheet of paper.

1. What kind of a presentation is this?

2. Who tells everyone to sit down?

3. Is this the first time this group has met?

4. Why doesn't the moderator introduce the speakers?

5. What does Professor Arm teach? Where?

6. What is Mr. Simone's problem?

7. How does he correct the problem?

8. Why is Mr. Simone talking about the origins of American law?

9. Is Mr. Simone an attorney?

10. What kind of American judges is Mr. Trommel writing about?

11. How is Mr. Trommel financing his work on his dissertation?

**APPLYING YOUR KNOWLEDGE**

In groups of two, fill in the parentheses (___) with appropriate items to create your own conversation that you will then present to the class. You may change anything, be anyone, or have any title you want. We have given you a few suggestions and done the first line for you, but you may change that.

*Speaker 1:* (<u>Good evening</u>). My name is (<u>Thomas Wang</u>). I am

(<u>president</u>) of ((1)_____). Welcome to our

((2)_____) meeting. Our ((3)_____),

((4)_____), will introduce ((5)_____) speaker.

*Speaker 2:* Thank you, (⑥_____). It's (⑦_____) to

introduce our speaker for (⑧_____) meeting.

(⑨_____) is currently (⑩_____) of

(⑪_____) at (⑫_____) and was also

(⑬_____) (⑭_____). (⑮_____)

me in welcoming ( ⑯_____).

*Speaker 3:* Thank you, (⑰_____), for that (⑱_____)

welcome. I'm pleased to (⑲_____) have the

(⑳_____) to (㉑_____) this group.

Suggestions for filling in the blanks:

| | | |
|---|---|---|
| 1. the Law Society | the International Club | the Defenders of Freedom |
| 2. annual | monthly | weekly |
| 3. vice president | founder | chair |
| 4. (choose any name) | John Drum | Dahlia Tran |
| 5. tonight's | this afternoon's | our first |
| 6. Tom | Mr. Wang | Mr. President |
| 7. a pleasure | an honor | a privilege |
| 8. tonight's | this afternoon's | this morning's |
| 9. He | She | Our speaker |
| 10. professor | president | director |
| 11. law | marketing | personnel |
| 12. DuVal Corporation | the University of Shelby | the Treasury Department |
| 13. UN representative | founder | on the Board of Trustees |
| 14. of mathematics | of Dragonfly Software | for ecological concerns |
| 15. Join | Help | |
| 16. him | our distinguished guest | Dr. Tao |
| 17. Fred | Madame Vice President | (you could leave it blank) |
| 18. kind | warm | generous |
| 19. once again | (you could leave it blank) | |
| 20. privilege | honor | chance |
| 21. speak to | address | talk to |

## Legal Thumbnail

# Founding of the U.S. Legal System

To begin to understand U.S. law, you must look at the founding of the United States and the uniting of the individual colonies into a single nation. The American War of Independence (1776–83) brought the original thirteen colonies together to fight a common foe, the British. The colonies, declaring themselves independent states, originally agreed to a very weak confederation in order to defeat their common enemy. This first federal constitution of the United States, The Articles of Confederation, was written in 1778 and was finally **ratified** [approved] by the states in 1781.

In this first form of American government, there were neither federal courts nor a president, and the single chamber of Congress had no way to enforce its laws. The individual states could and did ignore federal laws with **impunity** [without fear of consequences]. It quickly became clear that the United States would not remain united long unless the role of the federal government was strengthened.

In 1787, a constitutional convention was convened to form a stronger, more durable union. The primary concern of the participants, all European-American men, was the formation of a strong union without the disappearance of the states as individual powers in the system. The inevitable compromise among the delegates led them away from the earlier loose confederation of sovereign states toward a stronger central government. In the end this movement resulted in a central government, still protective of states' rights, but with broader federal powers over individuals.

Broadened powers, however, didn't mean unlimited powers. The Founding Fathers (women were not allowed to vote in the United States until ratification of the Nineteenth Amendment to the Constitution in 1920) designed the federal government with limited powers, which included the right to impose certain federal taxes, to wage war in the name of all the states, to regulate interstate and foreign commerce, and to make treaties with foreign governments or nations (such as the Native Americans or Indians, as they were called). The remaining powers belonged to the states.

This new constitution added two branches to the federal government: a federal system of courts with the Supreme Court as its head and the executive branch under the control of the newly created office of the president. Additionally, to help solve a major problem of representation between the large and the small states, the legislative branch was changed to its present bicameral [two chamber] form—the House of Representatives and the Senate, known collectively as Congress.

The Constitution established a series of checks and balances so that each of these three federal branches could maintain a watch on the other two. These checks and balances ensure that no one branch of the federal government becomes too powerful. Additionally, the states, ever mindful of retaining their powers, also provide an external check to ensure that the federal government as a whole doesn't become too powerful.

## Exercise A. Review and Discussion

Read the questions, and write your initial responses to them. Then, as a class, discuss the answers.

1. How might North America be different if the United States had retained the Articles of Confederation?

2. Why do you think there was originally no executive officer [president] in the United States? Is it possible to have a nation or state without an executive officer? If so, give an example or two.

3. What kinds of problems would arise if there were no federal courts and all disputes among states had to be decided by the Congress?

From our point of view today, it seems odd that the Constitution did not explicitly give the power of **judicial review** [the ability of a court to decide on the constitutionality of legislation] to the newly created federal judiciary. However, one of the first steps in that direction came not long after the adoption of the Constitution.

In his decision in the **landmark** [changes the law, extraordinarily significant] case *Marbury v. Madison*, 5 U.S. (1 Cranch) 137, 2 L.Ed. 60 (1803), the famous **Chief Justice** [head of the Supreme Court] John Marshall established that federal legislation was subject to judicial review in the federal courts. In this case, the Supreme Court refused **to give effect to** [authorize the use of] a section of a federal statute. The Chief Justice argued the Constitution had granted limited powers to the Congress. Therefore, it was the job of the federal courts to decide if Congress had adhered to the rules in the Constitution, which in this case the Court decided Congress had not done. Consequently, it was accepted by all branches of the federal government that the role of the judiciary was to determine if Congress had overstepped its powers and, if it had, to declare the legislation unconstitutional.

Not long after that decision, the Supreme Court successfully held that the federal Constitution (remember, each of the states has its own state constitution) gave the Court the authority to judge the validity of state **statutes** [codes] if they seemed in conflict with the federal Constitution. This judicial review of the state statutes has become one of the major unifying forces in the United States. The powers the Supreme Court gave itself and the federal judiciary have been crucial in the development of American law.

## Exercise B. System Comparisons and Discussion

A senior partner in your firm is meeting with a client who is lobbying for new legislation in your country to make it easier for the client's product to be sold there. The senior partner wants to know how legislation is reviewed in your system. If the law is passed, how could the law be challenged? Can the judiciary in your system tell the legislative branch that the new law is illegal even before it is passed?

Write a short, concise email explaining the process. The email must be fewer than 400 words. Remember, the senior partner is not asking for your advice, just an explanation of the process. See Part 2, Email (page 184), for models and directions for writing emails.

## Exercise C. Paraphrasing

This exercise is designed to give you practice in paraphrasing. First, individually review the sample section given to you. Then, in pairs, paraphrase the section in writing. Before you begin this exercise, review Part 2, Paraphrasing (page 180).

1. In many cases a lawyer must paraphrase [restate] or summarize a statute or legal document for a client. A summary includes only the most important ideas. A paraphrase includes everything found in the original but expressed in different, usually less complex, language. Look at this example of paraphrasing.

    **Original:** "The Senate of the United States shall be composed of two Senators from each State chosen by the Legislature thereof, for six Years; and each Senator shall have one Vote." [U.S. Constitution, Article 1, Section 3(1)]

    **Paraphrase:** Each state legislature will select two senators. Each senator will serve a six-year term and have one vote in the Senate of the United States.

Now, you try to paraphrase Section 3(3).

> **Original:** "No Person shall be a Senator who shall not have attained to the Age of 30 Years, and been nine Years a Citizen of the United States, and who shall not, when elected, be an Inhabitant of that State for which he shall be chosen."
> **Paraphrase:**

```
┌──────────────────────────────────────────────────┐
│                                                    │
│                                                    │
│                                                    │
│                                                    │
│                                                    │
│                                                    │
└──────────────────────────────────────────────────┘
```

2. Here is the text of the First Amendment to the U.S. Constitution. Try to paraphrase it in modern, simple English. Your instructor may choose to have you do this individually or in small groups. Remember, in a paraphrase we try to keep all of the ideas but change the wording so that it might be more understandable for others. We've given you three hints to help you.

   a. The word *Congress* now seems to mean any form or branch of government in the United States, whether local, state, or federal.

   b. **Redress** can mean "correction" or "remedy."

   c. In the United States, the word *government* means the executive, judicial, or legislative branches, not just the executive branch as it does in many systems.

   > **Original:** Congress shall make no law respecting an establishment of religion, or prohibiting the free exercise thereof; or abridging the freedom of speech, or of the press; or the right of the people peaceably to assemble, and to petition the Government for a redress of grievances.
   > **Paraphrase:**

```
┌──────────────────────────────────────────────────┐
│                                                    │
│                                                    │
│                                                    │
│                                                    │
│                                                    │
│                                                    │
└──────────────────────────────────────────────────┘
```

Because of our British origins, through the nineteenth century, U.S. judges, attorneys, and legal scholars relied on British law; today, however, British law is no longer as influential as it once was. There are a few British cases that are still mentioned in American law schools today, but far more importantly, there are fundamental concepts inherited from the English tradition that are still flourishing and continue to separate the English and American systems from other legal systems, such as the civil law systems of Germany and France. Three of the most important concepts that we have inherited from the English are supremacy of law, precedent, and the idea of the adversarial proceeding.

1. The fact that both the executive [the president] and legislative [the Congress] branches of the government are required to follow the law as set down in the U.S. Constitution is an indicator of the **supremacy of law** in the United States.

2. **Precedent** (which we will discuss in greater detail later) is the tradition that requires that courts follow the law as stated in decisions by earlier courts.

3. Finally, we all know from watching infamous American cases or courtroom dramas on television that the American trial is an **adversarial proceeding** [contest], like chess, in which the opposing attorneys seem to be more concerned with winning than with arriving at the truth. What is not clear from the televised cases or TV dramas is that in the U.S. 90 percent of the cases do not proceed to trial but are settled out of court in **settlements** [agreements] that are satisfactory to both sides. In other words, in most cases all sides work together to arrive at an agreement. The cases that one sees on television, whether actual cases or TV drama, are the exception rather than the rule in the American system.

Televised cases are not a fair depiction of the American legal system. Too often it looks as though the person with the most money to hire the cleverest attorney wins the contest. In these contests, the judge is often a referee who must wait for one of the attorneys to cry, "Objection!" before he or she can step in to decide if a piece of evidence or the questioning of a witness is valid. Normally, American judges don't gather evidence as judges do in many systems; instead they look only at what the attorneys bring them, so the evidence may be only as good as the attorneys care to make it. Unfortunately, TV trials rarely show that in the American system, judges can and do step in to ask for additional information or to limit questioning of a witness. It is true that the system is adversarial and that most of the questioning is done by the attorneys; however, to compare television courtroom drama to real life would be like comparing a pocket calculator to a powerful computer.

## Exercise D. System Comparisons and Discussion

1. Write a quick, informal email explaining the role of a judge in your system. Remember, an email must be brief and easy to understand. It should not be more than 300 words. See Part 2, Email (page 184) for models and directions for writing emails.

2. How does the role of the judge in your system differ from his or her role in the American system?

3. Why do you think American trials are so different from trials in countries with civil law systems?

# The Common Law System

Law students and lawyers from non–Anglo American countries learn that Anglo-American law is "case law" or "judge-made" law. That's true to an extent, but in reality a significant portion of the law of the United States is **codified** [written in the form of statutes]. Of course, it is true that in some cases no statutory or constitutional provisions will apply. Under those circumstances, attorneys must rely solely on earlier cases ("the common law") on the issue; however, constitutional provisions and statutes take precedence over case law.

American attorneys will search to find the case law relating to a statute before they can say they have thoroughly researched the problem. Without locating and reading the cases that explain the application of the statute or constitutional provision, they have not even begun their research.

Once cases pertaining to the issue have been found, they have to be analyzed to see if they are relevant. Or, if the attorney thinks that his or her case is different from previous cases, he or she must explain why those cases and their decisions are not applicable.

In this way, case law is not only judge-made but also attorney-influenced law. We can say that the common law is the law created daily through the interaction of judges and attorneys in the courtrooms across the United States at all levels, from local courts to the U.S. Supreme Court.

All types of judges, whether appointed or elected, have the legal right to make certain types of decisions. Once a judge makes a decision, that decision becomes a **precedent** [a guideline that is to be followed by courts in the line of appeal under that court in similar cases]. Of course, that judge's decision itself was based on the precedents taken from previous decisions of earlier judges. In that way, every decision can serve two purposes: to resolve the case that the judge is currently hearing and, if the decision is published, to provide other judges with precedent to follow.

# Precedent and *Stare Decisis*

In U.S. common law, some precedents have greater authoritative weight than others. The doctrine (or more accurately the tradition) of *stare decisis et non quieta movere* is the umbrella under which precedent stands. **Stare decisis** requires that courts follow common law precedents. But a court is **only** required to follow those precedents that are **binding on** [mandatory] that particular court. Binding authority is a ruling that was decided by a higher court in the direct line of appeal.

For example, a Tennessee state trial court in Memphis, Tennessee, must follow the precedents set by the Tennessee Court of Appeals for the Western District of Tennessee (which includes Memphis) and the Tennessee Supreme Court on state law issues. Cases decided by other courts, such as a court of another state or even the Tennessee Court of Appeals for the *Eastern* District of Tennessee, are **persuasive authority** [guidance only] only. Courts aren't required to follow persuasive authority, although persuasive authority from another district or court will generally be taken into consideration. Courts will give persuasive authority special consideration if the court that issued the precedent is closely related to one considering the precedent: for example, if both courts are in the same state but in different districts.

If a precedent is binding, judges have two options when they are looking at a case involving that precedent: they are either forced to decide the **pending** [started but not finished] case in accordance with the law of the earlier cases or to **repudiate** [overturn] the earlier decision. Only the original court that issued the decision or a higher court normally repudiates an original decision. For example, a Tennessee trial court in Memphis would in all likelihood never try to overturn a decision of the Tennessee Supreme Court. If a local Tennessee judge decided not to follow a binding precedent of the Tennessee Supreme Court, the losing attorneys in the case would most certainly appeal and would probably win the appeal.

For lawyers unfamiliar with common law, this ability to overrule a prior decision may be one of the most difficult concepts in U.S. law to grasp. Given sufficient legal grounds by an attorney, a judge may overturn a prior decision. Or, based on the facts of a particular case, a judge may decide the case in a way that seems to be at odds with precedent. Since a judge has the power to overturn a prior decision, American attorneys must review case law and then choose one of two possible courses of action:

1. reconcile the facts of the current case with prior decisions or
2. attempt to convince the judge to repudiate a prior decision

Of course, no matter how brilliant the attorney, rarely will a lower court repudiate a higher court's decision; the system must be stable.

The fact that a judge may overturn a decision doesn't mean that the law is uncertain. In only a few limited areas would most attorneys in the United States admit to legal uncertainty. Ninety percent of the cases in the United States are settled out of court. This datum allows us to infer that in 90 percent of the cases, attorneys for opposing sides reach a compromise based on an understanding of the law as a judge would see it. However, an attorney has the opportunity to **argue** his or her client's position before the court even if it would seem that the current law is relatively clear against his or her client. It could be time for a change. In fact, the U.S. Supreme Court intentionally chooses to hear cases that may be instrumental in changing laws.

### Exercise E. Case Hypotheticals and Discussion

Write an informal email outlining the differences you see that might help you and your partner **refute** this precedent case [show that this case is different from the case being cited as precedent] for the situation. Remember, an email must be brief and easy to understand. This email should not be more than 300 words. See Part 2, Email (page 184) for models and directions for writing emails.

1. For two weeks, a man has taken a prescription drug that carries a warning: "May Cause Dizziness. Do Not Drive or Perform Other Potentially Dangerous Tasks until You Know How This Medicine Affects You." As the man is driving down a crowded city street at 25 mph (10 mph below the posted speed limit), the steering column locks; the man applies the brakes, but the car lurches onto the sidewalk, striking and killing two pedestrians.

2. The attorney for the **executor** [the administrator of a deceased person's estate] cites the following case as precedent.

   A man is driving down a crowded city street at the speed limit (35 mph). When the steering column locks, the man immediately applies the brakes, but the car lurches onto the sidewalk, striking and killing two pedestrians. In a civil suit brought by the families of the victims, he is held **liable** [responsible].

## Exercise F. Paraphrasing and Discussion

1. Read the following opinion from the U.S. Supreme Court. Mr. Justice Black, with whom Mr. Justice Murphy and Mr. Justice Rutledge join, **dissenting** [disagreeing with the majority].

   *Francis v. Southern Pacific Co.,* 333 U.S. 445, 68 S. Ct. 611, 92 L.Ed.2d 798 (1948)

   It should be noted at the outset that tort law has been fashioned largely by judges, too largely according to the ideas of many. But if judges make rules of law, it would seem that they should keep their minds open in order to exercise a continuing and helpful supervision over the manner in which their laws serve the public. Experience might prove that a rule created by judges should never have been created at all, or that their rule, though originally sound, had become wholly unsuited to new physical and social conditions developed by a dynamic society. A revaluation of social and economic interests affected by the old rule might reveal the unwisdom of its expansion or imperatively require its revision or abandonment.

2. Rephrase in writing the following phrases or words from the text.

   a. at the outset     c. keep their minds open   e. social conditions

   b. it should be noted   d. dynamic society

3. Discuss this statement with a partner before you do #4 on your own. Traditionally, a child's mother is the woman who gave birth to that child. How might advances in science cause judges to review rules they might have established about "motherhood"?

4. Last night you were at a dinner party and met a scientist. You said that advances in science and medicine might cause judges and legislators to reexamine rules they had made about issues such as theft, copyright, murder, or abortion. Write a general email to her explaining your position more clearly. Remember an email must be brief and easy to understand. It should not be more than 300 words. See Part 2, Email (page 184) for models and directions for writing emails.

One additional factor that seems to make U.S. law opaque is that in addition to federal law, there is also the complexity of the interactions of 50 sets of state laws. However, **model codes** [for use in any of the states], such as the Uniform Commercial Code and the Model Penal Code, have been extremely helpful in

**reconciling** the laws of the states. Model codes are written by law professors, judges, and attorneys as guidelines for state and federal legislatures when **promulgating** [enacting] legislation. Unless specifically enacted by a state or the federal legislature, a model code has no force as law. Some states choose to enact only portions of a model code, some enact it in its entirety, and others choose not to accept any of a model code's provisions. However, use of the model codes by most states for at least some of the provisions has ensured some uniformity in U.S. law.

For attorneys, this complex system has an especially important consequence: in general, attorneys are licensed to practice only in their home states. If they wish to practice in another state, they must fulfill that state's requirements—such as taking a test on the specific features of that state's law [a part of the **bar examination**] before they can practice. Fortunately, there are some states that have **reciprocity** agreements [two or more states honor each other's rights or privileges, such as practicing law].

## Holding v. Dicta

Related to the concept of binding and persuasive authority is the distinction between holding and dicta. Law students in most countries won't have to undertake a long and detailed study into the distinctions between the two, but they should be aware that an important difference does exist. American law students, especially when writing a **legal memorandum** [information regarding the facts and the law on a particular issue usually written for courts], should understand the difference.

> **Holding**—the rule of law or legal principle that comes from the decision or the judgment plus the material facts of the case; binding authority
>
> **Dicta**—other statements in the decision that do not form part of the holding; persuasive authority

The precedent established by the case is the holding. In general, the holding of a case is binding authority, whereas the dicta are merely persuasive authority; arguments based on dicta are not binding. However, do not assume that dicta in a case are totally unimportant; sometimes the dicta become more important in later years than the actual holding. For example, the dicta in the famous Supreme Court ruling in *International Shoe Co. v. Washington*, 326 U.S. 310, 66 S. Ct. 154, 90 L.Ed. 95 (1945) are still cited in many cases.

In *International Shoe Co.*, the U.S. Supreme Court established the requirements for **personal jurisdiction** over a defendant in a civil action. Personal jurisdiction is important because it determines whether a court can force a defendant to appear before it in response to a civil lawsuit. The specific holding in this case relates to corporate agents in the state of Washington and the systematic conduct of business within the state. In its opinion, the court *discussed* but did not rule on traditional ideas of fairness. The dicta that arose from this discussion has become increasingly important in the jurisdictional decisions of other courts. The U.S. Supreme Court stated:

> It is evident that these operations [those of the corporation, International Shoe] establish sufficient contacts or ties with the state of the forum to make it reasonable and just according to our traditional conception of **fair play and substantial justice** [emphasis added] to permit the state to enforce the obligations which appellant [International Shoe] has incurred there.

Although the term *fair play and substantial justice* was part of the dicta of the Court's opinion, courts to this day use the term when making decisions regarding personal jurisdiction.

Let's look at a hypothetical example of how we might separate holding from dicta. In a case of armed robbery, the plaintiff, a short college professor, was robbed while walking down a dark, deserted street in downtown Memphis by an old Albanian man who waved a new Colt 45 pistol around and then fired one shot into the air.

If the judge says that all of these facts *(armed robbery, short college professor, walking, dark deserted street, downtown Memphis, old Albanian man, waving a gun, new Colt 45 pistol, fire one shot into the air)* are essential in making the decision, the judge's decision will be binding only in cases in which all the same facts are present and that will never happen. In other words, the decision will be binding in no other cases except where the same facts are present. However, if the judge leaves out some of the non-essential facts and makes broader descriptions, the holding will be binding on more cases. For example, was it important that it was an *old* man? Probably not. Was it important that it was a *man* and not a *woman?* Again, probably not. But do we broaden the term to *person* or *adult?* Would we want our holding to apply to children or just to adults?

After we answer these questions, we should be able to write a holding that would be binding on as many cases as appropriate. For this case we could write:

> The court held that for a person to be guilty of armed robbery
> that person must have threatened someone with a weapon.

Of course, that holding might be broadened or narrowed in future cases when the courts try to decide what a weapon is and what threatening is.

## Exercise G. Case Hypotheticals and Writing

In pairs, you will write a holding for the following case.

> In a case of armed robbery, the plaintiff, a young law student with bad eyesight, was robbed in the law library by a six-foot-tall blond woman who pointed a very realistic toy gun at the student while saying that she would shoot him in the leg if he didn't give her his law books.

1. Decide which of the facts you can either broaden or leave out completely.

| Fact | Leave Out or Broaden | Change To |
|---|---|---|
| armed robbery | neither | stays the same |
| young law student | broaden | *person* |
| bad eyesight | | |
| law library | | |
| six-foot-tall blond woman | | |
| very realistic toy gun | | |
| threaten to shoot him in the leg | | |
| law books | | |

2. Now write one sentence that would be binding on as many cases as appropriate. We have started the sentence for you

The court held that a person is guilty of armed robbery when. . . .

_____

_____

# Classification of Law in the United States

American attorneys do not normally see the broad general categories of law seen by their civil law counterparts. American attorneys would generally think in the more specific terms of torts, contracts, products liability, or criminal law rather than just public or private law. This is partly true because of the absence of specialized courts such as those found in some civil law countries. Nonetheless, U.S. law can be separated into three broad divisions:

1. law and equity
2. substantive and procedural law
3. public and private law

Although the most important distinction for an American attorney is the one between substantive and procedural law, let's begin with the development of a very old distinction.

### *Law and Equity*

In everyday English, equity means "fairness." In legal English it has a slightly different meaning, although it is still based on an idea that fairness sometimes means the courts must go beyond the strict legal codes. This distinction between actions **at law** and those **in equity** developed in England beginning in the thirteenth century. Eventually, separate courts of equity were established in the fifteenth century.

Basically, a "suit in equity" enjoyed more procedural flexibility, didn't have a jury, and could be reviewed in broader terms if it were appealed. More important for the plaintiff and defendant, a court of equity could order **injunctions** [order a defendant to do or not to do something specific that might cause further injury or harm to the plaintiff] or order **specific performance** [require the defendant to complete a contractual agreement], while a court of law normally can only use money as a remedy.

In the modern American legal system, the courts of equity and law have generally been merged. However, the concepts found in the two courts didn't always merge. In most cases, the right to a jury trial is available only for cases that are "triable at law" but not for those that historically are "triable in equity." Consequently, in some jury trials, the jury deals with a set of the issues, those at law, while the judge is responsible for other issues, those "in equity." However, it is important to remember that even today if legal remedies are sufficient, **equitable remedies** can't be used.

## Substance and Procedure

The distinction between substantive and procedural law is much more important for modern attorneys. Basically, **procedural law** establishes the rules for enforcing or administering law. It involves issues of jurisdiction, pre-trial actions, admissibility of evidence, and appeals. Procedural rules in part ensure that a trial is fair and timely. If a juror is biased, he or she can be dismissed. If evidence has been obtained improperly, for example, without a valid search warrant, procedural rules ensure that it will not be admitted in court. Procedural rules also govern whether or not the court has the power to hear a case.

For example, there are set procedures that normally must be followed before evidence can be used against a defendant in a trial. A police officer cannot just walk up to your house and demand to be let in to search for anything that might be illegal. The officer must get a warrant from a judge first that basically says what the officer is looking for and where the officer will look.

Another principle based in common law is that police officers, even with warrants, must knock on the door of a house and announce that they are police officers, as heard in many films and on television: "Open up. It's the police!" Let's look at a case taken to the Supreme Court in which the defense attorney tried unsuccessfully to argue that the "knock and announce" principle must always be enforced. In its decision the Supreme Court uses several English cases as precedent, including the famous seventeenth-century *Semayne's Case*, 5 Co. Rep. 91a, 91b, 77 Eng. Rep. 194, 195 (K. B. 1603), which contains a reference to a statute on the same subject from 1275 that was based on even earlier common law!

*Wilson v. Arkansas*, 514 U.S. 927, 115 S. Ct. 1914, 131 L.Ed.2d 976 (1995)

**Facts:** Arkansas undercover agents bought illegal drugs from Sharlene Wilson. Police officers were then given warrants to search Ms. Wilson's house and to arrest her. However, when the police officers arrived at Ms. Wilson's house, they discovered that the front door was open. The police officers opened the screen door, which was unlocked, and walked into the house. As they entered, they said they were police officers and that they had a warrant. "Once inside the home, the officers seized marijuana, methamphetamine, valium, narcotics paraphernalia, a gun, and ammunition. They also found petitioner [Wilson] in the bathroom, flushing marijuana down the toilet." *Id.* at 927.

**Attorney's reasoning:** Because the police had not knocked on the door and announced their presence, Ms. Wilson's attorney moved to **suppress** [not allow it to be used in the trial] the evidence (i.e., the drugs and gun) that the police found in their search. The attorney maintained the police had violated the common law knock and announce principle required by the Fourth Amendment's reasonable search and seizure clause.

**Ruling:** The Supreme Court agreed that knock and announce was a common law principle dating from at least 1275 and was part of the Fourth Amendment but noted that it was not a principle without exceptions.

> Nevertheless, the common law principle was never stated as an inflexible rule requiring announcement under all circumstances. Countervailing law enforcement interests—including, e.g., the threat of physical harm to police, the fact that an officer is pursuing a recently escaped arrestee, and the existence of reason to believe that evidence would likely be destroyed if advance notice were given—may establish the reasonableness of an unannounced entry. For now, this Court leaves to the lower courts the task of determining such relevant countervailing factors.

**Action:** The case was sent back to a lower court to decide if the facts in *Wilson* would support the reasonableness of the unannounced entry.

This case shows the importance of procedural law in the United States. On the other hand, **substantive law** concerns the law dealing with the facts of the case itself, such as the law of torts, products liability, corporations, or contracts. In the *Wilson* case, the possession of illegal substances would be an element of substantive law, but getting the evidence admitted into court would be a part of procedural law.

Some distinction between procedural and substantive law is familiar to all legal systems. There is even an International Association of Procedural Law. However, it seems in the United States that this distinction has taken on a heightened importance. The complex interactions among the 50 states, Puerto Rico, other territories, and the federal government have made procedure very significant. Each state has the right to make its own substantive and procedural law, but in some cases when the case reaches the federal level, the federal courts may use *state substantive law* but *federal procedural law,* which may vary from the procedural law of the state. Fortunately, many states now use uniform codes in these areas such as the Uniform Rules of Evidence, which has been adopted in whole or in part by most states. The issue becomes even more complex if there is any problem in determining what is substantive and what is procedural law, although fortunately that doesn't happen frequently.

## Exercise H. Case Hypotheticals and Role Play

In the *Wilson* case, the Supreme Court decided not to make a final judgment on what might be good reasons for unannounced entries. Let's see how you would handle this issue.

1.  Your instructor will assign one of the scenarios (a–e) to pairs or teams of students.

2.  Then your instructor will randomly tell your group to defend or attack verbally the stance that this scenario contains a good reason for an unannounced entry. Don't worry; there are no real right or wrong answers in this exercise.

3.  As a group, you will present your arguments to the court, your classmates.

4.  After each group presents its arguments, the entire class will act **en banc** [as a group] and decide if you proved your point or not.

*Fact Situations*

a.  A police officer is chasing a man who was shooting at people from his front yard into his house. The police officer doesn't knock and announce as he enters the man's house through the back door.

b.  Walking by a house, a police officer hears someone inside screaming, "Please don't shoot me!" She kicks in the door and rushes in without knocking and announcing and finds a man pointing a gun at a woman who turns out to be his wife.

c.  While checking doors of businesses to make sure they are locked for the night, a police officer finds one unlocked. He enters quietly thinking there might be burglars and discovers the owner of the business sitting in a chair smoking marijuana. He arrests the owner for possession of an illicit drug.

d.  The police have a warrant to raid the house at 132 Robin where a band of dangerous, armed counterfeiters are thought to be working. Without knocking and announcing, the police kick down the doors and break in through the windows at 123 Robin by mistake. Inside the wrong house, they discover hundreds of TV sets that all turn out to be stolen.

e.  The police think that a 78-year-old **con artist** [thief who tricks people out of their money] for whom they have an arrest warrant might be living at 4443 Arrol. At that house, they knock on the door and say, "Hello, pizza delivery." As the man opens the door to say he didn't order a pizza, the police arrest him.

## Exercise I. Case Comparisons

In a way, this case heard by the supreme court of Wisconsin asks the reverse of the question asked in *Wilson v. Arkansas*. After *Wilson* many courts assumed that exceptions to the knock and announce rule would need to be done on a case-by-case basis. Could there be a general type of search warrant that allows the police to dispense with knock and announce? Read the following case summary.

*State v. Richards*, 201 Wis.2d 845, 549 N.W.2d 218 (1996)

. . . Richards argues that because the police failed to 'knock and announce' prior to entering his motel room to execute a search warrant, any evidence seized must be suppressed. The issue is simply stated: whether the Fourth Amendment allows a blanket exception to the general requirement of 'knock and announce' (the rule of announcement) for entries into premises pursuant to a search warrant for evidence of felonious drug delivery. We conclude that exigent circumstances are always present in the execution of search warrants involving felonious drug delivery, [such as] an extremely high risk of serious if not deadly injury to the police as well as the potential for the disposal of drugs by the occupants prior to entry by the police. The public interests inherent in these circumstances far outweigh the minimal privacy interests of the occupants of the dwelling for which a search warrant has already been issued. Accordingly, we re-affirm *State v. Stevens*, 181 Wis.2d 410, 511 N.W.2d 591 (1994), *cert. denied*, 515 U.S. 1102, 115 S. Ct. 2245, 132 L.Ed.2d 254 (1995), and conclude that police are not required to adhere to the rule of announcement when executing a search warrant involving felonious drug delivery.

Write the answers to the questions based on the case.

1. What is the difference between a case-by-case exception and a blanket exception?

2. What are the two basic reasons for permitting police to ignore knock and announce in this particular case?

3. Why is this court not overly concerned with the privacy rights of Richards in this case?

4. The defendant maintains that an error was made in his trial. What was that error?

5. In what way is this case based on *Wilson v. Arkansas*?

## Exercise J. Oral Argument

Select a partner and work in pairs; one of you is a judge and the other is a prosecuting attorney who is trying to obtain a search warrant to search Sharlene Wilson's house. The judge agrees to issue a warrant. The attorney must attempt to convince the judge to issue a no-knock warrant based on this information from *Wilson v. Arkansas.*

During November and December 1992, petitioner Sharlene Wilson made a series of narcotics sales to an informant acting at the direction of the Arkansas State Police. In late November, the informant purchased marijuana and methamphetamine at the home that petitioner shared with Bryson Jacobs. On December 30, the informant telephoned petitioner at her home and arranged to meet her at a local store to buy some marijuana. According to testimony presented below, petitioner produced a semiautomatic pistol at this meeting and waved it in the informant's face, threatening to kill her if she turned out to be working for the police. Petitioner then sold the informant a bag of marijuana.

## Exercise K. Legal Vocabulary

When writing about the law, you need to be as precise as possible. Use the correct terms from the text to complete the following sentences. Pay attention to the right tense (if the term is a verb) and form as you fill in the blanks.

1. An amendment to the United States Constitution must be _____ by 3/4 of the states before it becomes part of the Constitution.

2. Ninety percent of the cases in the United States are _____ out of court.

3. Model codes, such as the Model Penal Code, have been helpful in _____ laws of the 50 states.

4. After attorneys practice law for five years in Tennessee, they may practice in Georgia because Georgia grants _____ to practicing Tennessee attorneys.

5. In *International Shoe Co. v. Washington,* the U.S. Supreme Court _____ the requirements for personal jurisdiction.

6. A case that is sent back to the trial court for a rehearing after an appeal has been _____ to the trial court.

7. The person responding to an appeal is called the _____.

8. In order to obtain a search warrant, a police officer must establish _____ (show the judge that there are reasonable grounds for the search).

9. If an attorney wishes to prevent the use of supposedly illegally obtained evidence during a trial, he or she must file a motion to _____ the evidence.

## *Public and Private Law*

The separation of U.S. law into public and private spheres is of little practical importance to a practicing U.S. attorney. However, this may help students from countries in which law is divided in this manner.

| Public Law | Private Law |
|---|---|
| Constitutional law | Civil law<br>Contracts |
| Administrative law | Family law<br>Property law |
| Labor law (government control of business activity) | Commercial law<br>Negotiable instruments |
| Trade regulation (government control of business activity) | Sales<br>Secured transactions |
| Criminal law (relationship between the individual and the government) | Business enterprises<br>Agency<br>Corporations |
| Tax law (controversial because of close relationship to corporation and property law, which are private law fields) | Partnerships |

# Legal Authorities and Reasoning

## Discovering Connections

In this chapter we will examine the ways lawyers apply their understanding of the U.S. legal system in preparing their cases.

Perhaps the simplest way to go about explaining legal reasoning in the American system is to examine it from two different angles—**legal authority,** which is the raw data that an attorney must gather through intensive legal research, and **legal reasoning,** which involves an ability both to read and to understand the sources that the research yields. The lawyer then uses these two different angles to assemble that information into a coherent whole used to represent his or her clients.

Lawyers in any jurisdiction in the United States rely on legal authority in order to win their cases. *Legal authority* is a very general term used to refer to a case, statute, regulation, treatise, law review article, or other legal reference source. These sources may either provide information that will be binding on a court, forcing it to follow the line of reasoning in a previous decision [**precedent**], or they may provide information that is merely persuasive information that may possibly sway a judge to decide in a client's favor but does not require the judge to act in accordance with the previous decision.

Legal authority is binding only when it is precedent. Precedent is a case opinion that guides a judge in subsequent cases because the prior case has similar facts or raises similar issues of law. Judges decide cases before them on the basis of principles established in prior decisions. This common law concept is called *stare decisis.*

## ACTIVITY

A. You are an attorney preparing an appeal for your client, who has been convicted of involuntary manslaughter. Keeping in mind the principle of *stare decisis* set out in the preceding paragraph and the concept of binding authority, rank the sources based on what you think their authoritative weight would be in the U.S. legal system:

_____ 1. a recent law review article discussing trends in involuntary manslaughter punishments

_____ 2. an article [**treatise**] on involuntary manslaughter written twenty years ago by a famous law professor

_____ 3. a five-year-old state statute defining the elements of involuntary manslaughter

_____ 4. a case decided last year in the same jurisdiction that is almost identical to your client's case and in which the defendant was found not guilty

B. Divide into groups and discuss your answers. Were there any significant differences in the rank order?

C. If so, discuss the differences and arrive at one group answer to be presented and supported for the rest of the class.

# Legal Listening and Writing

# Essential Terms

**plaintiff:** the **aggrieved** [wronged] party who institutes a legal action

**defendant:** the party against whom the **grievance** [complaint] is filed

**appeal:** a request by the losing party in a case to have a higher court review the application of law

**appellant:** the party appealing a lower court's decision

**appellee:** the prevailing party in a lower court against whom the appellant appeals

**jurisdiction:** the area(s) over which a court has the power to hear cases and impose its judgment

**remand:** An appellate court may send the case back to the lower court in certain circumstances for further action.

**trial court:** the court having initial jurisdiction over a case, hearing both facts and law, and basing its decision on an application of the law to the facts

**cert. denied:** the refusal of the Supreme Court of the United States to hear an appeal; the document filed to ask for the appeal is the **writ of certiorari**

**cause of action:** the legal basis for a court case; facts that trigger the application of a particular law; cases are sometimes dismissed for failure to state a cause of action

## Putting the Terms to Use

A. Listen to the conversation twice. The first time, just listen. The second time, try to answer the questions on a separate sheet of paper.

1. In which country is this conversation taking place?
2. What does "pulling something off the fire" mean?
3. When Simone says, "you might want to keep in mind," what does she really mean?
4. Can you address the judge from your seat?
5. What do you call an American judge in the courtroom?
6. Is there a special term for attorneys?
7. Why does Simone say, "Touché"?
8. How would you spell the American pronunciation of the last letter of the alphabet?
9. Can you use "Ms." for any American woman?
10. What is a general term for the judge?

B. Use the essential terms and the ones you learned from Jens and Simone on the audio to complete the memo started for you.

---

## Memo

Lee, Hall, and Barone, P.C.

To:       Jens Weihrauch

From:

Subject:  Preliminary Information on the Hradec Case

Date:

     Simone Fort has asked me to explain the facts and issues of the Hradec case to you. Our client, Loretta Hradec, a well-known dancer, sued the privately funded Maly Ballet of Prague (henceforth MBP) for breach of contract. As attorney for the _____, Ben Johnson attempted to show that MBP had breached the contract signed in New York by not paying Ms. Hradec following her car accident in which she broke her left arm. MBP maintained that it could not be sued in the U.S. since Ms. Hradec was to have performed in MBP's home theater in Prague, the Czech Republic. The _____ court, mistakenly interpreting this case as falling under the Foreign Sovereign Immunities Act, found for the _____. Ms. Hradec has chosen to _____ the decision. At that point Ms. Fort was given responsibility for the _____.

     As attorney for the _____, Ms. Fort must file an _____ brief outlining the grounds for the _____. Ms. Fort feels that our strongest ground for reversal is the jurisdictional issue: Were there sufficient minimal contacts within the United States to grant the court _____? As a jurisdictional expert, you will prove invaluable in convincing the appeals court to _____ the case to the lower court for a reevaluation of the jurisdictional issue.

---

## Legal Thumbnail

Normally, when we think of reason or reasoning, we think in terms of why. We watch our friend Paul push his piano out the window. What made him do that? Had he decided never to play again, or had he simply pushed the instrument too hard as he was cleaning his house?

The same need and search for a reason apply in the legal context, but the underlying motive is based both on statutes and on case law. In order to understand the legal reasoning in a particular jurisdiction, a practicing attorney must not only look at the codes/statutes but must also review the case law that has evolved through interpretation of the original statute or statutes. By understanding how to read cases, which in the American system are often interpretations of the statutes, a practitioner is able to research a point of law thoroughly and thereby effectively counsel clients.

**Case** in the legal sense has two meanings. First, it refers to a legal action between two or more parties that is initiated in a trial court, often with a **jury** [citizens who issue a **verdict** (decision by the jury on liability of the defendant) after hearing both facts and law]. The case may move through the various levels of the court system on a series of appeals in which there are no juries. Second, *case* is also a term used to refer to the written opinion of a judge articulating the rationale of the decision of the court through an explanation of the law and its application to the facts in that particular case.

## Understanding Legal Citations

A legal citation refers to the full text of a statute, a case, or some other source of legal information. The important thing to remember is that these citations are always unambiguous: they tell you exactly where you can locate the original document. If the legal citation is to a statute, the citation will direct you to the appropriate volume and section number of the code. For example, 18 U.S.C. §1001 would refer to the 1001st section of the 18$^{th}$ volume [**title**] of the United States Code.

If the citation is to a case, it will contain both the **style of a case** or **heading** [the names of the parties who are involved in the litigation] and sufficient information to locate the text of the case. Full texts of cases are found in volumes called **reporters,** which record and preserve decisions of a particular court or courts and are usually based on geography. There are **state reporters, regional reporters, federal reporters,** and **U.S. Supreme Court reporters.** In regional reporters, for example, cases heard in state courts in Delaware and Connecticut are reported in the Atlantic Reporter while cases heard in state courts in Alaska and Arizona are found in the Pacific Reporter. Other regional reporters for state cases include the South Eastern, the South Western, the Southern, and the North Eastern Reporters. Federal Reporters (F./F.2d/F.3d) report on appellate cases, and the Federal Supplement (F. Supp.) reports on cases heard in federal district courts. There are also special reporters of U.S. Supreme Court cases [U.S. Reporter (U.S.), Supreme Court Reporter (S. Ct.), and the Lawyer's Edition (L.Ed., L.Ed.2d)] and the various state reporters, which are often just excerpts from the regional reporters.

Of course, it would be impossible to report all cases heard at the federal and state levels in the United States. Statutes establish the criteria for inclusion of cases in the reporters. Once decisions are published, they serve as precedent for any future decisions in the same jurisdiction.

The style of case (the names of the parties involved) was mentioned earlier, and it is good to keep in mind that the order of parties may, in some states, switch back and forth through a series of appeals. This name changing can be very confusing unless you are able to decipher it. For example, in Alaska Sherrie Johnson sued Patrick Pletnikoff. The trial court designation (as in all states) was *Johnson v. Pletnikoff*. Sherrie Johnson won at the trial level, so Patrick Pletnikoff appealed the trial court's decision, at which time the style changed to *Pletnikoff v. Johnson* [*Pletnikoff v. Johnson*, 765 P.2d 973 (Alaska 1988)].

In most other states and in the federal system, the appellate courts retain the original trial court designations on appeal. In a Tennessee appellate case (one of the states that retains trial court designation), Sandra Kilpatrick sued James W. Bryant for medical malpractice. She lost at the trial court level and appealed. The style of the case on appeal was *Kilpatrick v. Bryant* [*Kilpatrick v. Bryant*, 868 S.W.2d 594 (Tenn. 1993)]. The same would have been true if she had won at the trial court level and Bryant had appealed.

How, then, does an attorney know what's going on? In the headnote, many states indicate after the party names the case history (e.g., Plaintiff-Appellant or Defendant-Appellee). If not, the attorney's next option is to read the summary of the case in the headnote or delve into the actual court opinion.

Actually locating the case in a reporter is simple once you understand the shorthand used in **case citations.** Let's look at one citation (often called just a **cite**) to see what we can learn: *Pletnikoff v. Johnson*, 765 P.2d 973 (Alaska 1988). The case is found in the 765th volume of the Pacific Reporter, Second Series, on page 973. The case was decided in Alaska in 1988.

### Exercise A. Citation Review

In pairs, review the following citations, and answer the questions for each.

*United States v. Alvarez,* 755 F.2d 830 (11th Cir. 1985)
42 U.S.C. §9401 (1988)
*Crompton v. Commonwealth,* 239 Va. 312, 389 S.E.2d 460 (1990)
*Davis v. Monsanto Co.,* 627 F. Supp. 418 (S.D. W.Va. 1986)
Kan. Stat. Ann. §59–102 (1983 & Supp. 1992)
*Hall v. United States,* 454 A.2d 314 (D.C. 1982)

1. What type of authority is cited?
2. In which publication and on which page would you expect to find the material?
3. Is it a state or federal decision/statute?

# Locating the Information

The first step in researching the legal authority in a jurisdiction is a general search using **descriptors** [words that represent general categories of information]. You may conduct a search using a computer if you have access to LEXIS or Westlaw, for example. Or you may conduct a manual search in which you go to shelves of law books and search for statutes, cases, and other types of legal authority that are **on point** [deal with the issue you are researching].

There are general information sources, also known as secondary sources, such as ***Corpus Juris Secundum*** [C.J.S.] or ***American Jurisprudence*** [Am. Jur.] [both forms of legal encyclopedias] that will lead you to specific cases. You may search by word descriptors (e.g., "wrongful death") in the indexes of the encyclopedias for references to specific sections in Am. Jur. or C.J.S. A general statement of the law is provided in the section, and case references interpreting prior cases and statutes are listed in footnotes. Be sure that you also check the **pocket parts** [updates that indicate the newest decisions]. In addition, there are also softcover updates that should be reviewed or you may find and use out-of-date decisions. You can also check other types of materials such as

1. *Words and Phrases:* an encyclopedic-type set that uses cases to define legal words and phrases;
2. **federal and state digests:** volumes with extensive case law summaries that can be located using a West Key number (discussed later in this chapter) or descriptive words; and
3. **annotated statute books:** code books with cases listed in footnotes, such as *United States Code Annotated* [U.S.C.A.].

# Understanding the Court System

In order to read cases and decipher case histories, it is necessary to understand the general framework of the American court system. When a **cause of action** [acts necessary to trigger a lawsuit] occurs, the plaintiff files a **complaint** [petition] with the court having jurisdiction over the matter. The cause of action is called a **claim for relief** in federal courts. The petition requests a review of the facts by the court. Every plaintiff who follows the procedure for submitting a petition receives his or her day in court regardless of the merits of his or her claim. However, trial judges may almost immediately dismiss cases they deem to be frivolous, or the matter may be settled out of court prior to or even during the actual trial of the case itself.

In a civil case, the losing party may appeal at least once as a matter of right. The court that has power to hear that appeal is called the appellate court. Normally this is the intermediate appellate court since most states and the federal system have three-tiered systems. Since the facts are considered to have been determined by the trial court, the appellate court will only hear questions of law. In other words, the question becomes whether the trial court understood and acted in accordance with the law in the jurisdiction.

This chart will help you visualize how the cases move from court to court.

| Level 1<br>*Trial Court →* | Level 2<br>*Appellate →* | Level 3<br>*Court of Last Resort* |
|---|---|---|
| **State system:** e.g., Circuit Court of Shelby County, Tennessee | e.g., Court of Appeals of Tennessee | e.g., Supreme Court of Tennessee |
| **Federal system:** District Court | U.S. Court of Appeals | U.S. Supreme Court |

## *State Courts*

Each of the 50 states and several territories has its own system so this chart and the explanations are very generalized overviews.

### LEVEL 1: TRIAL COURT

- Also referred to as the court of general jurisdiction, the court of record, or the court of original jurisdiction
- Plaintiff versus defendant: *Johnson v. Pletnikoff*
- Issues of fact: what happened?
  Jury is presented with evidence and renders verdict.
- Issues of law: was the defendant's action legal or illegal?
  Judge presides over case, instructs jury on law, enters judgment.
- The losing party has appeal as a matter of right to the next level.

**LEVEL 2: APPELLATE COURT**

- Intermediate appellate jurisdiction
- Appellant versus appellee or petitioner versus respondent losing party versus winning party in the previous trial or sometimes appellee versus appellant depending on the trial court designation
- Only issues of law may be considered by the appellate court

  a. prejudicial error—remand for new trial: start over
  b. reverse trial decision—judgment for appellant: loser in Level 1 becomes winner
  c. affirm trial court decision—judgment for appellee: winner in Level 1 stays winner

- An appeal from this level is normally at the discretion of the next higher court.

**LEVEL 3: STATE SUPREME COURT**

- Appellate jurisdiction or the court of last resort
- Appellant and appellee/petitioner and respondent
- Unless there is a conflict with the U.S. Constitution or federal law, no appeal is possible.
- The state supreme courts are the final arbiters of state law.

## Exercise B. Listening Comprehension

Listen to the attorney **counseling** [advising] her client. Then answer the questions.

1. What is the person called who brings the matter before the court?
2. What happens if a party loses at the trial court level?
3. What are depositions?
4. Who must follow the decision of the upper court in an appeal?
5. What is the docket?

## *Federal Courts*

The federal courts are divided into eleven geographic circuits, plus a circuit for Washington, **DC** [District of Columbia] and a federal circuit. 28 U.S.C. §41 gives the jurisdictions.

### §41. Number and composition of circuits

The thirteen judicial circuits of the United States are constituted as follows:

| Circuits | Composition |
| --- | --- |
| District of Columbia | District of Columbia |
| First | Maine, Massachusetts, New Hampshire, Puerto Rico, Rhode Island |
| Second | Connecticut, New York, Vermont |
| Third | Delaware, New Jersey, Pennsylvania, Virgin Islands |
| Fourth | Maryland, North Carolina, South Carolina, Virginia, West Virginia |
| Fifth | District of the Canal Zone, Louisiana, Mississippi, Texas |
| Sixth | Kentucky, Michigan, Ohio, Tennessee |
| Seventh | Illinois, Indiana, Wisconsin |
| Eighth | Arkansas, Iowa, Minnesota, Missouri, Nebraska, North Dakota, South Dakota |
| Ninth | Alaska, Arizona, California, Guam, Hawaii, Idaho, Montana, Nevada, Oregon, Washington |
| Tenth | Colorado, Kansas, New Mexico, Oklahoma, Utah, Wyoming |
| Eleventh | Alabama, Florida, Georgia |
| Federal | All Federal judicial districts |

This chart gives an overview of the structure of the federal courts and the various types of opinions the U.S. Supreme Court may issue.

**Level 1: U.S. District Court**

1. Made up of trial courts of original jurisdiction; 94 districts (including the District of Columbia and the territories)
2. One judge and, if desired, a jury
3. Appeal as a matter of right

**Level 2: U.S. Courts of Appeal**

1. Thirteen courts of appellate jurisdiction in the various circuits
2. Bank (also referred to as a panel) of three judges
3. Appeal to U.S. Supreme Court only via **petition for writ of certiorari** (request to the U.S. Supreme Court for review)

**Level 3: U.S. Supreme Court**

1. Nine members; nominated by the president and confirmed by the Senate; may serve for life
2. Appellants must petition for **writ of certiorari**—ask the Court to hear the appeal
   a. certiorari (cert.) granted if four members vote to hear the case
   b. cert. denied if less than four members vote to hear the case
3. Opinion types
   a. **per curiam** opinion [unanimous decision]
   b. **majority** opinion [opinion shared by the majority]
      *Example:* 6–3 decision—all six justices agree on one opinion
   c. **plurality** opinion [final outcome agreed to by majority but for differing reasons]
      *Example:* 6–3 decision—two justices write one concurring opinion, three justices write another concurring opinion, one justice writes his or her own opinion, and three justices dissent
   d. **concurring** opinion [agrees with the majority decision for different reasons]
   e. **dissenting** opinion [opinion given by a justice not agreeing with the majority]
4. No appeal is possible.
   Supreme Court decisions are binding in all jurisdictions in the United States. However, the Supreme Court may overrule its own earlier decisions.

## Exercise C. Reading for Details

1. At what level is a jury trial possible?
2. In what way is the Supreme Court different from all other U.S. courts?
3. How can a state case be appealed to the federal level?
4. What would *cert. denied* mean to an appellant?
5. Would a majority opinion carry as much authoritative weight as a plurality decision? Why or why not?

# Reading the Case

After locating a case in your jurisdiction, it is necessary to take a closer look to determine if it will prove helpful in answering your research question and providing precedent. To the uninitiated, cases appearing in any of the reporters can at first seem very confusing. However, once a few basic organizational concepts are mastered, the researcher will appreciate that the cases are arranged in a way that provides the maximum amount of data in the minimum amount of time.

The order and nature of information given usually follow the same or a similar format based on a system used by West Publishers, the primary legal reporter publisher. Cases obtained from the Internet will not normally have headnotes but will go immediately into the opinion. Headnotes from West's simplify reading of the case because they attempt to summarize the important information. So, let's look at *U.S. v. White*, 552 F.2d 268 (8th Cir. 1977), a criminal case, from a West publication.

## *Headnote*

### THE PARTIES

This section includes the names of the parties, identification of parties (plaintiff, defendant, etc.), an identification of the court in which the recorded case was heard, and the date of the opinion. In this chart, we've printed an actual headnote as it would appear in its vertical format in the left column and explanations of each of the lines in the right.

| | |
|---|---|
| UNITED STATES of America, Appellee | Prosecution |
| v. | versus |
| David Lee WHITE, Appellant | Defendant |
| No. 76-2047 | Docket Number the court's system for finding the case in its files |
| United States Court of Appeals, | the court hearing the case |
| Eighth Circuit | the federal circuit |
| Submitted March 24, 1977 | date appeal filed |
| Decided April 6, 1997 | date decision made |

**PROCEDURAL HISTORY**

The procedural history is a brief recitation of what the courts have done with this case. This section also includes the basis for review and an abbreviated recitation of the previous court's holding. There is also a single line indicating the court's **disposition** of the case [what the court decided to do with the case]. We have added explanatory statements in bold to the various sections of the procedural history.

Defendant was convicted in the United States District Court for the District of Nebraska, Warren K. Urbom, Chief Judge, of interstate transportation of a stolen motor vehicle **[previous court's holding—the District Court],** and he appealed. The Court of Appeals held that the evidence was sufficient to support the trial court's finding that defendant knew the vehicle was stolen and that he caused it to be transported across state lines **[basis for defendant's appeal implied— insufficient evidence to support lower court's decision].**

Affirmed **[Court of Appeals' disposition of the case].**

**WEST KEY NUMBER SYSTEM**

Sections numbered according to a system of key words provide references to legal issues. General topics discussed in the case (e.g., Labor Relations, Sales, or Civil Rights) are in bold print followed by a key symbol and a number reference to sections in the reporters' indexes that list similar cases—that is, cases that rely on similar legal principles. When there is more than one key number in the headnote, these key numbers are numbered 1, 2, 3, and so forth. The opinion is then divided into sections by West: [1], [2], [3], and so on. The numbers indicate the sections in which a discussion of the particular legal discussion can be located within the text of the opinion. In our example, there is only one key note; however, a complicated case may contain references to many points of law.

**Automobiles** 🔑 **355(12)** [*Note:* A section number would be before "Automobiles" if there were more than one key number in the opinion. Key and KeyCite© West Group.]

Evidence in prosecution for interstate transportation of stolen motor vehicle was sufficient to support trial court's finding that defendant knew vehicle was stolen and caused it to be transported across state lines. 18 U.S.C.A. §2312.

**LEGAL REPRESENTATIVES**

The names of the attorneys for both plaintiff and defendant, the attorneys' law firms, and the city within which the attorneys practice are listed.

Floyd A. Sterns, Lincoln, Neb., for appellant.

Daniel E. Wherry, U.S. Atty., and Robert F. Kokrda, Asst. U.S. Atty., Omaha, Neb., for appellee.

## *Opinion*

The opinion includes the names of the judges who heard the case, the holding, and the rationale. This section is the official court decision and is what is used by attorneys when writing legal memoranda. The headnote, which we discussed earlier, while useful for understanding the case, is not the official opinion. In *U.S. v. White* the disposition of the case comes at the beginning of the opinion. In other cases, the disposition of the case is found after the recitation of the procedural history/facts or at the end of the opinion.

### JUDGE OR JUDGES HEARING THE CASE

Before HEANEY, ROSS, AND HENLEY, Circuit Judges.
PER CURIAM.

### PROCEDURAL HISTORY

David Lee White was convicted by a jury of interstate transportation of a stolen motor vehicle in violation of 18 U.S.C. §2312. He appeals that conviction, contending that the evidence was insufficient to support the verdict. We affirm.

## Exercise D. Reading for Details

1. What is the first word that shows that this case is an appeal?

2. Who lost in the original trial?

3. Is this a federal or state case?

4. Which word shows that the appeals court agreed or disagreed with the trial court?

5. How many of the circuit judges agreed on the decision? How do you know?

**STATUTORY OR COMMON LAW BASIS FOR THE DECISION**
After the specific procedural history, the court will often summarize the statutory or common law basis for its decision. Sometimes at the end of the summary, the court will give the disposition of the case.

>     To sustain a conviction under 18 U.S.C. §2312, there must be some evidence before the jury which establishes that the defendant transported a motor vehicle in interstate commerce and that he knew that it was stolen. White concedes that the vehicle crossed state lines and was in interstate commerce. His principal contention is that the evidence did not establish either that he knew the vehicle was stolen or that he caused the vehicle to be transported.
>
>     When reviewing the sufficiency of the evidence to support a conviction, we must view evidence in the light most favorable to the government, *Glasser v. United States,* 315 U.S. 60, 80, 62 S. Ct. 457, 86 L.Ed. 680 (1942), and accept as established all reasonable inferences that tend to support the jury's verdict. *United States v. Overshon,* 494 F.2d 894 (8th Cir. 1974), *cert. denied,* 419 U.S. 853, 95 S. Ct. 96, 42 L.Ed.2d 85 (1974).

**FACTS/BACKGROUND**
A detailed recitation of the facts of the case is given. This includes identification of the parties, the series of events that precipitated the lawsuit, and often more detailed procedural history from the lower courts than the initial procedural information. In our case, *U.S. v. White,* the court is combining the facts with the legal conclusions to be drawn from the particular facts. This type of combining is not always done.

>     While in Connecticut, White and two acquaintances were in need of transportation. They located a station wagon which was unlocked with the ignition key inside. The three men got into the station wagon and drove away, traveled to Georgia, then Indiana, and finally abandoned the vehicle in Nebraska.

We conclude that a jury could infer from this evidence that White knew the vehicle was stolen. *United States v. Harris*, 528 F.2d 1327 (8th Cir. 1975); *United States v. Wilson*, 523 F.2d 828 (8th Cir. 1975).

White did not drive the vehicle during the journey. There was testimony by the other two men that White discovered some money in the station wagon which was used to pay for gas, that White read the road maps and instructed the driver as to the proper route, that he helped siphon gas from other vehicles, and that he was not coerced to remain in the vehicle. Based on these actions, the jury could find beyond a reasonable doubt that White had joint control over the vehicle and that he effectively transported it. *United States v. Williams*, 503 F.2d 480 (8th Cir. 1974); *United States v. Thomas*, 469 F.2d 145 (8th Cir. 1972), *cert. denied*, 410 U.S. 957, 93 S. Ct. 1429, 35 L.Ed.2d 690 (1973).

## Exercise E. Reading for Details

1. What kind of vehicle was stolen?
2. How did they get the car to start?
3. How did they get gas for the car?
4. Was White being forced to travel with the two other men?
5. What role did White play on the trip?
6. What is interstate transportation?

## Exercise F. Reading and Analysis

1. What are the two elements necessary for conviction under 18 U.S.C. §2312?
2. Are they present in *U.S. v. White?*
3. What's the difference between knowing and inferring that White knew the car was stolen?
4. What allowed the jury to determine that White transported the car across state lines?
5. Why is it important the car be transported across state lines and not just driven around in one state?

**REASONING (LEGAL DISCUSSION)**

A discussion of the point of law important to a final disposition of the case and the rationale for the court's decision normally follow the facts/background section of the opinion. When more than one issue is involved, the court normally discusses the rationale for each issue separately.

Although this evidence was not all uncontroverted and a great deal of the evidence supporting the verdict was testimony of White's accomplices, it is the province of the jury to determine the weight and credibility of the evidence. Even the uncorroborated testimony of an accomplice may be sufficient to sustain a conviction. *United States v. Knight*, 547 F.2d 75 (8th Cir. 1976); *United States v. Cady*, 495 F.2d 742 (8th Cir. 1974).

**FINAL DISPOSITION OF THE CASE**

The last section of each opinion contains the conclusion of the court regarding the case. In some instances, the holding of the court is found in this section; at other times, however, you must make a determination of the holding by combining key elements from the rationale of the court. Here is the holding in our example case.

The jury had sufficient evidence before it to determine that White knew the car was stolen, and that he caused it to be transported across state lines. For this reason, we sustain the conviction.

### Exercise G. Statutory Interpretation and Paraphrasing

1. Read 18 U.S.C. §2312.

   §2312. Transportation of stolen vehicles

   Whoever transports in interstate or foreign commerce a motor vehicle or aircraft, knowing the same to have been stolen, shall be fined under this title or imprisoned not more than 10 years, or both.

2. Look back at the holding. What's the difference between "transported across state lines" and "caused to be transported across state lines"?

3. Paraphrase the holding from this case to show that the elements of 18 U.S.C. §2312 necessary for conviction have been met. You may wish to review Part 2, Paraphrase (page 180) before doing the exercise.

# Case Briefings

Law students in the United States brief countless numbers of cases during their legal studies. One of the reasons for this is to enable them to learn how to read and understand the cases, especially those that are long and complicated. Briefing helps you capture the important elements of a case. For shorter cases of one to three pages, the "brief" is sometimes longer than the actual case itself. The point, however, is an amplified understanding of the law underlying the case and, once you have that understanding, the ability to read several cases and synthesize the cases to come up with a general rule of law.

Since there are many ways to brief a case, your instructor may give you a different format and instructions to follow. If not, follow the format given. Use the actual opinion for briefing the case rather than the headnotes.

## *Case Brief Elements*

1. **Citation**. You should be able to find the case again if you need to review it in full.
2. **Facts**. You will need for later synthesis if you are trying to show the court that the case you are working on is either similar to or distinguishable from the case that has been briefed and involves "similar" issues.
3. **Legal History** [procedural background]. To completely understand the case, you must be aware of what the lower courts have decided.
4. **Issue(s)** [in question form]. The questions of law as related to the facts of the case that the court must decide. What are the problems in this case?

5. **Holding(s) and Disposition**. The answers to the issues plus the material facts of the case. The holding differs from the rule of law because the essential facts of the particular case are included in the holding and not in the rule of law, which is developed from a synthesis of different holdings.

6. **Reasoning**. The court's discussion of why it decided as it did. This can be a mixture of cases and statutory law, as well as public policy, depending on the issues involved in the case.

7. **Rule of Law**. The law that is broadly applicable in this case. This is normally the holding without inclusion of the material facts. Other elements of the law that weren't applicable to the law might also be included here.

Now let's see how we can apply this format and brief *U.S. v. White*.

## *Brief*

### Citation
*U.S. v. White*, 552 F.2d 268 (8th Cir. 1977)

### Facts[1]
- White alleges that he and two accomplices found an unlocked station wagon with the key in the ignition.
- They got in the station wagon and took the car through Georgia and Indiana and abandoned the car in Nebraska.
- White did not drive the vehicle.
- His accomplices testified White read the map, found money in the car, gave directions, and helped siphon gas.

### Legal History
- White was convicted by a jury in the district court of interstate transportation of a stolen motor vehicle in violation of 18 U.S.C. §2312.

### Issue
- Was sufficient evidence presented to the jury to find White guilty of interstate transportation of a stolen motor vehicle?

### Holding
- Yes. Sufficient evidence was placed before the jury.

---

[1]The evidence does not prove that he knew the vehicle was stolen or that he caused the vehicle to be transported.

## Reasoning

- For a conviction under 18 U.S.C. §2312, the defendant must know that the vehicle was stolen, and the defendant must have transported the vehicle.
- All reasonable inferences for a jury's verdict must be accepted.
- The jury could find that the accomplices' testimony was of greater weight and credibility than that of White.
- The facts were sufficient to show that White knew the vehicle was stolen and that he had effective control over it.

## Rule of Law

- It is within the jury's province to ascertain weight and credibility of the evidence. All reasonable inferences that could be drawn by the jury from evidence presented at court will be accepted by the appellate court upon review.

## Exercise H. Writing and Reading for Details

Now that we've shown you how to read and brief a case, use the briefing format described to **brief** [summarize] the following case.

*Smith v. U.S.*, 385 F.2d 252 (8th Cir. 1967)

Appellant was convicted by a jury under the Dyer Act, 18 U.S.C. §2312, on two separate counts of interstate transportation of a stolen motor vehicle. He brings this appeal on two grounds. First challenged is the sufficiency of the evidence to sustain the requisite intent to commit a violation of the Act under either count; secondly, appellant suggests error in the trial court's refusal to admit certain conversations relating to his intent to steal. We affirm.

On the two occasions charged, appellant obtained automobiles from rental car agencies. On April 14, 1966, he rented a vehicle in Bridgeport, Connecticut, and then after abandoning this car in Chadron, Nebraska, on April 27, 1966, he secured a vehicle in Chadron from another rental agency. He was arrested in Long Beach, California, on June 7, 1966, in possession of the latter car. In the first instance, he gave a check at a time when his account contained insufficient funds to cover it, and in Chadron, he gave a bad check for a deposit on the rented car. Without belaboring the facts involved, in each instance appellant flagrantly violated the rental agreements, converting the car to his own use beyond any reasonable period of time. After being notified that the second car was turned in as stolen, he nevertheless continued to drive it across state lines and use it as his own.

Evidence of larceny by false pretenses has long been held by this circuit to be evidence of guilt under the Dyer Act. See *Stewart v. United States,* 151 F.2d 386 (8ᵗʰ Cir. 1945). And we have held that giving of an insufficient funds check to obtain a motor vehicle will substantiate a charge of stealing under this Act. *Landwehr v. United States,* 304 F.2d 217 (8ᵗʰ Cir. 1962). Appellant, however, argues that he did not intend to take the cars permanently. But whether he formed a specific intent to permanently deprive the owner of his property, or intended simply to deprive him for so long as it suited appellant's purposes, is immaterial. Either form of guilt is sufficient. *Schwab v. United States,* 327 F.2d 11, 14 (8ᵗʰ Cir. 1964). See also *United States v. Turley,* 352 U.S. 407, 77 S.Ct. 397, 1 L.Ed.2d 430 (1957).

Appellant is not the first to challenge the applicability of the Dyer Act to conversions of rental cars. See *United States v. Jones,* 340 F.2d 599 (4ᵗʰ Cir. 1965); *Dixon v. United States,* 295 F.2d 396 (8ᵗʰ Cir. 1961); *United States v. Dillinger,* 341 F.2d 696 (4ᵗʰ Cir. 1965); *United States v. Welborn,* 322 F.2d 910 (4ᵗʰ Cir. 1963); *Jarvis v. United States,* 312 F.2d 563 (9ᵗʰ Cir. 1963). In *Blum v. United States,* 348 F.2d 141, 144 (5ᵗʰ Cir. 1965), the rule is well stated:

> Where a person lawfully obtains possession of an automobile by a rental arrangement, and later forms an intention to convert it to his own use, and in furtherance of that intention transports it across a state boundary, a Dyer Act violation has occurred.

Without setting forth the detailed facts, we have read the record and find sufficient evidence to support the jury's finding of the requisite criminal intent necessary for conviction as to either count.

... [Second issue omitted.]

Judgment affirmed.

❖ ❖ ❖

# Shepardizing

The American legal system relies heavily on the development of law through cases. Flexibility, a benefit of that system, is a disadvantage to the legal research novice. Since there are many influences on the court, both legal and societal, a decision with basically the same facts may be decided in two different ways at different times because of statutory or policy changes. Though legal researchers do not usually encounter this problem with more recent cases, it is important to be thorough. Merely locating cases is not enough. It is also necessary to make sure that the cases found are still considered "good law." The cases may have been reversed, overruled, or reinterpreted in ways that make them inappropriate or even dangerous to the case you are researching.

In order to make sure that the cases cited as precedent are truly precedent, you should use **Shepard's Citators** from LexisNexis®, either as hard-copy books or as an online service. West has another citator service—KeyCites—that provides the same information as Shepard's Citators. These citators give the history of the case in a concise form and identify other cases and authorities that cite the case as precedent or note that the case is no longer considered precedent. Looking up a case in this work is so crucial that the term **sheparizing** has become an integral term and concept in American legal English.

# Legal Reasoning

Earlier in the chapter a distinction was drawn between legal authority and legal reasoning. To simplify it even more, legal authority is the *what* and legal reasoning is the *how*. In other words, it does no good to have located sources if there is no understanding of how to make them work for your client. Though there may be only one section of a code that is relevant to a particular set of facts, there is very rarely only one case that can serve as precedent. A legal researcher or practitioner must find some way in which to relate the statute and the case law in order to understand how the law is applied.

## *Synthesis*

One can approach legal research from one of two directions depending on the type of law in question. Civil law is code based, and attorneys do not rely on cases to clarify statutes; they rely instead on legal commentaries. Common law relies heavily on case law to clarify the statutes. Because the American legal system is based on common law, the ability to read and synthesize cases is crucial.

In order to understand how the precedent (cases) and statutes work together, it is often necessary to do a legal synthesis of both precedent and statutes. There are several different types of works that provide syntheses of law: C.J.S., Am. Jur., and hornbooks (treatises) on various legal subjects such as contracts, torts, products liability, or corporations. However, these sources are only for background work; no American attorney should ever cite these in legal memoranda or in court. Think of them as basic encyclopedias.

The series *Restatements of the Law* (on torts, contracts, etc.) also provides a synthesis of law but is considered to be a more valuable authority than general legal encyclopedias. These volumes are a compilation of law by various legal authorities, including judges and law professors, who synthesize the law on various issues and put it in a statutory form. These "statutes" are not considered law in the United States, but occasionally references to Restatements can be found in court opinions or legal memoranda submitted to the courts.

To understand what is meant by a legal synthesis, consider the following "statute" from the Restatement (Second) of Torts §493 (1965), relating to classes of individuals who may be beneficiaries in wrongful death actions, which was developed from a compilation of various cases, and the comments to the statute that follow. First, however, you need to know that **contributory negligence** means partial responsibility for whatever happens, in this case, a death.

§493 Beneficiary Under a Death Statute

(1) Unless otherwise provided by statute the contributory negligence of one beneficiary under a death statute does not bar recovery for the benefit of any other beneficiary.

(2) Whether the contributory negligence of a beneficiary under a death statute bars or reduces recovery to the extent of his own benefit depends upon the statute.

a. *Different kinds of death statutes.* A "death statute" is a statute which gives a right of action against one who has wrongfully killed another. . . . Death statutes vary in form and purpose. The purpose of the more usual form of statute is to compensate the survivors for the benefits which they could have derived from the earning power of the decedent had his life not been cut short. . . . Where the statute is of this type, the fact that a beneficiary is himself guilty of negligence which contributed to the death of the decedent does not prevent recovery unless he is the sole beneficiary.

After reading through such a passage, it is easier for the beginning researcher to have some sense of the area in which he or she will research. The writers of the Restatement have researched and synthesized the statutes and the cases that interpret those cases.

Though synthesis looks relatively effortless, it requires putting the skills that you have acquired so far in this chapter to their ultimate use. To be unable to synthesize cases in legal research is like being a painter who only knows the color chart but cannot blend its components to produce new colors.

Synthesizing cases can be a rather complicated process. Let's take a look at four cases from Louisiana and try to deduce a general rule of law from the cases. Continuing with the idea of contributory negligence of a parent, let us see what determination can be made about parental contributory negligence in wrongful death cases. Louisiana courts agree with this general rule.

> A parent is required only to use reasonable precautions with regard to a child under his supervision, as judged by common-sense standards for a reasonably prudent person under similar conditions and circumstances. *Argus v. Scheppegrell*, 472 So.2d 573 (La. 1985).

The question is what constitutes reasonable care.

1. A mother allowed her three-year-old son to go to a swimming pool under the supervision of ten-, nine-, and eight-year-old cousins. Returning from the pool, the child was hit by a truck while crossing the street and killed. Ms. Anderson's child had been taken away from her before for lack of supervision. The mother was found contributorily negligent. *Anderson v. New Orleans Public Service, Inc.*, 572 So.2d 775 (La. 1990).

2. A mother, realizing that her nineteen-year-old daughter was high on prescription drugs, sent her to bed. She then searched the daughter's purse and removed the drugs from it. When the daughter came out of her room, the mother sent her back to bed and left her under the supervision of a younger child while the mother attended a meeting in the apartment building. While the mother was away, the nineteen-year-old daughter found the drugs her mother had hidden, took them, and died of a drug overdose. The mother was not found contributorily negligent. *Argus v. Scheppegrell*, 472 So.2d 573 (La. 1985).

3. A six-year-old child drowned in a gravel pit 100 feet from his family's trailer while under the supervision of his mother, who was in the trailer. The mother was found contributorily negligent. *Humphries v. T. L. James & Co.*, 468 So.2d 819 (La. 1985).

4. A nine-year-old child drowned in a neighbor's swimming pool. Neither the mother, who was in her house nearby, nor the grandfather, who was babysitting, knew that the neighbors had a pool. Neither the mother nor the grandfather was found contributorily negligent. *Simmons v. Whittington*, 444 So.2d 1357 (La. 1984).

This chart might help in your analysis of these cases.

| Case Name | Age of Child | Supervision | Cause of Death | Negligent |
|---|---|---|---|---|
| Anderson | 3 years | minor cousins—prior lack of supervision by mother | hit by truck crossing street | yes |
| Argus | 19 years | young child | drug overdose | no |
| Humphries | 6 years | mother | drowned in gravel pit | yes |
| Simmons | 9 years | mother and grandfather | drowned in neighbor's pool | no |

## Exercise I. Reasoning

1. In pairs, decide what factors seem to be the most important in determining whether a parent was contributorily negligent or not.

2. Read the excerpt from Am. Jur. in Student Resources, Text 5, page 283.

3. Does the excerpt aid in your analysis of the cases? Did you draw the same conclusion from the cases? Is it possible that other factors should be included?

## Distinguishing Cases

Sometimes an attorney wishes to show how his or her case is different from previous cases that provide the general rule. In this situation, the researcher will attempt to provide reasons why the facts of a case allow the general rule to be modified or even ignored. Making explicit what is different about a particular case from other apparently similar cases is known as **distinguishing** a case.

For example, as the attorney for the father of an eight-year-old child killed in an automobile accident, you could use the cases on contributory negligence to help build counter-arguments when the defendant attempts to use the defense of contributory negligence to lower or eliminate the damage award.

Let us say that the child was struck by an automobile and killed on a Saturday afternoon while riding his bicycle on the quiet residential street where he lived. The father, who was watching a football game on television, had told his son that it was okay to ride the bicycle on their street but not to go any further.

As the attorney for the father, you would want the court to use the *Simmons* and *Argus* cases. *Simmons* would probably be the best precedent, since the child is much closer in age to the child in this case, assuming your case is being heard in Louisiana. Of course, the age of the child will not be all that is considered by the court when determining what a reasonably prudent parent would do, but the *Simmons* case might be a good place to start

## Exercise J. Reasoning and Paraphrasing

Before liability in a wrongful death case (or any tort case) can be assessed, **proximate cause** must be determined. In other words, who is directly responsible for the accident with no **intervening causes** [an action that happens after the initial accident and changes the natural order of events]? To help determine proximate cause, the **"but for"** test is used by courts: but for the defendant's actions, the plaintiff would not have suffered harm.

1. Use the cases to fill in the chart, which will help you distinguish the cases. We've done the first two for you.

| Case Name | Type of Accident/Action | Cause of Death | Intervening Cause | Outcome |
|---|---|---|---|---|
| Jackson | auto accident | auto accident | none | for plaintiff |
| Janovitch | auto accident | tuberculosis | none | for defendant |
| Janus | | | | |
| Ji | | | | |
| Jade | | | | |
| Johansson | | | | |
| Jerod | | | | |

*Cases*

**Jackson:** A janitor suffering from fatal lung cancer is killed in an auto accident caused by a cement truck. His wife sues the cement company. She wins.

**Janovitch:** A teacher suffering from tuberculosis dies from that disease several weeks after being hit by a car. His injuries were slight. His estate loses.

**Janus:** A judge with severe heart problems and limited chances of surviving a heart transplant dies during the heart transplant operation because the anesthesiologist uses the wrong mixture. Her heirs win.

**Ji:** A lawyer dies several weeks after a car accident after catching pneumonia caused by the injuries. The lawyer's estate wins.

**Jade:** A musician's son is killed in an airplane crash for which the defendant, an airline, is responsible. The musician commits suicide after learning of her son's death. Her heirs sue the airline based on the musician's suicide. The musician's estate loses.

**Johansson:** In a crash caused by the driver of the other vehicle, a young motorist dies of smoke inhalation because he is pinned against the steering column in his own smoking car and is unable to escape before losing consciousness, even though he sustained no injuries directly in the crash. His domestic partner wins the claim.

**Jerod:** A young man with no history of mental illness was arrested on a public intoxication charge and placed in jail. He suffered no abuse from the police, and it was clear that he would be released the next day. While in jail he hanged himself. It was later discovered that Jerod suffered from occasional bouts of depression. His heirs lose.

2. Write a general rule that covers all of the cases.

# Criminal Law

---

## Discovering Connections

People around the world have a peculiar fascination with law as it relates to crimes and the criminals who commit them. Open any U.S. newspaper or turn on the television news any day of the year, and no doubt a story involving a crime will be discussed. In law we should only be concerned with legal responsibility for the crime, but moral issues will always play a role in the development of the law (as in the legalization of abortion) and defenses to the commission of a crime (such as mental incapacity). How do we reconcile the moral and legal issues involved in the commission of a crime?

### ACTIVITY

Your instructor will place you in groups for this activity. In the story that follows, there are six characters:

| | | | |
|---|---|---|---|
| the Bar Owner | _____ | Carl | _____ |
| Jack | _____ | Joan | _____ |
| Man Leaving the Bar | _____ | Gail | _____ |

1. Using this list, individually rank the characters (from 1 to 6 with 1 being the most and 6 the least responsible) in the order of their *moral* responsibility for Joan's death.

2. Now, work with other members of your group and decide on the ranking of the six characters as a group. You must reach a unanimous decision.

3. Explain the group answers to the class and try to reach a class consensus.

### The Bluebird Bar

Around 5 PM one evening, a man and his wife entered the Bluebird Bar. The man, Jack, ordered a whiskey for himself and a cola for his wife, Gail. Jack continued to order the same drinks about every 1/2 hour.

At 11 PM the bar owner refused to serve Jack any more drinks because he was obviously extremely intoxicated and bothering other customers. Gail was used to Jack's behavior and never asked her husband to quit drinking.

"Are you driving him home or should I call a taxi?" the bar owner asked Gail. Jack shouted, "Get out of my face! I'm driving home, and neither of you can stop me!" Jack then shoved the owner aside and walked out the door. The owner just shrugged his shoulders and walked off. Gail went to the pay phone in the corner to call her sister for a ride.

As Jack left the bar, a man walking by the bar shouted to him, "Hey Buddy, call a taxi!" When Jack drove off, the man simply shook his head and walked down the street.

Meanwhile, Joan and Carl were having a lovers' quarrel on the next corner. The quarrel soon escalated into a major fight, and Carl struck Joan, saying, "Don't ever tell me not to touch you again. I'll show you who's boss here." At that point, Joan, crying hysterically and paying no attention at all to the traffic, ran into the street directly in front of Jack's car. Jack was not able to stop in time, and Joan was killed instantly.

## From Morality to Law

## Simplification and Interpretation

In order to find someone guilty of a crime, the prosecution has to prove the defendant guilty of all elements of the crime (as defined by statute or at common law) beyond a reasonable doubt. Three essential elements of all crimes are

1. *mens rea* (replaced by culpability in some states under the Model Penal Code) [the mental state—the intent]
2. *actus reus* [the act—a wrongdoing that can be an act or an omission]
3. causation [the act is the cause of/related to the harm done]

A. In the same groups used for Discovering Connections, determine if the party you found morally responsible for Joan's death could also be found legally responsible from the aspect of criminal law. Are the common elements of crime present? [Hint: In determining whether *mens rea* is present or not, use the MPC terms *purposely, knowingly, recklessly,* or *negligently.*]

B. There is no *criminal* liability for tavern owners who continue to sell drinks to patrons who are obviously intoxicated when those patrons later commit crimes such as **vehicular homicide** [killing of another person through dangerous use of a motorized vehicle]. However, some states do have **dramshop** or **civil damage** statutes that place *civil liability* on a tavern owner in some instances. In your groups, look at the statute that follows regarding civil liability of a tavern owner for acts committed by a patron who is intoxicated. Would the tavern owner in Discovering Connections be civilly liable for the death of Joan?

> Every person who is injured in person or property by any intoxicated person, has a right of action in his own name, severally or jointly, against any person who by selling or giving alcoholic liquor, causes the intoxication of such person. [*Lopez v. Maez,* 98 N.M. 625, 651 P.2d 1269 (1982)]

Following is a dramshop statute from the state of Iowa written in formal legal English. Using everyday English, rewrite this statute.

> Iowa Code §123.92. Civil liability for sale and service of beer, wine, or intoxicating liquor (Dramshop Act)—liability insurance
>
> Any person who is injured in person or property . . . by an intoxicated person or resulting from the intoxication of a person, has a right of action for all damages actually sustained, severally or jointly, against any licensee or permittee, whether or not the license or permit was issued by the division or by the licensing authority of any other state, who sold and served any beer, wine, or intoxicating liquor to the intoxicated person when the licensee or permittee knew or should have known the person was intoxicated, or who sold to and served the person to a point where the licensee or permittee knew or should have known the person

would become intoxicated. If the injury was caused by an intoxicated person, a permittee or licensee may establish as an affirmative defense that the intoxication did not contribute to the injurious action of the person. . . .

Now compare the Iowa statute with the New Mexico statute given on page 55 and answer these questions.

1. Is the civil liability the same for tavern owners under both statutes?
2. Is the host at a party liable for drunk guests under either of the statutes?
3. Is the owner of a liquor store liable if a customer buys alcohol which he or she drinks at a later time under either of the statutes?
4. If a tavern owner is civilly liable under both statutes, does he or she have a defense under either of them?
5. If a defense is available, could a tavern owner take advantage of the defense in the scenario used in "Discovering Connections"?

## Legal Thumbnail

# Theories of Punishment

The basic difference between criminal and civil law is punishment. Criminal law is designed to punish a wrongdoer for an action against society. Civil law, on the other hand, is designed to compensate an injured party with damages (usually money) for the injury. In deciding what criminal punishment is appropriate, the basic questions to be asked are the following.

1. How much has the defendant injured society?
2. How can you best punish this individual?

The question of how best to punish an individual depends to a great extent on which theory of punishment a society finds most effective. What is society trying to accomplish with the punishment? The four basic theories on which punishment is based are as follows.

• **Reformation.** This concept involves teaching a criminal how to function in society without committing any further wrongdoings: helping the criminal become a "good" citizen. While few people would disagree with the notion that prisoners should be rehabilitated, the question of whether reformation works is more debatable due in part to the high degree of **recidivism** [committing of further crimes after release] among released prisoners.

- **Restraint.** This refers to the need to keep criminals "off the streets" (i.e., imprisoned) so law-abiding citizens are free from potential harm. While this is not as noble of a concept as reformation, the idea of protecting citizens is important. The question becomes, however, whether restraint works unless it is permanent or combined with some form of rehabilitation.
- **Retribution.** This is the theory that a wrongdoer should pay for his or her crime: getting even with the criminal. Many people find this idea barbaric; however, it seems to be one of the major factors in determining punishment, as seen in the sayings *the criminal owes a debt to society, make the punishment fit the crime,* and *an eye for an eye.*
- **Deterrence.** There are two types:

  1. *Individual:* The aim is to keep a particular individual from committing another crime. If he or she is punished for a wrongdoing, perhaps it will help to keep him or her from committing another offense.
  2. *General:* The basis here is that punishing one person for a crime will keep others from committing the same crime. The question is whether people are aware of the sentences that are imposed on criminals. Of course, proponents of the deterrence theory believe that punishment does, at least to some extent, deter crime.

## Exercise A. System Comparisons and Discussion

In groups, decide which theories of legal punishment are used in your legal system. Do you think one theory predominates?

Criminal court judges don't make decisions about punishment solely on the basis of public policy and social welfare. The judges are guided by legislative or case guidelines that have classified offenses based on their severity. Punishments have to be meted out in accordance with the law. The next sections provide a brief introduction to the classification and elements of criminal law. A discussion of all types of crimes, including the intricacies of practice in criminal law, is beyond the scope of this chapter. However, statutory law and cases for a few of the different crimes will be discussed.

# Classification of Offenses

Because not all crimes are equal, punishments vary; the degree of the seriousness of a crime determines its category, which in turn determines the punishment that can be imposed.

**Misdemeanors** constitute a minor class of offenses that are punishable by a fine or imprisonment for up to one year. Examples of misdemeanors are **disturbing the peace** [an act that interrupts the peace of an area] or **reckless driving** [poor driving that endangers others]. Some states further divide misdemeanors into classes (A, B, etc.) based on the level of punishment imposed for the offense.

**Petty offenses** are often considered a subset of misdemeanors and are the lowest classification of crimes. Examples include parking tickets or violations of building codes. Depending on the state law, punishment can be a **fine** [monetary payment], imprisonment in the **county jail** [local jail for minor offenders or for holding convicted **felons,** people who have been found guilty of a more serious crime, prior to transport to another prison] or both, depending on state law.

A **felony** is any crime that is punishable by death or imprisonment in a state or federal **penitentiary** [prison for felons] for more than one year. Each state and the federal government further classify felonies into various degrees of harm. Virginia, for example, has six degrees of felony, classified according to the punishment for each class of felony.

Class 1—death or life imprisonment

Class 2—life imprisonment or a sentence of more than 20 years

Class 3—imprisonment between 5 and 20 years

Class 4—imprisonment between 2 and 10 years

Class 5—imprisonment for 1–10 years or less in the discretion of the court

Class 6—imprisonment for 1–5 years or less in the discretion of the court

Whether crimes are first-, second-, third-, or even sixth-degree felonies depends on the circumstances of each case. Factors that raise or lower the degree of felony are given in the statutes. For example, kidnapping under the MPC is a felony in the first degree unless the kidnapper voluntarily releases the victim unharmed in a safe location. If those conditions are met, then kidnapping becomes a felony in the second degree.

# Criminal Liability

Recall that there are three common elements in all crimes: *mens rea, actus reus,* and causation. Many jurists would also include **concurrence** [the *mens rea* and *actus reus* must be connected]. In other words, the **prosecution** [attorney representing the state, also commonly referred to as the **prosecuting attorney, district attorney,** or **DA**] has to prove that these elements were present before he or she can obtain a conviction.

The primary standard of proof in a criminal trial is that the prosecution must prove all elements of an offense "beyond a reasonable doubt"—the facts as proven establish guilt. Public policy requires that the burden on the prosecution be a heavy one because in the U.S. system every person must be considered innocent until proven guilty. Determining which standard is appropriate is a legal decision based on case and statutory law.

## *Mens Rea*

*Mens rea* or the intent is often the most difficult aspect of the crime to prove. If the required mental state for the offense is lacking, no crime has been committed. The mental state required to commit a crime varies with the crime. In *Commonwealth v. Woodward,* 7 Mass. L. Rptr. 449 (1997) (the trial of a British au pair accused of killing an infant in her care), for example, the state of Massachusetts charged Woodward with second-degree murder. In Massachusetts, that charge requires "**malice,**" which has been interpreted to mean an intentional act that creates a substantial risk of death. Woodward was convicted of second-degree murder by a jury, a verdict that was later reduced to involuntary manslaughter by Judge Zoebel. (A reduction of a jury verdict is possible in a limited number of states and is an extraordinarily rare use of power by a judge.) Judge Zoebel did not find that the circumstances surrounding the case supported a finding of the intent required to commit second-degree murder.

The test for malice (in the circumstances here) is whether, under the circumstances known to Defendant, a reasonable person would have known that her intentional act created a substantial risk of death to Matthew Eappen. . . .

Viewing the evidence broadly, as I am permitted to do, I believe that the circumstances in which Defendant acted were characterized by confusion, inexperience, frustration, immaturity, and some anger, but not malice (in the legal sense) supporting a conviction for second degree murder. . . .

> This sad scenario is, in my judgment after having heard all the evidence and considered the interests of justice, most fairly characterized as manslaughter, not mandatory-life-sentence murder. I view the evidence as disclosing confusion, fright, and bad judgment, rather than rage or malice, . . . [citation omitted].

❖ ❖ ❖

For the prosecution to prove intent in a **personal property theft** [stealing property belonging to another] case, he or she must prove that the defendant *knew* that the property belonged to someone else and that the defendant *intended* to deprive the owner of rightful use of the property (in other words, the defendant knew it didn't belong to him or her and meant to steal it). The Model Penal Code §2.02(2) divides intent into four categories:

a. **purposefully,** conscious desire to engage in the conduct or desire to cause the result
b. **knowingly,** person is aware of his or her conduct and is aware that his or her conduct is practically certain to cause the result that it did
c. **recklessly,** person must be aware of a substantial and unjustifiable risk that he or she consciously disregards
d. **negligently,** person should be aware of a substantial and unjustifiable risk that a reasonable person would have perceived in the circumstances

With those definitions, the MPC can avoid the distinction between general and specific intent, which has been subject to some controversy. However, the distinction hasn't disappeared, and in some jurisdictions intent is still divided into three categories:

1. general intent
2. specific intent
3. strict liability

**General intent** commonly means that the prosecution is not required to prove the intent to cause the specific result. In the *Woodward* case, the prosecution, in order to prove second-degree murder, had to prove only a general intent to commit an act [in this case, rough handling]. It was not required to prove a specific intent to harm the baby, Matthew Eappen. Judge Zoebel stated: "The only intent the government need prove is the intent to perform the act, not any particular intent as to the act's consequences." The rough handling demonstrated a disregard for the well-being of the baby but no specific intent to actually harm him.

**Specific intent** concentrates on the actual thoughts of the defendant at the time of the offense. The defendant must have intended to do the particular act that is prohibited. **Kidnapping** [unlawful restraint and movement of a person by another] is an example of a crime requiring a specific intent. Crimes involving **strict liability** require no intent. A person is guilty simply by having committed the act. Examples include **statutory rape** [having sex with a person who is by statute defined as underage] and crimes against the public welfare, such as selling altered food and drug products.

### Actus Reus

Perhaps the easiest of the elements to understand is the *actus reus* or the "wrongful deed." It is simply the act that the defendant has committed that has caused harm. Normally the act involves the **commission** [doing something] of an act. Sometimes not performing an act, an **omission,** such as failure to pay your income tax, can also be the act or *actus reus* element of the offense. One of the premises of criminal law is that harm has been done to society, hence the requirement of an act. Thinking about robbing a bank is not normally a crime (however, see the section on inchoate crimes later in this chapter), but actually robbing the bank is. In the latter, harm has been done to society; in the former, no harm has been done.

### Causation

Causation is also an element of every offense. It becomes part of the *actus reus* whenever the crime requires a result, such as **shoplifting** [removing property from a retail store without paying for it]. A prosecutor has two steps to prove causation. First, he or she must show **causation in fact**—the defendant's conduct was the cause of the incident. This test is usually phrased as a question.

> Would this have happened if the defendant had not acted?

Second, **proximate cause** must be shown. Proximate cause is sometimes referred to as the "but for" test. That is, it must be shown that the defendant acted in a continuous sequence of events, unbroken by any **intervening cause** [any other action], that harm resulted, and that without the action by the defendant ("but for"), the result would not have occurred.

### Concurrence

Concurrence simply means that the *actus reus* and *mens rea* must be connected. The results of a crime can occur later. Concurrence doesn't require simultaneous action and intent, but the two must be connected. That is, you can commit murder even though your **victim** [person injured by a criminal act] dies a month later. Courts have created the doctrine of **transferred intent** to handle cases in which intent is present and an act occurs; however, the harm hurts a person other than the intended victim. For example, if Cristo shoots at Mustafa and misses him but hits and kills Thierry, he can still be found guilty of murder. Cristo has used unlawful force against a person, so the courts hold that his unlawful intent (to kill Mustafa) is transferred to his act against a third party (killing Thierry) even though he did not intend to harm the third party.

# Specific Crimes

Criminal law is further divided into broad categories, each having specific crimes associated with the categories: crimes against persons, crimes against property, and **inchoate** [attempted] crimes. Each specific crime, such as theft, has additional elements that must be proven before a defendant can be found guilty.

## *Crimes against Persons*

### Exercise B. Close Reading

1. Carefully read the provision on kidnapping in the MPC.
2. To whom does the *his* refer in the statute?

*Kidnapping*

Model Penal Code §212.1 defines kidnapping as follows:

A person is guilty of kidnapping if he unlawfully removes another from *his* [emphasis added] place of residence or business, or a substantial distance from the vicinity where he is found, or if he unlawfully confines another for a substantial period in a place of isolation, with any of the following purposes:

(a) to hold for ransom or reward, or as a shield or hostage; or

(b) to facilitate commission of any felony or flight thereafter; or

(c) to inflict bodily injury on or to terrorize the victim or another; or

(d) to interfere with the performance of any governmental or political function.

## Exercise C. Case Hypotheticals and Pair Work

1. Working in pairs, review the scenarios that follow and determine if the actor is guilty of kidnapping under the MPC.

2. Pay particular attention to the language of the code itself and be prepared to defend your answer in class.

*Fact Situations*

a. During a bank robbery, one of the robbers holds a gun to the bank president's head while her cohorts are getting the money from the safe. She tells the president he is her "hostage." The robbery takes ten minutes to complete, after which the robbers leave the bank president unharmed.

b. A farmer picks up a mentally ill hitchhiker and takes him to his farm, which is 50 miles from the nearest town. The hitchhiker is told he has to work at the farm until he is able to pay the farmer back for the ride. Because the hitchhiker is mentally ill, he doesn't realize that he can simply walk away from the farm and find another ride to town.

c. A thirteen-year-old girl agrees to go to an out-of-state concert with a sixteen-year-old boy from her high school. They attend the concert without letting her parents know and don't return for three days, during which time her parents have informed the police that their daughter is missing.

d. A father, who was granted the right during a divorce proceeding to see his daughter on the weekends **(visitation rights),** doesn't bring the girl back on Sunday night. He and his daughter have gone to Mexico for two weeks without obtaining prior approval of the mother, who was granted custody by the court.

e. During a divorce proceeding, a mother takes her daughter and flees the state, remaining in hiding with the child because she fears that the father will be granted joint custody even though the mother believes that the father has been abusing the child.

## Exercise D. Case Hypotheticals and Pair Work

Not every state has enacted the MPC as written in the draft code itself. Colorado is one of the states that chose to change the kidnapping statute.

1. Read the Colorado statutes on kidnapping in the first and second degree. Pay close attention to the language of the statutes.

   Colo.Rev.Stat. §18-3-301. First degree kidnapping

   (1) Any person who does any of the following acts with the intent thereby to force the victim or any other person to make any concession or give up anything of value in order to secure a release of a person under the offender's actual or apparent control commits first degree kidnapping:

      (a) Forcibly seizes and carries any person from one place to another; or

      (b) Entices or persuades any person to go from one place to another; or

      (c) Imprisons or forcibly secretes any person. . . .

   Colo.Rev.Stat. §18-3-302. Second degree kidnapping

   (1) Any person who knowingly seizes and carries any person from one place to another, without his consent and without lawful justification, commits second degree kidnapping.

   (2) Any person who takes, entices, or decoys away any child not his own under the age of eighteen years with intent to keep or conceal the child from his parent or guardian or with intent to sell, trade, or barter such child for consideration commits second degree kidnapping. . . .

2. Working in pairs, decide if the answers you reached in Exercise C would be true in Colorado.

Closely related to the crime of kidnapping are the crimes of **false imprisonment** [interfering with the liberty of another] and **interference with custody** [child custody questions]. The *interference with custody* statutes are relatively recent innovations in response to problems that arise in custody hearings as in scenarios *d* and *e* from the exercise on kidnapping. Some state legislatures have thought it best to enact specific child custody provisions rather than rely on kidnapping statutes that may be inappropriate or inadequate.

## Crimes against Property

Common property crimes include **larceny** [taking of property of another with intent to permanently deprive the person of the property], **embezzlement** [fraudulent conversion of the property of another—an accountant takes money belonging to his or her employer for his or her own use], **robbery** [which is larceny with two additional elements—the property must be taken from the victim's person or presence and the taking must be by violence or intimidation], **arson** [malicious burning of the dwelling of another—many modern statutes define arson as including nonresidential buildings], and **burglary**.

### BURGLARY

At common law, burglary was defined as the breaking and entering of a dwelling at night for the purpose of committing a felony. The "breaking" element included entry through use of force, fraud, or threat of force in addition to actually opening a door or window. The "entry" element was defined as the entry of any part of the body or an instrument that was to be used to commit the felony. For example, an "entry" would have included a thief breaking open a window and using a coat hanger to reach a purse on a chair in the house. Even though only the thief's hand and the coat hanger "entered" the room, it was still an entry. Modern statutes have eliminated several of the elements needed at common law:

1. No breaking is required; simple entry is enough.
2. Any time of day suffices.
3. Structures other than dwellings are included.

Model Penal Code §221.1 defines burglary as follows:

> [1] (1) . . . A person is guilty of burglary if he enters a building or occupied structure, or separately secured or occupied portion thereof, with purpose to commit a crime therein, unless the premises are at the time open to the public or the actor is licensed or privileged to enter. [2] It is an affirmative defense to prosecution for burglary that the building or structure was abandoned. [bracketed numbers added]

## Exercise E. Statutory Interpretation

1. Reread Model Penal Code §221.1. We have numbered the sentences for you as [1] and [2].

2. In pairs or groups of three, break the rule down bit by bit to understand its meaning. See Language Activity 9, page 207, for an example.

   a. First write each sentence on the board or a piece of paper. Erase all but the absolute minimum you need to understand the central message of this rule.

   b. When you as a group have agreed on the basis of the sentence, you may go on to the next step.

   c. Clause by clause or even phrase by phrase, add parts back to the sentence in the order of importance.

3. What are the essential elements of burglary under the MPC?

Now, let's look at the burglary statutes from two different states, New Mexico and Alaska, as reported in *State v. Sanchez*, 105 N.M. 619, 735 P.2d 536 (1987)

In New Mexico, the crime of burglary is defined by Section 30-16-3, which reads:

Burglary consists of the unauthorized entry of any vehicle, watercraft, aircraft, dwelling or other structure, movable or immovable, with the intent to commit any felony or theft therein.

A. Any person who, without authorization, enters a dwelling house with intent to commit any felony or theft therein is guilty of a third degree felony.

B. Any person who, without authorization, enters any vehicle, watercraft, aircraft or other structure, movable or immovable, with intent to commit any felony or theft therein is guilty of a fourth degree felony.

In Alaska, burglary is defined under Alaska Stat. §11.46.310(a) (1986), which reads:

A person commits the crime of burglary if the person enters or remains unlawfully in a building with intent to commit a crime in the building.

## Exercise F. Statutory Comparisons

Working on your own, compare the statutes and answer the questions. Then compare your answers with a partner.

1. In what ways do the statutes of New Mexico and Arizona differ from the MPC? From each other? Use the method described in Exercise E if you are having trouble understanding the statutes.

2. Is the Alaska statute more like the MPC or the New Mexico statute? Why?

The New Mexico Court of Appeals explored the differences between the statutes, including legislative history and policy, in order to distinguish two burglary cases in New Mexico from one in Alaska. In the Alaskan case [*Arabie v. State of Alaska*, 699 P.2d 890 (Alaska Ct. App. 1985)], the defendant was **apprehended** [caught] in a walk-in cooler with a case of beer in his hands. The cooler section was not open to the public, but the 24-hour store was open to the public. He was convicted by the trial court but appealed, contending that the statutory elements for burglary were not met. On appeal he argued that because the building was open to the public, the "unauthorized entry" element of the offense had not been proven. The Court of Appeals agreed and reversed the conviction, holding that the "unauthorized entry" requirement under the statute had not been met.

In the New Mexico case, two convictions were consolidated for purposes of appeal. One case involved facts substantially similar to those in *Arabie*. The defendant was found, with the intent to steal, on the loading dock of an auto parts store. In the second case, the defendant entered a hospital office and stole a purse. Both defendants cited *Arabie* and requested that the New Mexico court reverse the convictions because their acts did not fall within the statutory definition of burglary.

## Exercise G. Statutory Interpretation

With a partner, decide on the answers to the following questions. Be prepared to defend your answers orally.

1. Which of the three statutes (MPC, Alaska, and New Mexico) include breaking into a parked car as burglary?

2. Is a person who enters his own house in order to commit a crime guilty of burglary under any of the statutes? Why or why not?

3. Would breaking into an *RV* (recreational vehicle) be burglary under any of the statutes?

4. Look at Alaska's definition of a building:

> Alaska Stat. §11.81.900 (b) (3) Cum.Supp.1986: "[B]uilding," in addition to its usual meaning, includes any propelled vehicle or structure adapted for overnight accommodation of persons or for carrying on business. . . .

Now, how would you answer Question 3?

## Exercise H. Writing

Write your answers to Questions 1 and 2. Then compare answers with a partner.

1. It's not clear whether a backpacking tent is a structure or not. Write two different definitions of *structure.* Write the first version so that it includes backpacking tents, but write the second so that it excludes backpacking tents from structures.

2. Using your first definition of *structure* or one provided by your instructor, decide which of the following would be included:

   a. a large box used by a poor person to sleep in at night

   b. a hammock used by mountain climbers to sleep in at night on a multiday climb

   c. the doorway of a house used by homeless people to sleep in at night

   d. a beach hut built of natural materials on a public beach used regularly by various people

   e. the area under a bridge where homeless people regularly live and sleep

## *Inchoate Offenses*

*Black's Law Dictionary* 505 (3ᵈ pocket ed., 2006) defines inchoate crimes as

> A step toward the commission of another crime, the step in itself being serious enough to merit punishment.

### ATTEMPT

The policy behind the punishment of attempted crimes is to correct or reform persons who represent a danger to society. In other words, it is better to punish someone (with a lighter sentence) who has exhibited criminal intent rather than allow the person to go free and actually succeed in the commission of a crime on a second or third attempt. Four elements are necessary to be convicted of an attempt:

1. an act in furtherance of a criminal intent to commit a crime that remains uncompleted
2. intent to commit the crime
3. apparent ability to commit the crime
4. the legal possibility to commit the crime

Both *mens rea* and *actus reus* are required for conviction of an attempted crime. The state of mind requirement has been stated to be that the defendant must have the specific intent to commit the intended crime. For example, to be convicted of attempted burglary, the defendant must have intended to commit burglary or the *mens rea* element is missing. The *actus reus* element must be satisfied by showing that the defendant has taken a "substantial step" toward completion of the crime that he or she intended to commit [*United States v. Jackson,* 560 F.2d 112 (2d Cir. 1977), *cert. denied,* 434 U.S. 941, 98 S. Ct. 434, 54 L.Ed.2d 301 (1977)].

## SOLICITATION

As with attempt, the specific crime (such as burglary) does not have to be completed to convict a party of solicitation. Solicitation in and of itself is a crime. **Solicitation** is the act of convincing another person to commit a crime. The persuader doesn't have to take part in the crime to be guilty of solicitation. A common example might be the hiring of a thief to steal business records from a competitor. If Bill solicits James to break into Bauxite Corporation and steal the latest profit reports, and James reports the conversation to the police, Bill cannot be charged with burglary, but he can be charged with solicitation. Under the MPC, the solicitor of a crime can also be charged at the same level as the person actually committing the crime if the crime is successful. In this example, if James had stolen the records, both James and Bill could have been charged with burglary.

## *Homicide*

Current homicide law differs greatly from the common law offense of murder because at earliest common law, no degrees of murder were recognized and all murders were punishable by death. Now, however, all states recognize different categories of homicide ranging from the most heinous, murder, to the lesser crime of manslaughter. Murder has further been divided into degrees by state legislatures (first- or second-degree murder), and manslaughter has been divided into voluntary and involuntary manslaughter. Additionally, some state legislatures have created new categories, such as negligent or vehicular homicide.

The most important thing to remember is that homicide is now a statutory offense; therefore, there will be differences from state to state. What is second-degree murder in Massachusetts may be voluntary manslaughter in Tennessee. Again, the MPC provides draft statutes for the states to use when promulgating legislation, but there are differences among the states reflecting state legislative policy.

## MURDER

A **legal term of art** [term with a specific legal meaning] is used to distinguish between murder and manslaughter: *malice aforethought.* You must remember, however, that it is a legal term of art and cannot be explained by use of ordinary dictionary definitions. For example, a woman who kills her terminally ill husband because she cannot bear to see him suffer is guilty of murder, even though it is obvious that no "malice" was intended in the killing. The four states of mind that are said to make up malice aforethought are:

1. intent to kill
2. intent to inflict great bodily injury
3. intent to commit a felony
4. awareness of a high risk of death or serious bodily injury

So the woman had an *intent to kill* and is therefore guilty of at least second-degree murder. In the ordinary meaning of the words, she did not act *maliciously,* but in the legal sense she exhibited *malice aforethought.* Second-degree murder is any homicide with *malice aforethought* that is not specifically first-degree murder.

First-degree murder is considered a more heinous crime than second-degree murder; therefore, an additional element indicating such heinousness is required. Degrees of murder are statutory, and there are substantial differences between states. However, in many states, first-degree murder includes malice aforethought and the additional element of one of the following: (a) deliberation and premeditation (after reflection); (b) a killing committed during the **res gestae** of a felony (the *res gestae* includes all acts in the immediate preparation, actual commission, and immediate escape); or (c) murder by poison, lying in wait, or torture.

Differences in state law include differences in interpretation of premeditation. In some states, no appreciable amount of time is needed for reflection; it can be a matter of minutes. In other states, evidence of reasonably calm consideration is required. In *State v. Bingham,* 40 Wash.App. 553, 699 P.2d 262 (1985), the court refused to accept the inference of premeditation from the fact that it took several minutes to strangle the victim to death. The dissent, however, stated that the defendant, during the minutes it took for death to occur, had ample time to deliberate on what he intended to accomplish.

On the other hand, the Court of Appeals for the District of Columbia in *Bostic v. United States,* 68 App.D.C. 167, 94 F.2d 636 (1937), *cert. denied,* 303 U.S. 635, 58 S. Ct. 523, 82 L.Ed 1095 (1938) stated that the government is not required to show "a lapse of days or hours, or even minutes." The jury must decide if there has been sufficient time for deliberation.

In 1987, the Washington Supreme Court reviewed an appeal by the state of Washington [*State v. Ollens*, 107 Wash. 2d 848, 733 P.2d 984 (1987)] of a **pretrial review** [review of legal issue prior to trial] to determine whether the jury should be allowed to consider whether premeditation was present or not. When the trial court refused to allow the jury to decide on the issue of premeditation, the state appealed.

## Exercise I. Listening

1. Review these facts before listening to a summary of the Ollens judgment. William Tyler, a taxicab driver, was fatally stabbed during a robbery. Lawrence Ollens has been charged with aggravated murder.

| Order of Wounds | Injury Caused | Fatal |
|---|---|---|
| 1 | perforated left lung and heart | not immediately |
| 2 | perforated right lobe of liver and kidney | not immediately |
| 3 | penetrated right lobe of liver | not immediately |
| 4 | penetrated right thigh | no |
| 5 | slashed throat | potentially |

The struggle between Tyler and Ollens was estimated to have lasted approximately two to three minutes after Tyler's neck was slashed. Numerous defensive wounds were also noticed by the county **medical examiner** [doctor who examines bodies of people suspected of dying under suspicious circumstances], indicating that there had been a struggle.

2. Now listen to the extract that summarizes the judgment in *State v. Ollens.* Then answer the questions.

   a. What was the disposition of the case?

   b. What arguments were made by the state?

   c. What arguments were made by Ollens?

   d. What reasoning does the court use to find *Bingham* distinguishable from *Ollens?*

MANSLAUGHTER

Most states distinguish between voluntary and involuntary manslaughter. Others add additional degrees of manslaughter such as negligent or vehicular manslaughter. A homicide that would otherwise be second-degree murder may be reduced to voluntary manslaughter if it was committed in response to adequate provocation, sometimes referred to as killing in the "heat of passion." In general, four requirements must be met.

1. The provocation must be reasonable, that is, judged by the standard of the reaction of an objective, reasonable person, not a subjective standard that relates to the actor.
2. The provocation must be what actually caused the actor to kill.
3. The interval between the provocation and the killing must be short (a reasonable person would not have had time to "cool off").
4. There must have been no actual cooling off between the provocation and the killing.

### Exercise J. Discussion

Think about these questions for two minutes. Then discuss your answers as a class.

> Should the fourth factor listed above be judged by an objective or a subjective standard? How can you tell if someone has cooled off?

Involuntary manslaughter is an unintended killing if it is caused by reckless (or negligent in some jurisdictions) conduct or if it is caused by the commission of an act not amounting to a felony.

In *State v. Williams*, 4 Wash. App. 908, 484 P.2d 1167 (1971), an infant died because his parents didn't obtain medical care in time to save the child. The parents were charged with involuntary manslaughter. The court specifically found that the parents loved their child and had no intention of harming him. However, under the Washington statute, simple negligence was enough to convict the defendants. The court stated:

On the question of the quality or seriousness of breach of the duty, at common law, in the case of involuntary manslaughter, the breach had to amount to more than mere ordinary or simple negligence—gross negligence was essential [citations omitted]. In Washington, however RCW 9.48.060 (since amended by Laws of 1970, ch. 49, s. 2) and RCW 9.48.150 supersede both voluntary and involuntary manslaughter as those crimes were defined at common law. Under these statutes the crime is deemed committed even though the death of the victim is the proximate result of only simple or ordinary negligence [citations omitted].

## Exercise K. Writing a Memorandum

In pairs, prepare a memorandum. See Part 2, Legal Memoranda (page 194), and Part 2, Active and Passive Voice (page 234), before writing the memorandum.

1. You are working in the district attorney's office in Bangor, Maine. You have recently been informed of a case involving a death in a hunting accident (based on an actual case). As the prosecuting attorney, you have to decide if the **perpetrator** [person accused of committing a crime] has indeed committed a crime, what the crime is, and if you should prosecute.

2. Write a memorandum for the file (informal but informative) discussing your options and your decision.

3. The facts are as follows.

> David Roth, 45, went deer hunting in the Maine woods with a friend. He fired at what he thought was a deer but instead killed Marjorie Weston, who was standing in her backyard. Ms. Weston was wearing white mittens and did not have on an orange blaze jacket, which hunters are required to wear.
>
> Mr. Roth was hunting in a lawful area and alleges that he shot at a deer and did not know that a house was in the area. He is a scoutmaster, father, husband, and hard worker. No traces of deer have been found in the area.

4. The following statute will be of use in your determination. The statute was in effect at the time of the incident but has since been repealed.

> Me. Rev. Stat. Ann. 17A §203 (1964)
>
> A person is guilty of manslaughter if he . . . recklessly, or with criminal negligence, causes the death of another human being.

# Defenses to Crimes

If the prosecutor establishes a *prima facie* case [provides enough proof on the elements of the crime for the case to be sent to a jury for deliberations] of wrongdoing, then the defendant may offer a defense to the crime, such as self-defense or insanity, that would relieve the defendant of legal responsibility for the crime with which he or she has been charged even if the defendant actually committed the act.

## Self-Defense

Self-defense and its related defenses (e.g., defense of others or defense of property) are only applicable when crimes against persons are involved (murder, kidnapping, robbery, etc.). In general, a person may use whatever reasonable force is necessary to protect him- or herself, short of deadly force. **Deadly force** [that likely to kill or cause serious bodily injury] may generally only be used where it appears to be reasonably necessary in three instances:

1. to prevent immediate death or serious injury
2. to prevent the commission of a felony
3. to catch a felon

The "retreat rule" of the MPC has been adopted by a number of states and says that if it is possible to run away safely, that should be done rather than using deadly force. The policy justification is that it makes more sense to run rather than to take a life. There are, of course, limitations to the necessity to retreat.

1. A person only has to retreat if he or she would otherwise be forced to use deadly force.
2. The person must know that he or she can retreat safely.
3. It doesn't normally apply to the defense of one's own home.

There are other defenses that are applicable to all crimes, including insanity, necessity, duress, and entrapment.

## *Insanity*

A defendant may be found not guilty of a crime if, at the time the defendant committed the crime, he or she was insane. In all criminal trials, there is a general presumption of sanity; however, a defendant may raise the defense if appropriate. States differ as to procedural requirements for standards and burden of proof at trial. Some states require that the prosecution prove sanity of the defendant beyond a reasonable doubt, whereas others require that the defendant convince the jury that he or she was insane by a preponderance of the evidence. There are also differing methods for determining insanity that vary from state to state.

The three major attempts to define insanity are the M'Naghten test, the irresistible impulse test, and the Durham test. The traditional method is the M'Naghten test, which requires that the accused must show that due to his or her mental illness, the defendant either

1. did not know the nature and quality of the act, or
2. did not know whether the act was right or wrong.

Courts have not always defined the word *know* for juries but have simply left it to the jury to decide what *know* means. This test has been criticized in modern times because someone who is mentally ill might know that what he or she is doing is wrong but may not be able to resist the act. This led to the irresistible impulse test.

The focus with the irresistible impulse test is not the defendant's knowledge of whether an act is right or wrong but whether the defendant can maintain self-control. States that permit the use of this test use both the irresistible impulse and M'Naghten test when instructing the jury on the insanity defense. Any of the three factors is a complete defense (the perpetrator cannot be convicted of the crime) to the commission of the crime for which the defendant has been charged.

The final major attempt at defining insanity was the Durham or product test, which was first used by a court in *Durham v. United States,* 94 U.S.App.D.C. 228, 214 F.2d 862 (1954) and has since been abandoned as being too broad. It rejected both the M'Naghten test and the irresistible impulse tests as too narrow and restrictive. A defendant could be acquitted by reason of insanity if the defendant could show that the crime was the product of a mental illness.

### Exercise L. System Comparisons and Discussion

As a class discuss the answers to the questions.

1. Is insanity a defense in your country?
2. Which of the tests is more like the test used to determine insanity in your country? How does it differ?

## *Necessity*

If an act is committed that is illegal because it is necessary to prevent a greater harm, then the defense of necessity is applicable. For instance, if you tie your boat to a dock in a storm in order to prevent loss of life or property, you might be guilty of the offense of trespass. However, your defense to a trespass action is necessity. It was necessary for you to dock there in order to prevent a greater harm (the loss of human life or property) from occurring.

## *Duress*

Duress is similar to the defense of necessity except it does not involve an act of nature but an act of a person. If you are threatened and forced by another person to commit a crime (the *actus reus* only), then you cannot be held criminally liable for the commission of the crime. Although there is not much case law in this area, courts have held that the person under duress must believe that death or great bodily harm is imminent and the submission to coercion must be reasonable. Courts have generally held that the defense of duress does not apply to intentional killings.

## *Entrapment*

Entrapment involves public officers inducing someone to commit a crime that the person would not normally have considered committing with the intent of later prosecuting the person for that crime. The policy behind the use of entrapment as a defense is to keep government officials from inventing crimes. There are two approaches to the entrapment defense. The first is the traditional (subjective) approach, which examines the defendant's character and predisposition to commit the crime. This approach is still followed in the majority of states. The modern (objective) approach examines the behavior of the police rather than the predisposition of the defendant. The modern approach finds that entrapment occurs when the police activity was reasonably likely to have convinced a reasonable but unpredisposed person to commit the crime.

### Exercise M. Case Hypotheticals and Discussion

In pairs, decide which of the defenses might be applicable. Be prepared to defend your answers orally.

1. An undercover police officer convinces a reformed drug dealer to return to drug dealing by offering the former drug dealer a large sum of money for drugs.

2. An inmate just released from the psychiatric hospital where she was under treatment for schizophrenia commits a bank robbery after voices

tell her that it is necessary for her to rob the bank because the people working there are evil and need to be punished. At the time she commits the bank robbery, she knows that it is illegal.

3. A minor begins to work for a prostitution ring (remember, prostitution is legal only in a few counties in one state—Nevada—in the United States) after being told that if she does not, she will be severely beaten, and that if she tells anyone about the conversation or threat, she will be killed.

4. John Jones threatens to shoot Mrs. Myers if she does not help him rob a bank. Mrs. Myers runs away from Mr. Jones and enters a stranger's house and telephones the police.

5. Martin stabs Jacob during a barroom brawl that Jacob started by hitting Martin after he saw Martin talking to his wife. Martin claims that Jacob had a gun, and he was afraid that Jacob was going to use it to kill him.

## Criminal Law and Moral Values

The imposition of penalties in criminal proceedings is society's way of making sure that the values it considers important are followed. That is why, from time to time, criminal law changes, usually through statutory enactments but also through judicial decisions. For example, abortion was illegal in the United States for many years and punishable under criminal law, but after the Supreme Court case *Roe v. Wade*, 410 U.S. 113, 93 S. Ct. 705, 35 L.Ed.2d 147 (1973), which invalidated a state abortion statute, that is no longer true.

A controversy that has not yet been resolved is the "right to die." Do terminally ill patients have the right to choose to die? If they so choose, does someone have the right to assist them if they are unable to commit suicide on their own? Dr. Jack Kevorkian has been tried for murder for assisting in suicide and in 1999 was found guilty of second-degree homicide in Michigan. He was sentenced to serve a 10–25 year sentence and was paroled in June 2007. Although the laws regarding assisted suicide are still in flux, his act is not yet legislatively acceptable. In 1997, the U.S. Supreme Court upheld the validity of legislation in Washington that makes it a crime for a doctor to give lethal drugs to patients who want to end their lives [*Washington v. Glucksberg*, 521 U.S. 702, 117 S. Ct. 2258, 138 L.Ed.2d 772 (1997)]. According to the Supreme Court, there is no constitutional guarantee of the right to assisted suicide, but the justices also made it clear that the question is one for the state legislatures to decide. The legislatures have the power to ban doctor-assisted suicide or to legalize the practice. The decision is one that no doubt will be based on the moral values of the **constituency** [voters].

# The Cultural Defense

The conformation of criminal law to societal values is one reason why criminal law differs from state to state and country to country. Cultures have different concepts of what is right and wrong as a reflection of their moral values.

Courts in the United States have begun to take notice of the idea of differing moral values between cultures. In general, an immigrant or a visitor to the United States is required to conform to the laws of the United States. However, in some instances, prosecutors either reduce the charge that is brought against a defendant or ask for lighter sentences after conviction in response to recognition of different cultural values.

For example, in the *Columbia Law Review* (June 1996) Doriane Lambelet Coleman reports on a murder case involving a Chinese immigrant. In 1989 Dong Lu Chen, after bludgeoning his wife to death with a hammer after learning she had been unfaithful, was convicted of second-degree manslaughter instead of first-degree murder. Moreover, he was sentenced to only five years probation after the judge accepted a cultural defense. An expert on Chinese culture testified that it is appropriate in China for a husband to publicly announce that he intends to kill an unfaithful wife, and the community then acts to stop him. Unfortunately, in this case, the community, not understanding the nature of the threat, did not act, and the wife was killed.

Another case involving the use of the cultural defense involved Vietnamese refugees in Connecticut. Vietnamese refugee Binh Gia Pham set himself afire to protest policies of the Vietnamese government. His friends who had assisted in and videotaped the suicide were charged with second-degree manslaughter, a charge with a maximum penalty of ten years in prison. During the sentencing phase, it would appear that the judge took cultural factors into account because he sentenced the five friends to probation after determining that they had no idea that they had done anything wrong and that Binh Gia Pham would have committed suicide with or without the assistance of his friends.

## Exercise N. System Comparisons and Discussion

1. In groups of three, discuss the questions that follow. Be prepared to defend your answers orally during class discussion.

2. In the cases of Chen and Bing Gia Pham, do you find the use of the cultural defense more acceptable in one of the cases? If so, why? If not, why not?

3. Are subjective factors, such as lack of a prior criminal record, ever used in your system for sentencing factors? List three examples.

4. Are cultural factors less valid than some of the examples you listed?

## Exercise O. Role Play

1. Read the scenario, which is similar to that of the Binh Gia Pham case.

   A monk from Shangra La (an imaginary country) **immolates** [setting oneself afire] himself with the assistance of two friends in Hartford, Connecticut, in protest of current policies in Shangra La. His two friends videotape the incident, which they then provide to a news agency in Hartford. After giving the videotape to the news agency, they report the incident to the city police. The two friends were aware of the penalty for assisted suicide in Connecticut because of the publicity that the Binh Gia Pham trial received. Indeed, the two friends wrote about the case for the newsletter of the Shangra La community in the United States. They have no prior record and have been model citizens since their arrival in the United States three years ago. The state attorney decides to prosecute, and the trial has reached the **closing argument** [summation of the case] stage.

2. Divide into teams. One team should prepare the closing argument for the prosecution and the other team the closing argument for the defense. You may need to add additional facts. If so, make sure that your instructor is aware of the information you are adding.

   This information about closing arguments may help in your preparation.

   A closing argument is an attorney's chance to tell the entire story. Until this point in a trial, the judge or jury has only heard the story in bits and pieces from the witnesses and evidence presented at trial. Now the attorneys get to draw it all together into a coherent whole, applying facts to law. The attorneys have to point out vital details, weave the witnesses' stories together, and explain connections that are significant for their case and the law that applies.

   The rules about what an attorney may or may not say are not as stringent as those for **opening statements** [attorneys' introduction of the case to the court]. You can argue and draw conclusions, but your argument needs to be logical and well organized. Your job is to help the judge or the jury believe your evidence and not that of your opponent. Successful trial attorneys approach the entire trial with a "theory" of the case in mind. This theory of the case is designed to show the judge and jury why a particular verdict is legally and morally necessary. Everything that is done in a trial is done with this theory in mind. So, in your closing argument, think about the theory you want to present to the judge or jury and prepare accordingly.

3. Choose one of the group members to present your group's argument. Prosecution always begins, followed by the defense. Most courts allow a short amount of time for **rebuttal** after both closing arguments have been presented [response to the closing argument of the opposing side]. In this case, closing statements should be limited to ten minutes for each side, with five minutes of rebuttal time.

# *Civil Procedure*

## Discovering Connections

Civil procedure deals with the rules, methods, and practice used in taking a civil (as opposed to criminal) case or action through the courts. Each court system has its own civil procedure. The United States has separate court systems for each state and the federal government. This means there are more than 51 different court systems in the United States even if we don't take into account special courts such as the U.S. Claims Court. The state systems and the federal system are separate but related.

### ACTIVITY

1. Fill in the chart on page 82 with these terms commonly used in the United States to refer to the various courts in both the federal and state systems.

> appellate court
> Appellate Divisions (NY)
> Court of Appeals (NY)
> court of first instance
> first appellate court
> highest appellate court
> supreme court (not NY)
> Supreme Court (NY)
> trial court
> U.S. Courts of Appeal
> U.S. District Court
> U.S. Supreme Court

| Lowest Court | Mid-Level Court | Highest Court |
|---|---|---|
|  |  |  |
|  |  |  |
|  |  |  |
|  |  |  |

2. Two attorneys are discussing the recent progress of a lawsuit through the court system. Listen to the conversation, and see if you can tell whether the suit was filed in state or federal court.

## Legal Listening

## Essential Terms

**jurisdiction:** the power of a court to hear and decide a case

    **original:** the first court to hear the case; decides facts and law

    **appellate:** a court that hears a case if a party is unsatisfied with the original decision

    **subject matter:** power over the particular issue in the case

    **concurrent:** Both state and federal courts have original jurisdiction to hear the case.

    **exclusive:** Either the federal or state court has sole power to hear the case.

    **personal:** *in personam*—power over the parties in the case

    *in rem:* power over property

    *quasi in rem:* primarily power over property rights with elements of personal rights also

**venue:** the geographic location of the actual trial of the case

**pleadings:** the statements filed in court that detail plaintiff's and defendant's cases

    **complaint:** the statement filed by the plaintiff stating the cause of action

**answer:** the response filed by the defendant listing defenses to the complaint

**demurrer:** a statement by the defendant attacking the legal sufficiency of the plaintiff's complaint [in most jurisdictions now called a motion to dismiss]

**discovery:** the process of obtaining information about the other party's case prior to the actual trial

## Putting the Terms to Use

Listen to the following conversation between a man and his lawyer. After you hear the recorded conversation, you will be given ten questions to answer.

# Legal Thumbnail

# Jurisdiction

### *Subject Matter Jurisdiction*

Attorneys must be able to determine which court has the power to decide the matter that their clients have entrusted to them. In other words, the first decision an attorney must make prior to filing a complaint is to decide which court has subject matter jurisdiction. This might simply refer to the subject matter of the case, such as torts or contracts. However, subject matter jurisdiction also relates to the question of exclusive or concurrent jurisdiction of state and federal courts.

In **diversity of citizenship** [citizens of different states or even another country] cases, either a state court or the federal court has the power to hear the case. The table that follows provides a few examples of the subject matter jurisdiction of state and federal courts.

| Jurisdiction | | |
|---|---|---|
| **Exclusive Federal** | **Concurrent (federal and state)** | **Exclusive State** |
| bankruptcy | federal questions* | probate |
| patents and copyright | diversity of citizenship** | divorce |
| suits against the United States | | |

\* "The district courts shall have original jurisdiction of all civil actions under the Constitution, laws, or treaties of the United States." 28 U.S.C. §1331.

\** "The district courts shall have original jurisdiction of all civil actions where the matter in controversy exceeds the sum or value of $75,000, . . . and is between—
   (1) citizens of different States;
   (2) citizens of a State and citizens or subjects of a foreign state; . . ."
28 U.S.C. §1332.

## Exercise A. Case Hypotheticals and Pair Work

Working in pairs, read the scenarios, and decide which courts would have subject matter jurisdiction over your case.

1. Your client, Sue Little, feels that portions of her book were used in a television program without the producers of the program first obtaining her permission to use the material.

2. Mr. Marvin, a resident of Ohio, and your client, Ms. Ching, a resident of Massachusetts, were involved in an automobile accident in Ohio. Mr. Marvin is suing Ms. Ching for $76,000.

3. Mr. Forster wants to divorce his wife, Margaret Forster-Simms. Ms. Forster-Simms is your client. Both parties are residents of Illinois.

4. Your client is **executor** [administrator] of the estate of her mother, who has just died. The mother died in a nursing home in Olympia, Washington. Your client is a resident of Seattle, Washington.

5. Mr. Batson, a resident of Massachusetts, has been injured by a product manufactured by your client's company, which is incorporated and has its principal place of business in Munich, Germany.

Let's follow the attorneys in an actual case as they make decisions regarding jurisdiction. The facts of the case of *Bybee v. Oper der Standt* [sic] *Bonn*, 899 F.Supp.1217 (S.D.N.Y. 1995) are as follows.

Bybee is an opera singer residing in New York City. She became acquainted with defendants Bonn Opera Company and its "Intendant"— General Manager—del Monaco in March 1991 when she auditioned in New York for a position with that opera company. Del Monaco conducted the audition....Bybee alleges that she was subsequently offered a position by del Monaco to perform for the Bonn Opera Company in Germany. [Bybee's husband was also offered a position with the opera company, which he turned down.] Bybee claims that the defendants refused to honor her contract as a result of her husband's decision....

## Exercise B. Reading for Details

1. Answer the questions.

   a. Where does the plaintiff reside?

   b. Where do the defendants reside? A corporation is considered a resident of the state in which it is incorporated or where it has its principal place of business.

   c. What legal theory is the case based on? Torts? Contracts? Products liability?

2. Does the federal district court in the New York area have subject matter jurisdiction? On what basis? If you need more information, what is it?

3. Does the New York Supreme Court (the name of trial courts in New York State) have subject matter jurisdiction? On what basis?

In the *Bybee* case, an additional complication arose because defendants (the Opera Company) claim that they are immune from subject matter jurisdiction because under the Foreign Sovereign Immunities Act (FSIA) **instrumentalities** [agencies] of a foreign state are not subject to U.S. jurisdiction unless they fall within one of the exceptions listed in the FSIA (28 U.S.C. §§1602–11).

## Exercise C. Pair Work and Oral Presentations

1. Read the excerpts from the United States Code that form part of the FSIA.

   ### 28 U.S.C. §1603. Definitions

   (a) A "foreign state", . . . , includes a political subdivision of a foreign state or an agency or instrumentality of a foreign state as defined in subsection (b).

   (b) An "agency or instrumentality of a foreign state" means any entity—

      (1) which is a separate legal person, corporate or otherwise, and

      (2) which is an organ of a foreign state or political subdivision thereof, or a majority of whose shares or other ownership interest is owned by a foreign state or political subdivision thereof, and . . . ,

(3) (d) A "commercial activity" means either a regular course of commercial conduct or a particular commercial transaction or act. The commercial character of an activity shall be determined by reference to the nature of the course of conduct or particular transaction or act, rather than by reference to its purpose.

(c) . . .

(d) . . .

(e) A "commercial activity carried on in the United States by a foreign state" means commercial activity carried on by such state and having substantial contact with the United States.

### 28 U.S.C. §1604. Immunity of a foreign state from jurisdiction

Subject to existing international agreements to which the United States is a party at the time of enactment of this Act a foreign state shall be immune from the jurisdiction of the courts of the United States and of the States except as provided in sections 1605 to 1607 of this chapter.

### 28 U.S.C. §1605. General exceptions to the jurisdictional immunity of a foreign state

(a) A foreign state shall not be immune from the jurisdiction of courts of the United States or of the States in any case—

(1) . . . ;

(2) in which the action is based upon a commercial activity carried on in the United States by the foreign state; or upon an act performed in the United States in connection with a commercial activity of the foreign state elsewhere; or upon an act outside the territory of the United States in connection with a commercial activity of the foreign state elsewhere; or upon an act outside the territory of the United States in connection with a commercial activity of the foreign state elsewhere and that act causes a direct effect in the United States.

2. In pairs, decide whether the court should grant the defendants' motion to dismiss the action due to lack of subject matter jurisdiction. Which provisions of the FSIA, if any, will help the judge in making the decision? Questions to consider that may help you in your decision are the following:

a. Is the Bonn Opera Company an instrumentality of the state?

b. Did it carry on commercial activities in the United States?

3. Present your decision orally to the class.

## Exercise D. Listening

1. Listen to the judge reading her decision on the subject matter jurisdiction issue in the *Bybee* case. As you listen, circle the provisions the court used to make its decision on the defendant's motion to dismiss the action due to lack of subject matter jurisdiction.

   **FSIA provisions:**
   28 U.S.C. §1603 (a)   (b) (1) (2) (3)   (c)   (d)   (e)

   28 U.S.C. §1604

   28 U.S.C. §1605 (a) (1) (2)

   **Motion:**          Granted          Denied

2. Does the decision of the court match your decision? Did the court use the same provisions you used when making your decision?

### *Personal Jurisdiction*

The next question that must be decided by attorneys when choosing where to file a complaint is the issue of personal jurisdiction.

Does the court have the power to decide a case involving this particular defendant? This question is of major importance in American law. Note that the question asks about the defendant, who is the important party as far as personal jurisdiction is concerned. The plaintiff, by filing the complaint, has submitted to the jurisdiction of the court. There is a two-prong test used by a court to determine if it has personal jurisdiction over the defendant:

due process + a long-arm statute = personal jurisdiction

DUE PROCESS
Section one of the Fourteenth Amendment to the U.S. Constitution requires due process: ". . . nor shall any State deprive any person of life, liberty, or property, without due process of law; . . ." The U.S. Supreme Court in *International Shoe Co. v. State of Washington,* 326 U.S. 310, 66 S. Ct. 154, 90 L.Ed. 95 (1945) clearly set forth the rules relating to due process for personal jurisdiction purposes. The defendant must have "minimum contacts" with the state in order to satisfy the traditional notions of "fair play and substantial justice."

Let's see how this was defined in *International Shoe*. The state of Washington, in a state court, attempted to collect unemployment contributions from International Shoe Company for commissions paid to sales agents who lived and made sales in Washington. International Shoe contended that it did not have a sufficient presence in the state and, therefore, the state court could not exercise personal jurisdiction over it.

International Shoe stated that

1. it had no office in Washington,
2. no actual sales were completed there though it did employ eleven to thirteen sales representatives in the state, and
3. no stock was maintained in the state.

Therefore, suing International Shoe in the state of Washington constituted a violation of due process.

The Washington Supreme Court held for the state; International Shoe appealed to the U.S. Supreme Court, which held in part as follows.

> To the extent that a corporation exercises the privilege of conducting activities within a state, it enjoys the benefits and protection of the laws of that state. The exercise of that privilege may give rise to obligations; and, so far as those obligations arise out of or are connected with the activities within the state, a procedure which requires the corporation to respond to suit brought to enforce them can, in most instances, hardly be said to be undue.

The U.S. Supreme Court went on to state that the activities of International Shoe within the state of Washington were "systematic and continuous" and that International Shoe had sufficient ties with the state. Additionally, the Court held that the **forum** [court] must be a fair one in which the defendant will have the full opportunity to be heard; a condition that was also met in this particular case.

### LONG-ARM STATUTE

A long-arm statute is codified law that permits state or federal courts to exercise personal jurisdiction over nonresident defendants. The essential requirement in American law, that a defendant be properly notified of an action that has been filed against him or her, presented a problem. Normally, a **process server** [a person appointed by the court to deliver court materials] is sent by the court to the defendant's address with the appropriate court documents. This is known as **service of process.** Service of process outside a state's boundaries can be an expensive process, so various statutes have been enacted to resolve the service of process requirement. Of course, the requirements vary from state to state.

## Exercise E. Information Gap

An incomplete summons form similar to those used in many courts in the United States when requesting a response or answer to a complaint follows. In order to complete the form, you will have to work with a partner to gather the additional information. Partner A should use the form on this page. Partner B has the additional information on the Part B form as Text 3 in the Student Resources section (page 280). Working together, fully complete the summons without showing each other the information on your forms.

**Part A**

---

### SUMMONS

Civil No. __6547/2006__

IN THE ___District Court of Provo___ (name of court)

_____ (county)　　STATE OF _____

_____
Petitioner/Plaintiff

vs.

___Hamilton Jacobsen, CEO, Software Systems, Inc.___
Respondent/Defendant

THE STATE OF UTAH TO THE RESPONDENT:

_Mr. Jacobsen_____ (respondent)

You are hereby summoned and required to file an Answer to the attached Complaint for _breach of contract_____ on file with the Clerk of the above entitled Court at:

_____

_____

_Provo, UT_____ (court address)

and to serve upon, or mail to Petitioner's/Plaintiff's attorney, at

_____

_1023 West Court St._____

_____ (attorney's address)

a copy of said Answer, within 20 days if you are served in the State of Utah or within 30 days if you are served outside the State of Utah, after service of this Summons upon you. If you fail to do so, judgment by default will be taken against you for the relief demanded in said Complaint, which has been filed with the Clerk of the above entitled Court and a copy of which is hereto annexed and herewith served upon you.

READ THESE PAPERS CAREFULLY. These papers mean that you are being sued for failure to meet the terms of your agreement with _____ to develop a new _____ for her import business. The system was due _____ ago and is not yet operable. (brief case description).

_Rose Connors_____　　DATED: _____
Attorney for Petitioner/Plaintiff
_987 W. Court Ave._____ (street address)
_Provo_____ (city) _UT_____ (state) _____ (zip)

---

The important question of personal jurisdiction is even more complicated. Perhaps the most difficult of the factors is the determination of whether or not the **minimum contacts** test has been met. It would appear that the courts now use a two-prong test:

purposeful contacts + balancing test = minimum contacts

Purposeful contacts can basically be defined to mean that if the defendants knew or should have known that their activities might give rise to lawsuits within the forum state, then purposeful contacts have been established.

Additionally, a court must balance factors to determine if "fair play and substantial justice" will be met if a defendant is required to appear before it. A Colorado appellate court, *Trans-Continent v. A Little Bit of Sweden,* 658 P.2d 271 (Colo.App. 1982), citing *World-Wide Volkswagen Corp v. Woodson,* 444 U.S. 286, 100 S. Ct. 559, 62 L.Ed.2d 490 (1980) set forth the balancing factors.

The test, however variously stated, seeks to balance the burden on the defendant with the forum state's interest in obtaining convenient and effective relief and the interstate judicial system's interest in obtaining the most efficient resolution of controversies.

## Exercise F. Using the Casebook

Expert legal readers use the headings in a casebook to help them understand what they should look for in a case. In an LL.M. program, students need to learn to read as experts. By using the headings, readers begin with an understanding of what the author of the casebook uses the cases to explain. Readers then do not have to struggle to decide on the specific topic for a case, but can read the case looking for information pertaining to the specific topic.

Look at the table of contents from a casebook on Civil Procedure. Then answer the following questions.

1. What chapter and section will most likely include the *International Shoe* case?

2. Where is information on how people or corporations are made aware of a pending lawsuit?

3. What chapter contains information on what court has the jurisdiction to hear the content of a case?

4. A U.S. Supreme Court case clarifies the minimum contacts test as compared to territorial restrictions. Where would you most likely find this case in the book?

5. Where would you find an explanation of exercise of jurisdiction over people or corporations located in another state?

## Exercise G. Statutory Interpretation

Read the following scenario.

> Shane Cerny, a resident of Montana, is driving his brand-new car 10 mph over the speed limit on a two-lane street in Bucksnort, Tennessee. Ashley Monterra, coming from the opposite direction, is driving at the speed limit of 35 mph. Shane turns to look at the beautiful sunset over the rolling hills and crosses the center lane, crashing into the side of Monterra's pickup truck. Monterra dislocates her shoulder and breaks a leg in the crash. She later sues Cerny in a Tennessee state court for damages in excess of $100,000. Tennessee's long-arm statutes for this action, Tenn. Code Ann. §§20-2-224 and 20-2-223 (1997), read as follows.

> ### §20-2-224 Service outside the state.
>
> When the exercise of personal jurisdiction is authorized by §§20-2-221–20-2-225, service may be made outside this state in the manner provided by the Tennessee Rules of Civil Procedure or as otherwise provided by law.

> ### §20-2-223 Personal jurisdiction based on conduct.
>
> (a) A court may exercise personal jurisdiction over a person, who acts directly or indirectly, as to a claim for relief arising from the person's:
>
> (1) Transacting any business in this state;
>
> (2) Contracting to supply services or things in this state;
>
> (3) Causing tortious injury by an act or omission in this state; . . .
>
> (b) When jurisdiction over a person is based solely upon this section, only a claim for relief arising from acts enumerated in this section may be asserted against that person.

1. Reviewing the two-prong minimum contacts test for torts, determine in writing if the Tennessee state court would have personal jurisdiction over Cerny.

2. Does the Tennessee state court have subject matter jurisdiction?

3. Write a brief email message to your client, Mr. Cerny, explaining the jurisdictional issues in Tennessee and their impact on him.

The growth in use of computers and contracting via the Internet creates an added dimension to the questions of personal jurisdiction. Courts in recent cases have decided personal jurisdiction issues using the standard measure of minimum contacts, but as more cases arise involving personal jurisdiction and contracts via the Internet, new laws may develop.

In *Compuserve v. Patterson,* 89 F.3d 1257 (6th Cir. 1996), the court held that contacts that were primarily electronic were sufficient to give a court personal jurisdiction over a person doing business online. Patterson, a Texas attorney who entered into a distribution agreement with Compuserve, which does business in Ohio, was sued in Ohio by Compuserve. Patterson had filled out the standard distribution agreement in Texas and transmitted it electronically to Compuserve in Ohio.

The agreement stated that it was entered into in Ohio and that Ohio law governed the contract. A dispute between the parties arose after Compuserve began distributing a product similar to Patterson's. In a letter to Compuserve, Patterson demanded $100,000 in damages from Compuserve, whereupon Compuserve filed an action in Ohio seeking a **declaratory judgment** [judgment of the court on an issue of law without an actual order for enforcement of the judgment] that its product did not infringe upon that of Patterson. Patterson moved to dismiss the action for lack of personal jurisdiction. The trial court found in Patterson's favor, but the Court of Appeals for the Sixth Circuit reversed after finding that the defendant had met the tests that the court set forth for personal jurisdiction.

First, the defendant must purposefully avail himself of the privilege of acting in the forum state or causing a consequence in the forum state. Second, the cause of action must arise from the defendant's activities there. Finally, the acts of the defendant or consequences caused by the defendant must have a substantial enough connection with the forum to make the exercise of jurisdiction over the defendant reasonable.

The court found that the minimum contacts test had been met: purposeful contacts and balancing factors.

## Exercise H. Reading for Details

1. Who was the plaintiff in the Ohio action?
2. Why did Patterson ask the trial court to dismiss the case?
3. Who appealed the trial court's decision?
4. Patterson lived in Texas; what gave Ohio personal jurisdiction over him?
5. Why was Patterson demanding damages from Compuserve?

## *Venue*

In contrast to jurisdiction, which relates solely to the power of the court to hear and decide a case, venue concerns the physical, geographical location of the hearing. A court can have jurisdiction and then decide that the venue is improper. In deciding whether venue is appropriate or not, courts normally consider two primary factors:

1. litigant or witness convenience
2. the availability of an impartial jury

Venue, while important, is not as important as the jurisdictional question. A judgment can be declared invalid if jurisdiction is improper; however, if venue was improper but jurisdiction correct, the judgment will stand. If the defense attorney objects to venue (for instance because he or she feels that the jury will not be impartial), the attorney must make the objection at the beginning of the action or venue will be deemed waived.

There have been several criminal trials in the news in the 1990s that involved questions of venue. Usually, the defendant(s) felt that an impartial jury would not be available in the county/state where the action was filed. For example, the defense attorneys for the four police officers accused of beating motorist Rodney King requested a change of venue, which was granted, because the attorneys felt that the officers would not receive a fair trial in Los Angeles County. Also, for the same reasons, the venue in the Timothy McVeigh Oklahoma City bombing (in Oklahoma) was changed to Denver (in Colorado) in a search for an impartial jury.

There has been some criticism of venue issues in recent years. With expanded media capabilities from radio to television news coverage and the Internet, it is difficult to find jury members in any part of the United States who haven't had prior exposure to information on the case in some form or another.

*Fact Situation*

Marya Callais, a citizen of Tennessee, was walking near a busy street in Nashville, Tennessee, one day when a large concrete block fell off a passing truck and hit her, resulting in numerous injuries to Ms. Callais. In addition to incurring pain and suffering and medical expenses, she could not work for more than a year. She wants to sue the trucking firm for $300,000 in damages. The firm's headquarters are in Oklahoma, although the firm does business in Tennessee. In which courts can Marya bring suit? A Tennessee state court, an Oklahoma state court, a federal court in the Sixth Circuit (Tennessee), or a federal court in the Tenth Circuit (Oklahoma)?

# Parties and Pleadings

## *Parties/Claims*

The simplest form of lawsuit has two parties and only one claim is involved. The party bringing a civil action is the plaintiff, and the party against whom the action is brought is the defendant. On appeal, the party appealing an action is the appellant or petitioner, and the party answering the appeal (the winning party in the lower court) is the appellee or respondent.

As you have also learned, law is not that simple. More than one party can be injured, and those injured parties can join together to sue the defendant. There can also be more than one defendant. The defendant can also have a claim against the plaintiff. **Joinder rules** have been established that set out the procedures and rules for the joining of parties or claims in an action. There can even be an entire group of people who have been affected by an action.

When parties are joined in an action, they are called either **co-plaintiffs** or **co-defendants,** which simply means that more than one party is involved on either side of the action. For example, if Pekka Lukonen and Juha Arnheim are injured in an automobile accident with Jason Denbreeijen, the injured parties can be joined; Pekka and Juha would then be co-plaintiffs. If three cars were involved in the accident, and Pekka and Juha sue Jason and the driver of the third car, Marushka Valentova, then Jason and Marushka would be co-defendants.

*If Pekka and Juha decide to sue both Jason and Marushka, the parties would then be called co-plaintiffs or co-defendants.*

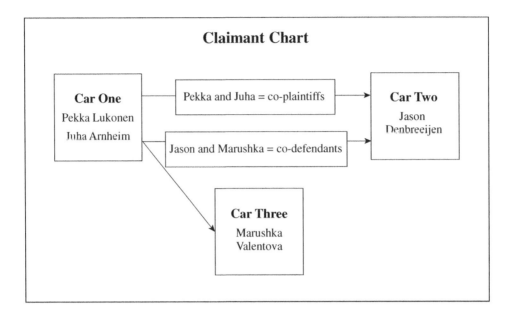

## Claim Joinder

A **cross-claim** is a claim filed by a co-defendant against another co-defendant, who for that particular action would be called **cross-claimants**. If, for instance, in the example, Marushka decided to sue Jason, she would file a cross-claim against Jason, and then, in addition to being co-defendants, they would become cross-claimants.

A defendant can file a **counterclaim** against the plaintiff if another cause of action is involved. The counterclaim must be other than simply an answer or a response to the claim of the plaintiff. In federal procedure a counterclaim is either **compulsory** [arising out of the transaction in the suit] or **permissive** [arising out of actions outside the present claim by the plaintiff]. In the example, if Pekka repeatedly calls Jason a liar and a maniac in public after the accident, Jason could file a counterclaim for defamation against Pekka.

## Exercise I. Claimant Chart

Draw a claimant chart for this section. Who are cross-claimants and/or counterclaimants in the car accident fact situation?

## Exercise J. Statutory Interpretation

1. Read Rule 13(g) of the Federal Rules of Civil Procedure that governs cross-claims in federal proceedings. We have numbered the sentences for you as [1] and [2].

> **Rule 13. Counterclaim and Cross-Claim—(Federal Rules of Civil Procedure) (g) Cross-Claim Against Co-Party.**
>
> [1] A pleading may state as a cross-claim any claim by one party against a co-party arising out of the transaction or occurrence that is the subject matter either of the original action or of a counterclaim therein or relating to any property that is the subject matter of the original action. [2] Such cross-claim may include a claim that the party against whom it is asserted is or may be liable to the cross-claimant for all or part of a claim asserted in the action against the cross-claimant. [bracketed numbers added]

2. In pairs or groups of three, break the rule down bit by bit to understand its meaning. See Language Activity 9, page 207, for an example.

    a. First write each sentence on the board or a piece of paper. Erase all but the absolute minimum you need to understand the central message of this rule.

    b. When you as a group have agreed on the basis of the sentence, you may go on to the next step.

    c. Clause by clause or even phrase by phrase, add parts back to the sentence.

    d. Keep track of when you added each part. Compare your result with the other groups.

## Pleadings

**Pleadings** are the documents filed with the court by plaintiff and defendant that detail the facts, charges, and possible defenses to the action. The action commences with the filing of a **complaint** (also called a petition or a declaration) by the plaintiff that states the alleged wrongdoing of the defendant. Three requirements for the complaint are:

1. facts leading to the court's jurisdictional competence,
2. facts that show that plaintiff should be granted a remedy, and
3. the remedy requested.

### Exercise K. Listening

Listen to the attorney talking to his client about an automobile accident in which the client was injured. Then fill in the pleading form that has already been partially completed for you (on pages 99–101).

# CIRCUIT COURT OF SHELBY COUNTY
## MEMPHIS, TENNESSEE

_____,
      Plaintiff,
         v.              }       No. _____
_____,       [court docket number—a number
      Defendant             the court assigns to each case]
and
_____,
      Defendant.

## I
## PLAINTIFF'S DOMICILE

Plaintiff _____, is resident of _____
County, State of _____, residing at _____
_____ [street address], _____[city], _____[zip code],
_____[telephone number].

## II
## DEFENDANTS' DOMICILE

Defendant _____, resides at _____
[street address] in the City of _____, _____ County,
State of _____.

Defendant _____, resides at _____
[street address] in the City of _____, _____ County,
State of _____.

## III
## FACTUAL ALLEGATIONS

Plaintiff _____ on _____,
20_____, at approximately _____ was driving west on Jefferson Avenue in
Memphis, Tennessee. She was proceeding at about _____ miles per hour in the
_____ lane of the four-lane street when _____, the defen-
dant, driving _____ on Jefferson Avenue, went into a spin and swerved into her
lane of traffic, striking the plaintiff's vehicle on the front driver's side. At no time did
Plaintiff's car leave the _____, westbound lane of traffic. Defendant,

_____, was backing out of a _____ on Jefferson Avenue into Jefferson Avenue at the time Defendant _____'s car was proceeding _____ on Jefferson Avenue. He alleges that he swerved to miss Defendant _____'s car and thereby lost control of his vehicle, spinning into Plaintiff's lane of traffic.

As a result of the negligence of defendants, Plaintiff _____ was thrown forward sharply, striking various parts of _____ body, and causing serious and permanent injuries to the Plaintiff.

IV
CAUSES OF ACTION

The collision on _____, 20_____, resulted from the negligence of the Defendant, _____, in failing to keep _____ vehicle under control, in driving at excessive speed in a _____ area, and in failing to guide _____ vehicle so as to avoid colliding with the vehicle of _____ in violation of Tenn. Code Ann. §55-8-123 of the State of _____, which provides:

> Whenever any roadway has been divided into two (2) or more clearly marked lanes for traffic, the following rules, in addition to all others consistent herewith, shall apply:
> (1) A vehicle shall be driven as nearly as practicable entirely within a single lane and shall not be moved from such lane until the driver has first ascertained that such movement can be made with safety; . . .

And from the negligence of Defendant, _____, by making an improper move into traffic in violation of Tenn. Code Ann. §55-8-150 of the State of Tennessee thereby causing Defendant, _____, to swerve into Plaintiff's lane of traffic, striking Plaintiff's vehicle. The statute provides as follows:

> The driver of a vehicle within a business or residence district emerging from an alley, driveway or building shall stop such vehicle immediately prior to driving onto a sidewalk or onto the sidewalk area extending across any alleyway or driveway, and shall yield the right-of-way to any pedestrian as may be necessary to avoid collision, and upon entering the roadway shall yield the right-of-way to all vehicles approaching on the roadway.

V
INJURIES SUSTAINED

As a proximate result of the negligence of Defendants, Plaintiff, _____, suffered serious injuries, including a broken _____, pain in her knees, hip, and chest, and trauma to her sternum. As a result of such injuries, Plaintiff _____ has incurred hospital and medical expenses and has sustained physical pain and mental anguish. _____ has been unable to attend to _____. Plaintiff _____ was employed at the time of the collision and, as a proximate result of the negligence of Defendants, is now unable to work and has been placed on long-term disability. _____ will sustain physical pain and mental anguish for the remainder of _____ life.

Plaintiff _____ alleges that all charges sustained for medical services are the usual, reasonable, and _____ charges for similar services rendered in _____ County, State of _____. _____ injuries, and the effects thereof, are in all reasonable probability of a lasting nature and will handicap _____ for the remainder of _____ life. By reason of the negligence of the Defendants, Plaintiff _____ has been damaged in the sum of $_____.

VI
TOTAL DAMAGES SUSTAINED

Plaintiff's automobile was damaged and _____ in the sum of $_____. Plaintiff's total damages are in excess of the sum of $_____.

Plaintiff avers that she is entitled to recover from Defendants the amount of _____ Dollars, and requests this court to grant such _____, and demands a _____ to try the cause, and further requests such other relief as this court deems proper.

_____
Signature of Plaintiff

Attorney for _____

_____
Attorney's Address

Once the defendant is notified of the allegations against him or her through delivery of a **summons** [notice that legal action has been instituted and that defendant must appear in court on a certain date] and a copy of the complaint, he or she has several options.

The defendant can file an **answer** in response to plaintiff's complaint denying some or all of the allegations set forth in the complaint and setting forth **affirmative defenses** [new facts intended to absolve defendant of liability for the wrongdoing]. The answer may also set forth any permissive or compulsory counterclaims.

The defendant can also file a **motion to dismiss** or a **demurrer,** in this instance, a pre-answer response stating that even if the facts in the complaint are true, they are insufficient to support a cause of action—in other words, that the defendant is guilty of no legal wrongdoing. If the court agrees and dismisses the complaint, then the defendant is not required to file an answer. Plaintiff is normally given additional time to file an amended complaint alleging additional facts sufficient to support a cause of action. Motions to dismiss may also be based on the court's lack of subject matter or personal jurisdiction, improper venue, or insufficient process, among others.

A final option is to simply not respond to the complaint at all. If defendant chooses to do this, the court will award a **default judgment** to the plaintiff that will grant plaintiff the relief requested in his or her complaint.

# Discovery

The purpose of pre-trial discovery is to ensure that all relevant information is disclosed to all parties prior to the trial. With full access to the relevant facts prior to trial, parties have time to prepare fully, and the trial becomes less of a contest of wits and a fairer procedure. If during the discovery process the parties discover that there are no contested issues of fact, the path for a **motion for summary judgment** is opened. A motion for summary judgment is a motion by one of the parties, when facts are uncontested, for the court to decide the issue(s) of law without the necessity for a full-blown trial, which is normally expensive and time consuming.

There are various devices used by the parties in the discovery process. The Federal Rules of Civil Procedure provide for discovery devices, two of which are discussed here:

1. depositions of parties and witnesses (oral and written)
2. interrogatories

## *Depositions*

Depositions function as mini-trials and are the most expensive and perhaps most useful of the discovery devices. Generally attorneys from both sides are present, and there are **direct examinations** [questioning by your own attorney] and **cross-examinations** [questioning by the opposing attorney]. The witness or party testifies in front of a court official, under oath, and the testimony is taken down.

Depositions upon written questions are subject to the same rules as oral depositions regarding what information may be sought and who may be deposed. The difference is that attorneys exchange a series of written questions prior to the actual deposition (direct/cross-examination and **redirect/recross-examination;** *redirect* refers to questions that the attorney who conducted the direct examination asks after the cross-examination of the opposing attorney; *recross* are the questions asked by the opposing attorney after the redirect), which are then answered by the witness before a court reporter. The court reporter then transcribes the answers, and the party/witness signs the transcription and swears to its accuracy.

## *Interrogatories*

**Interrogatories** are a series of written questions for which written responses are then prepared and signed under oath. Interrogatories may only be directed to the parties and not to witnesses, whereas depositions upon written questions can be directed to either parties or witnesses. Also, the questions are not limited to the party's personal knowledge as in depositions but may require that the party search his or her records for the answers. Interrogatories are not normally used as evidence in court and can be extremely burdensome on the parties because they are unlimited in the number of questions that can be asked and the number of interrogatories that can be served on the parties.

## The Trial

After the completion of discovery, either party or the court may request a pre-trial conference that, though still part of the pre-trial process, serves to determine the direction of the trial. The parties and the judge, in an informal discussion, identify the matters in dispute and plan the course of the trial. Throughout the entire pre-trial procedure, parties have been "bargaining" to see if an **out-of-court settlement** [agreement between parties outside the court] is more appropriate than an actual trial. But if the negotiations haven't been concluded satisfactorily, the parties prepare to go to trial.

## *The Jury*

Not every trial in the United States is a jury trial. In many civil law cases, especially in the field of torts, there are juries, however. If so, the first thing that must be done is to **impanel** [choose] a jury. This is done by means of the **voir dire** [questioning of prospective jurors by attorneys] prior to the actual trial on the issues. During the questioning, the attorneys attempt to discover if jurors might be in any way prejudiced against their clients, and if so, the attorneys exercise **challenges** [requests for jurors to be removed from the jury panel].

There are two types of challenges: **peremptory challenges,** for which no cause must be stated, and **challenges for cause,** for which an attorney must show a reason for the removal of the juror. For example, if the juror and one of the parties to the action are neighbors, an attorney may exercise a challenge for cause. Of course, the judge may refuse to accept the challenge. In general, peremptory challenges are limited in number and challenges for cause are unlimited.

Juries traditionally consisted of twelve members who had to reach a unanimous decision. In recent years, however, that rule has been modified somewhat, and a few states accept juries with as few as six members, whereas others no longer require a unanimous verdict in civil trials.

Attorneys and students from civil law systems often have trouble understanding the use of a jury in common law systems. While there are certainly disadvantages, there are also advantages to having a jury of six to twelve citizens decide your fate rather than one judge.

### Exercise L. Juries through Moral Dilemmas

Jason Ciapala, a Ciapalese LL.M. student, is in an advanced civil procedure seminar. At the beginning of the semester, each student was told to submit a twenty-page research paper for the class. Jason was not that sure of his research and writing ability, so he kept postponing starting the assignment. Two weeks before the paper was due, Jason got a severe case of the flu and was out of school about ten days.

Two days before the paper was due, Jason asked Professor Dicker, his seminar professor, for an extension due to his illness. After talking to Jason, Professor Dicker realized that Jason had not started on the paper prior to getting sick, so he decided that an extension was unwarranted. After all, Jason had had the entire semester to write the paper. Why had he waited until the last minute?

Jason did not understand Professor Dicker's attitude, but knew he had to do something. Without the course, he would not finish the LL.M. program. So he started to work. That night, the only one in the computer lab, he saw some paper in the waste paper basket from one of his fellow seminar students. As he looked over the thrown away paper, he realized that a partial rough draft of a paper had been thrown away.

Because the paper was not complete, he thought it would be okay to use the rough draft to start his own paper. Using this research and rough draft, he completed his assignment and turned it into Professor Dicker.

Much to his surprise, he and Jennifer Mason, the student whose paper he had found, were called into the Dean of Students' office. The Dean said that both students were to go before the disciplinary council for a hearing on plagiarism. Jennifer was shocked and asked why. Jason said nothing. What he had done was not considered plagiarism in his country, so he was also confused.

The law school disciplinary board decided that Jason was guilty of plagiarism. The most difficult decision the board faces, though, is what to do with Jason. He explained what he had done and the fact that using other people's notes is not plagiarism in his country. What should the board do? Should Jason have (1) a failing grade for the paper, (2) a failing grade for the class, (3) expulsion from the class, (4) expulsion from the LL.M. program, (5) a reprimand and note in his file, or (6) an explanation of the cultural ramifications of plagiarism in the United States.

1. In the order of most appropriate response to least appropriate, rank what the law school should do about Jason and the research paper problem. One is the most appropriate response; six the least appropriate.

    _____ failing grade for the paper

    _____ failing grade for the class

    _____ expulsion from the class

    _____ expulsion from the LL.M. program

    _____ a reprimand and note in his file

    _____ an explanation of the cultural ramifications

2. After you have ranked the disciplinary actions, check your responses with two partners. The three of you must agree on the order of "punishments" for Jason. Once the three of you have agreed, check with another group of three and reach consensus. You must have unanimous agreement. One person who does not agree with you "hangs" your jury.

    In deciding Jason's punishment as a unanimous vote, you have acted similarly to how a jury might act when reaching decisions in lawsuits. The jurors will first reach their own conclusions, then have to support their conclusions in discussions with the other jurors. Eventually, the jury must come to a unanimous decision. If one person does not agree, then the jury cannot reach a verdict, and the trial, if the parties decide to continue, must start again.

3. Think about what you and your partners did when trying to decide Jason's punishment. Were there advantages to a decision by his peers (fellow students)? Were there disadvantages?

List four advantages and disadvantages of the jury system based on your recent experience as a "juror."

Once the jury has been impaneled, the trial can begin. The figure that follows outlines the progress of a trial. (We will assume a female plaintiff in this example.)

---

**Plaintiff's opening statement**
[introduction of case by plaintiff's attorney]

↓

**Defendant's opening statement**
[introduction of case by defendant's attorney]

↓

Plaintiff's case (plaintiff always presents case first)
Direct examination of Johann Strauss, the first witness
Cross-examination of Strauss by defense (optional)
Redirect by plaintiff (optional)
Recross by defendant (optional)
Continues until all witnesses have been examined

↓

Plaintiff **rests** case
[tells the court that she has proven her cause of action].

↓

Defense moves for a **directed verdict** (optional). Elements required:
1. Judgment as a matter of law
2. Request by defense for judge to decide in favor of defense because plaintiff presented insufficient evidence to prove her case
3. Judge views case in light most favorable to plaintiff

↓

Defense case
Same order of presentation as with plaintiff
Defense rests case

↓

Plaintiff may move for a directed verdict (optional).
Same process as with the defense motion

↓

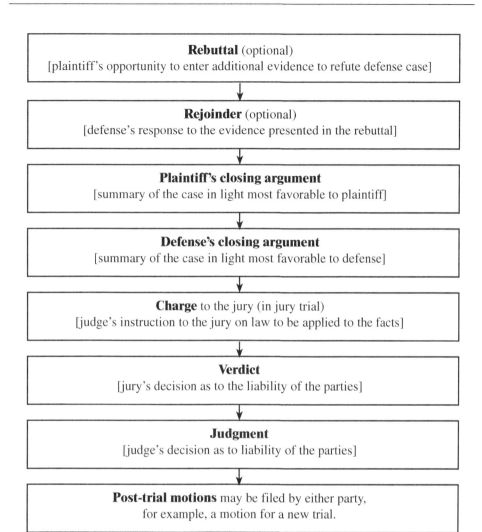

**Rebuttal** (optional)
[plaintiff's opportunity to enter additional evidence to refute defense case]

**Rejoinder** (optional)
[defense's response to the evidence presented in the rebuttal]

**Plaintiff's closing argument**
[summary of the case in light most favorable to plaintiff]

**Defense's closing argument**
[summary of the case in light most favorable to defense]

**Charge** to the jury (in jury trial)
[judge's instruction to the jury on law to be applied to the facts]

**Verdict**
[jury's decision as to the liability of the parties]

**Judgment**
[judge's decision as to liability of the parties]

**Post-trial motions** may be filed by either party,
for example, a motion for a new trial.

Appeal process may begin.

## Exercise M: Progression of a Lawsuit. Fill in the Chart

Margaret Smith, an opera singer, was hired to sing for the Metropolitan Opera Company by Mason Jenkins, the managing director of Metropolitan. Jenkins was fired by Metropolitan, which then refused to honor the contract between Smith and Jenkins. Smith wants to sue for breach of contract.

1. Working in pairs as attorneys for Smith, chart the progress of the court case. We have filled in portions of the chart for you. If no more information is needed, draw an X in the box.

| Date | Activity | Expected Result | Parties |
|---|---|---|---|
| May '05 | Smith is "injured"—breach of contract | | Smith/Jenkins/ Metropolitan Opera (Opera) |
| June '05 | Smith hires Pearson as her attorney | filing of lawsuit | Smith/her attorney |
| July '05 | | eventual damages | Pearson/court |
| July '05 | | | Pearson/Opera and Jenkins's attorney (Morris) |
| Aug '05 | | Summary judgment | Pearson/Morris |
| Sept '05 | Court denies motion for summary judgment | | |
| Nov '05 | Discovery process begins | | All parties |
| Dec '05 | Pearson to depose Jenkins | Obtain information about the alleged contract | Pearson/Jenkins/ Morris/court reporter |
| Jan '06 | | Obtain information from the plaintiff, Smith | |
| Feb '06 | | | |
| Feb '06 | | | |

| Mar '06 | Trial date set for August '06 | | |
|---|---|---|---|
| Aug '06 | Trial begins | Someone will "win." | All parties and judge/jury |
| Aug '06 | Verdict rendered | | |
| Aug '06 | Judgment entered | | |
| Sept '06 | Post-trial motions filed | Appeal | "Losing" party |

# *Torts*

---

## Discovering Connections

Tort law is the body of law that deals with civil wrongs, except those that arise from contract problems. The purpose of torts is to compensate an injured party through the award of damages for the injuries incurred during a **tortious** [a violation of tort] act. Policy considerations—such as maintenance of a peaceful society, deterrence, social responsibility, and the balancing of economic interests against societal benefits—play vital roles in tort law because it attempts to find a balance between the harm caused to individuals and the benefit to society. Of course, societal wrongs are also dealt with in criminal law. The difference is that a tort is a wrong against an individual, whereas a crime is a wrong against society as a whole. However, some acts or omissions may be both criminal offenses and tortious ones. A simplified equation to explain the elements of a tort action is

$$\text{act/omission} + \text{personal/property interest} +$$
$$\text{intent/negligence/inadvertence/mistake} = \text{tort}$$

Obviously, it would be impossible for any body of law to address every injury, so the questions then become: Under what conditions should liability be imposed? What factors affect liability? What types of damages/remedies are presumed sufficient under the law to redress these wrongs?

## ACTIVITY

1. Review the fact situations, and decide what "crimes" or torts, if you have them, might have been committed under the laws of your country.

2. Are there any situations in which both criminal and tort law might apply?

*Fact Situations*

a. A research scientist developed an injectible vaccine for AIDS. Unfortunately, one in a million doses causes instant death. In the United States that would mean that 300 people would be killed by this vaccine. The children of a woman killed instantly wonder what actions they might take.

b. Extended-wear contact lenses are very comfortable and can be worn during sleep. However, wearers of these lenses are repeatedly told by their optometrists that these lenses increase their risks of developing serious medical conditions of the eye. Adnan loses the sight of one eye as a direct result of wearing extended-wear lenses.

c. Mary is shopping for a new coat at Markham's Department Store when she is approached by a security guard who insists that she accompany him to the manager's office. Mary repeatedly asks to leave, but the manager and security guard refuse her request and question her for more than an hour about merchandise they allege she has stolen. Finally, a second security guard approaches with a woman who looks slightly like Mary and who is indeed the culprit. The manager apologizes and lets Mary go.

## Legal Discussion

## Essential Terms

**tortfeasor:** person who is guilty of tortious conduct

**trespass:** an unlawful interfering with the property or property rights of another

**intentional infliction of emotional distress:** causation of severe mental suffering or physical injury through highly aggravated acts or words. The acts or words must be done with (1) intent to cause an injury or (2) a reasonable certainty that those acts or words will result in the injury

**false imprisonment:** interference with the freedom of or restraining the movements of an individual. There must be the intent to detain, and the detention must be without privilege or consent.

**defamation:** interference with one's interest in his or her good reputation and name; defamation encompasses two torts, slander (spoken) and libel (written)

**wrongful death action:** suit brought by the beneficiaries of a decedent against a person who allegedly caused the decedent's death through negligence

**battery:** the unlawful interference with another's person, such as hitting someone on the arm with a handbag

**negligence:** failure to use such care as a reasonably prudent and careful person would use under similar circumstances; applies to either an act or an omission

## Putting the Terms to Use

1. After familiarizing yourself with these terms, return to the activity in Discovering Connections and see if you can find situations that meet any of the definitions you have been given.

2. Next, read the story, and indicate the appropriate tort in the blank spaces provided.

   _____ Jennifer and Giorgio were classmates at Cleghorn Community College in Pocahontas, Arkansas. Though Giorgio, a male student from Greece, thought he and Jennifer, a female student from Michigan, were only friends, unbeknown to him, she had become obsessed and determined to marry him at all costs. She began to slip into his yard every night and watch him sleeping through an open window. She never hurt or disturbed anything in the yard; she merely watched him.

_____ Unfortunately, Jennifer did not know that Giorgio and his fiancée, Mary, whom he met while an exchange student in North Dakota, had already decided to marry but had not announced their engagement. Because Mary was completing her studies at the University of Texas, Jennifer never saw Mary—that is, until the holiday break, when her midnight vigil revealed that Giorgio was not alone anymore. Jennifer was distraught—her dreams dashed. Then she decided if she could make Mary see reason, all was not lost. She cornered Mary in the ladies' room at the local movie theater, locked her in a toilet stall, and would not let her out, all the while making a plea for Giorgio's affection. After twenty minutes or so, Mary agreed to give up Giorgio, and Jennifer released her. Mary had lied, as Jennifer's moonlight vigil soon revealed.

_____ Jennifer became incensed and stopped Giorgio and Mary at church the next day. She shouted terrible insults at Mary, calling her vile names and calling on the minister to impose religious sanctions on Mary. Mary was so distressed that she experienced severe panic attacks, developed hives, and lost her beautiful blonde hair.

_____ Not satisfied with that, Jennifer typed up a scornful letter about Mary, complete with picture, and stuck a copy on every car in a department store parking lot.

_____ Finally, Jennifer began following Mary and bumping, shoving, or tripping her whenever possible, though it always appeared to be an accident on Jennifer's part.

Mary can take no more; she seeks legal advice from you, the new lawyer in town.

3. Finally, as a class, discuss the answers. Did you all reach the same conclusion? If there were differences, what caused them?

---

## Legal Thumbnail

---

Tort law has developed over the centuries and lacks statutory organization; consequently, it is helpful to discuss torts by categorizing them in terms of the degree of fault inherent in the tortious conduct/liability.

1. **Intentional torts** require fault in the form of intent; it must be shown that the actor knew that there was a substantial certainty of harm.
2. **Negligent torts** require that the act create an unreasonable risk of harm.
3. **Strict liability** requires no showing of intent/negligence or fault by the actor. The doctrine was developed to cover situations in which a party was engaged in ultrahazardous situations, such as use of explosives or dealing with wild animals.

## Intentional Torts

Proof of an intentional tort requires showing that a protected right has been intentionally breached. Obviously, the difficulty here lies in proving another's state of mind, since for obvious reasons the statements of the defendant regarding his or her own intent are questionable. Therefore, intent is most often proved through **circumstantial evidence:** the defendant's conduct, in the context of his or her surroundings and what he or she presumably knew and perceived. The law makes presumptions regarding the defendant's intent in light of these considerations, assuming that the defendant intends the natural and probable consequences of his or her acts.

Intentional torts include actions that the layperson often associates with criminal law but are actually also covered by tort law. Two major types of intentional torts are

1. personal torts such as **assault, battery,** and **false imprisonment** [unlawful confinement] and
2. property torts such as **trespass to land** [unlawful entry on property of another] and **trespass to chattels** [interference with or damage to the belongings of another]

Since it is beyond the scope of this text to deal thoroughly with all of these torts, one example from each category, beginning with the personal tort of false imprisonment, will be examined.

### *False Imprisonment*

The tort of false imprisonment involves cases in which the plaintiff has allegedly been unlawfully confined by the defendant. For false imprisonment to be proven, these elements must be present:

1. intent to confine a person within a certain area;
2. actual confinement;
3. awareness of plaintiff of the confinement or injury to plaintiff due to confinement; and
4. prevention of exit or no safe exit possible by plaintiff.

Of course the elements as in all legal descriptions must be clarified. What, for example, is a legal exit or what constitutes confinement?

Consider the case of *Big Town Nursing Home, Inc. v. Newman*, 461 S.W.2d 195 (Tex. Civ. App. 1970). The plaintiff, Newman, was confined in a nursing home without a **commitment order** [court order requiring placement in an institution] after his nephew took him to the nursing home and paid for a one-month stay. Newman had health problems, including Parkinson's disease and alcoholism. Shortly after his placement in the home, Newman tried to leave; however, he was stopped by employees of the nursing home, who placed him in the section of the nursing home reserved for senile patients. Apprehended several times during several escape attempts, Newman was taped to a chair to prevent his further escape attempts. Approximately seven weeks after being placed in the home, Newman successfully escaped. He then sued the nursing home for false imprisonment and won **actual (compensatory)** [the losses that are readily provable and actually sustained] and **exemplary (punitive)** [damages designed to punish the wrongdoer] **damages.** Although the nursing home appealed the case, the trial court's decision was upheld on appeal; the appellate court held that a nursing home cannot force a patient to stay when there is no legal justification.

If the plaintiff agrees to the detention, obviously there is no false imprisonment. What happens, however, if the plaintiff has no knowledge of the confinement at all? The majority of the jurisdictions hold that the plaintiff must have been aware of the confinement in order for there to have been a false imprisonment. In Newman's case, he was obviously aware of the confinement despite his illness, so that argument (lack of awareness) could not be raised by the nursing home.

## Exercise A. Case Hypotheticals and Discussion

In groups of three, look at these scenarios, determine whether or not there has been false imprisonment in these scenarios, and give reasons for your decisions. Be prepared to defend your answers in class.

*Fact Situations*

1. The captain of a fishing boat agreed to let one of his crew leave the trawler at the next port of call. However, once they reached port, the captain refused to allow the crew member to use the rowboat to get

ashore. Since it was the only way ashore, the crew member had to remain with the fishing boat for two more months until the fishing season ended and the home port was reached.

2. Jane, who was clearly under the influence of alcohol or drugs, was found wandering around the city streets at 2 AM one morning by a security guard. He drove her to a beach area outside of town and left her there in an abandoned hut. Jane went to sleep. When she awoke the next morning, she had no recollection of what had happened the night before. However, after being told the story by an acquaintance who knew both the security guard and Jane, she sued the security guard for false imprisonment. During the trial it was unclear whether Jane had gone willingly to the beach hut or had requested that the guard let her out elsewhere.

## *Trespass*

Trespass, the most familiar of the property torts, prohibits the unauthorized entry of a person or thing onto the property of another. The right to exclusive possession of the land is the basis for this tort, a right that had its origin in feudal times and was most fiercely defended. Unlike in other countries where citizens may have the right to temporary access to all undeveloped lands (such as *allemansrätt* in Sweden), U.S. law allows landowners to close off land completely to others.

A *prima facie* [basics that must be proven] case of trespass must include an act, coupled with the intent to cause entry by the defendant, and an invasion of the plaintiff's land. In other words, the person must have intended to enter another's land.

Damages are not required to be proven for intentional trespass. Only when the entry onto another's land is negligent (and then falls under negligent torts) is there any requirement for showing actual damages.

The intent to cause entry does not mean that the defendant must have knowledge that the land he or she enters belongs to another but only that he or she intends the act that would effect an entry. In most U.S. jurisdictions, it does not matter whether a defendant's presence on another's land is a mistake caused by ignorance of the ownership or the boundaries, or even that the trespass may have benefited the land. In all cases, it has been held to be trespass. For example, if Jan builds a small lake to attract migrating ducks and the pond extends over onto Alfred's property, Jan has trespassed even though Alfred has a benefit because he can use the lake water to irrigate one of his fields. It's of no matter that Jan thought he was building the lake only on his own property; Jan has committed trespass.

Property interests are such that failure to remove something from the land can be considered a trespass. If, for example, you had been given permission to leave your car parked on your neighbor's property for six months and you didn't remove it at the end of six months, that could be considered a trespass. Trespass can even be remaining on another's land after a privilege (either the owner's consent or a legal privilege irrespective of consent) expires; for example, because the privilege to be on the campus in a classroom building generally expires when the university closes for the night, it might be possible in some states to charge a student who is studying in an otherwise empty classroom building with trespass. Causing another to enter plaintiff's land may also be held a trespass. It is also interesting to note that the rights inherent in the possession of land extend above and below the surface.

### Exercise B. Listening

1. Listen to the two discussions. The first time, just listen to each conversation. The second time, decide if a tort has been committed or not.
2. In pairs, review your answers and list the reasons for your decisions.

# Negligence

The central factor in negligence is determining what the standard of care imposed upon the public should be, as a general rule, all persons are under a duty to conduct themselves in such a manner as not to create unreasonable risks of physical harm to others. During a trial, the conduct of the defendant is reviewed to determine if he or she has met the reasonable person standard. That is, would a reasonable person have acted similarly under similar circumstances? For the court to impose liability for negligence, the following elements must be proven:

1. that the defendant had a duty of care;
2. that there was a breach of that duty by negligent conduct (act or omission);
3. that the act or omission caused injury (proximate cause); and
4. that the act or omission is not subject to the defenses of assumption of the risk or contributory negligence.

Although the elements are isolated for discussion, they are interrelated to the extent that it is almost misleading to speak of them separately.

### Standard of Care

The standard of care that must be exercised is that which a reasonable person would use under similar circumstances. It is important to note that this standard is an external, objective one in which all people are deemed to use certain minimal levels of care in all of their activities.

## Proximate Cause

Proximate cause is one of the most difficult and elusive of the concepts associated with tort law. Proximate cause is related to the concept of duty. If the defendant is found to have had a duty to protect the plaintiff from the consequences of the harmful act, and breached that duty, then there is proximate cause. Determinations of proximate cause by courts are true exercises in the use of precedent and legal reasoning; case law, public policy arguments, and common sense all play a part in the court's decision.

However, a person does not have the same duty of care to all persons. Basically, a person only has a duty of care to someone with whom that person logically would be likely to interact. In other words, we are obligated only to those people or that property that our actions or inactions would foreseeably have an effect on. This issue of foreseeability is enormously complex since the courts have held that the duty of care is owed only to a plaintiff who is reasonably foreseeable. The question then becomes, who is foreseeable? A landmark case on foreseeability is *Palsgraf v. Long Island R.R.*, 248 N.Y. 339, 162 N.E. 99 (1928). The facts of the case were set forth by Chief Justice Cardozo, a distinguished American jurist, in his opinion.

> Plaintiff was standing on a platform of defendant's railroad after buying a ticket to go to Rockaway Beach. A train stopped at the station, bound for another place. Two men ran forward to catch it. One of the men reached the platform of the car without mishap, though the train was already moving. The other man, carrying a package, jumped aboard the car but seemed unsteady as if about to fall. A guard on the car, who had held the door open, reached forward to help him in, and another guard on the platform pushed him from behind. In this act, the package was dislodged, and fell upon the rails. It was a package of small size, about fifteen inches long, and was covered by a newspaper. In fact it contained fireworks, but there was nothing in its appearance to give notice of its contents. The fireworks when they fell exploded. The shock of the explosion threw down some scales at the other end of the platform many feet away. The scales struck the plaintiff, causing injuries for which she [Palsgraf] sues.

# Writing a Summary

The scope and length of the summary is determined by the purpose and context for writing it. In legal writing you may be asked to summarize an article/case or to synthesize several articles/cases into a summary. A summary is a shorter version of the original text that clearly conveys the overall meaning of the original text.

We will focus on writing short summaries of a sentence to several sentences in length. In writing such short summaries, brevity obviously is critical. In order to write in such a concise manner, you will need to be sure you completely understand the meaning of the main text. From there, you need to be able to formulate in your own words the main idea(s) and purpose of the original text. It is also important to remember to reference the original source.

Let's take a look at writing the summary step-by-step.

1. Read the original text carefully in order to fully understand the author's meaning.
2. Highlight text and/or take notes on the main ideas.
3. Rewrite these notes in your own words.
4. Based on the required length of the summary assignment, synthesize the ideas and write out your summary.

As an example, review the text in this chapter under False Imprisonment. Highlight the main ideas. Now rewrite them in your own words in a brief summary. Text 4 in the Student Resources Section (page 282) is a sample summary for you to look at after you've done your own.

## Exercise C. Summarizing

1. Review the *Palsgraf* decision, and underline the words or sections that indicate whether or not the court will find that the plaintiff, Palsgraf, was or was not a foreseeable plaintiff.

2. On your own, as if you were explaining the case to another attorney to clarify a point of law, write a four-sentence summary of the facts. Not all the facts are essential for the explanation of who is a foreseeable plaintiff. You must decide which facts can be omitted.

Cardozo resolved the issue of foreseeability as follows.

❖❖❖

> The conduct of the defendant's guard, if a wrong in its relation to the holder of the package, was not a wrong in its relation to the plaintiff, standing far away. Relatively to her it was not negligence at all. Nothing in the situation gave notice that the falling package had in it the potency of peril to persons thus removed. Negligence is not actionable unless it involves the invasion of a legally protected interest, the violation of a right.

❖❖❖

In simple terms since the plaintiff was not foreseeable, the railroad owed her no duty and therefore did not act negligently.

Another area that causes problems in determining proximate cause is the issue of intervening causes. The courts have to determine if another act, either by a person or a natural force, comes between the tortious act committed by the defendant and the plaintiff. Foreseeability is also an issue in making this determination. If the defendant should have foreseen the intervening act, then lack of foreseeability is not a defense. For example, Tracy lights a campfire in windy weather in the Sierra Nevada mountains after a four-month dry spell. She leaves the fire burning and goes off to take a short hike. The wind spreads the fire, and Martina's house is destroyed by the resulting forest fire. Tracy will not be allowed to rely on intervening forces (the strong wind and dry conditions) as a defense because it was foreseeable that strong winds in dry woods could cause a forest fire. She was negligent in leaving the fire burning when she left the campsite.

## Strict Liability

Strict liability is liability without fault—it is based on the policy of law that under certain circumstances a plaintiff may be allowed recovery even though there is no fault on the part of the defendant. It should be noted here that a finding of no legal fault is not the same as a finding of no moral blame. You can be legally innocent but morally guilty. Legal fault stems from a deviation from a standard of conduct needed to protect society and its citizens. Historically, strict liability covered situations in which activities—blasting, storing inherently dangerous substances, keeping wild animals—were abnormally dangerous ones. These activities were and are still allowable as long as no harm occurs; in other words, the activities may be carried on but only if the actor is willing to insure the public against harm.

Sellers and manufacturers can be held responsible under strict liability even if the seller or manufacturer exercised all reasonable care in production and sale of the product and even if there is no **privity of contract** [contractual relationship between the parties].

## Exercise D. Analysis and Collaboration

1. Divide into groups. Read the scenarios and reach a group consensus as to whether the cause of action should be based on intent, negligence, or strict liability. The causes of action are not mutually exclusive. For example, you can file a suit based both on negligence and strict liability.

2. List the reasons for your decisions. Select one group member to present your list.

*Scenarios*

a. Fletcher owned coal mines on property next to Rylands's property. Rylands had a reservoir built on his property. During construction of the reservoir, workers discovered old mining shafts that weakened the reservoir structure. The reservoir, once filled with water, burst and flooded Fletcher's coal mines. Fletcher sued. *Fletcher v. Rylands,* L.R. 1 Exch. 265 (1866).

b. The Arizona Public Service Company hung copper wire along poles that were irregularly placed. In the autumn, Brittain flew his helicopter into the wire because the copper color blended with the landscape. Brittain's wife sued for wrongful death. *Arizona Public Service Co. v. Brittain,* 107 Ariz. 278, 486 P.2d 176 (1971).

c. Sutherland, from property not belonging to Herrin, repeatedly shot at ducks and other game birds. The shots were fired over Herrin's property and disturbed his cattle and his peace and quiet. Herrin sued. *Herrin v. Sutherland,* 74 Mont. 587, 241 P. 328 (1925).

d. Connie Francis Garzilli, a well-known singer, was criminally assaulted in her motel room at Howard Johnson's Motor Lodge in Westbury, New York, when the attacker came in through a sliding glass door. Proof was offered at the trial that the door could be easily forced open from the outside. Francis and her husband sued the motel chain for, *inter alia,* mental suffering and deprivation of companionship. *Garzilli v. Howard Johnson's Motor Lodges, Inc.,* 419 F.Supp. 1210 (E.D.N.Y. 1976).

# Intellectual Property

We have discussed torts that address interference with the person or property of another and his or her right to a good name. There is yet another category of tort, which relates to the intellectual property of an individual or a business. Intellectual property rights are often included in the category of business torts. These rights have their basis in the public policy concept of competition as the approved form of economic activity. Most people would agree that competition results in significant benefits to consumers. It encourages businesses to keep prices low and product quality high while encouraging innovation and product diversity. Unlike other torts, which evolved through common law, the law of intellectual property lies in federal statutes. Included in this category are trademark, patents, and copyright infringement.

## *Trademarks*

A **trademark** is a symbol used by merchants to identify their goods and distinguish them from those of others that may be similar but not identical in quality or composition. By ensuring that no other merchant can imitate a trademark, the law provides a strong incentive for the merchant to invest in goodwill. In other words, if the company improves its products and makes them commercially attractive, then consumers will reward the company by seeking out products bearing its trademarks because from the consumer's point of view, he or she can rely on getting a product of the same quality from the manufacturer each time he or she returns to the marketplace.

There are both advantages and disadvantages to trademark protection. On one hand, a company motivated to improve its products and establish a broad consumer base is protected from the unscrupulous behavior of a competitor who tries to sell an inferior product under the same trademark as the original. However, where trademark protection is strong, merchants invest heavily in advertising and promotion in order to cultivate brand loyalty on the part of the consumer. When this happens, it is harder and more expensive for new companies to break into the market, which consequently reduces the incentives for established firms to maintain product quality and keep prices down.

Occasionally, companies use names that are so similar to one already in use that a suit is brought for **trade name infringement** [unauthorized use of a trade name already in use]. In the following case, *Tri-County Funeral Service, Inc.,* (d/b/a Howard Funeral Home) *v. Eddie Howard Funeral Home, Inc.,* 330 Ark. 789,957 S.W2nd 694 (1967) that is exactly what happened. The facts, which are rather complicated, and the court's judgment are set forth in Judge Newbern's opinion:

❖ ❖ ❖

This is a trade-name infringement case. The appellant, Tri-County Funeral Service, Inc. ("Tri-County"), which does business as Howard Funeral Home in Melbourne, sought an injunction pursuant to Ark.Code Ann. 4-71-113 (Repl. 1996) to prohibit the appellee, Eddie Howard Funeral Home, Inc., also located in Melbourne, from using the name "Howard" in connection with its funeral business. The Chancellor declined to issue the injunction. Our determination in this de novo review is that Tri-County was entitled to the relief sought; thus we reverse the Chancellor's decision.

In 1949, Roman and Wilma Howard began working for the Roller Funeral Home in Melbourne. At some point in the 1950s they left that employment. The funeral home changed hands several times, and Mr. and Mrs. Howard returned as employees in 1961. A Mr. Robinson purchased the business while it was being operated as "McCollum Funeral Home," and in 1968 Mr. Robinson asked the Howards for permission to operate as "Howard Funeral Home," although the Howards owned no interest in the business. Permission was granted.

In 1974, Billy Howard, Mr. and Mrs. Howard's son, joined them as an employee of Howard Funeral Home. In 1978 the business was sold to Justine Jones who, in 1984, sold it to Rhodes-Madden, Inc., the parent company of Tri-County. In the sales agreement, there was a provision selling the name, "Howard Funeral Home." The ensuing bill of sale, however, did not mention the sale of the name. Tri-County continued to operate the business as Howard Funeral Home.

Roman Howard retired sometime during the 1980s. Billy Howard left his employment with the business in 1984. Wilma Howard remained until 1989 when her employment was terminated because of rumors that Billy Howard was attempting to open a competing funeral business.

In 1991, Billy Howard was rehired by Tri-County to manage the business, and he rehired Wilma Howard as an employee. In 1992, Billy Howard hired his younger brother, Eddie Howard, to work in the business. Billy Howard died, and Eddie Howard became the manager in 1994. In 1996, Eddie Howard's employment was terminated due to his apparent efforts to begin a competing business. Wilma Howard then resigned from her employment with Tri-County.

Eddie Howard established "Eddie Howard Funeral Home, Inc.," a corporation of which he and his wife are the only shareholders. Tri-County sued to prevent that corporation from using the Howard name, alleging that the name had acquired a secondary meaning and that it constituted an interest protectable in accordance with §4-71-113. . . .

❖ ❖ ❖

## *Patents*

**Patents** are protected by federal statute in order to stimulate desirable creativity and to reward those creators with limited monopolies. In general, monopolies are not allowed under American law; however, patents are rewards to a creator, giving him or her a strong financial incentive. This incentive of the monopoly, however, is of a limited duration and is only renewable under exceptional circumstances, such as delay in issuance or because of appellate review. In all instances, the extension can total no more than five years. Read the following section from Title 35 of the United States Code, §154.

> Contents and term of patent
>
> (a) In General.—
>
>> (1) Contents.— Every patent shall contain a short title of the invention and a grant to the patentee, his heirs or assigns, of the right to exclude others from making, using, offering for sale, or selling the invention throughout the United States or importing the invention into the United States, and, if the invention is a process, of the right to exclude others from using, offering for sale or selling throughout the United States, or importing into the United States, products made by that process, referring to the specification for the particulars thereof.
>>
>> (2) Term.—Subject to the payment of fees under this title, such grant shall be for a term beginning on the date on which the patent issues and ending 20 years from the date on which the application for the patent was filed in the United States. . . .

### Exercise E. Reading for Details

Carefully review the statute, and answer the questions.

1. What is the holder of a patent entitled to?
2. What must the patent holder do to secure his patent?
3. What is the standard term of a patent?

Before being granted the privilege of patenting his or her invention, an inventor must satisfy three statutory tests of novelty, non-obviousness, and usefulness. To meet the novelty test, an item must be new, a departure from what has gone before. Thus, if a product were already patented abroad, it could not satisfy the novelty requirement and therefore would not be patentable.

The non-obviousness test simply means that the differences between what is sought to be patented and prior knowledge must not have been obvious to people of ordinary skill in the field in which the patent is sought (35 U.S.C. §103). The patent applicant must also show usefulness. Title 35 U.S.C. §101 states:

> Whoever invents or discovers any new and useful process, machine, manufacture, or composition of matter, or any new and useful improvement thereof, may obtain a patent therefor, subject to the conditions and requirements of this title.

What will satisfy this requirement is a question of fact. It is interesting to note that regardless of the infringing party's intent, the owner has a cause of action. Thus an innocent subsequent inventor who unknowingly makes, uses, or sells a device that was previously patented is liable, and he or she may be punished with the same severity as an intentional infringer.

It is possible to be liable for patent infringement even if one does not actually make, sell, or use the device. A person who induces another to infringe a patent may be held liable. In addition, a person who provides an ingredient that permits another to infringe may be held liable for **contributory infringement.** The penalties for relief include **injunctive relief** [court order requiring a person to do something or stop doing something] and damages. Though the damages are generally the reasonable **royalties** [payment for right to use a product, process, creation, etc.], 35 U.S.C. §284 allows damages to be increased up to **treble** [three times] the amount of actual damages.

### Exercise F. Analysis

Consider the scenarios and determine if there has been an infringement of someone's intellectual property rights and, if so, whether that infringement is a trademark or patent infringement.

*Scenarios*

1. The owner of Solar Tortilla Chips, a product well known to consumers by its logo of a bright red sun wearing a sombrero, is surprised on his weekly trip to the grocery store to find products that he has not manufactured being sold under the name of Solar Tortilla Chips and sporting the same logo.

2. Mehdi is an electrical engineer who has been working at home for years on a new type of electrical circuit that will revolutionize electronics. He begins to produce and sell these circuits and makes an enormous profit. Amir, another engineer, had previously patented a process that was substantially similar to the process Mehdi discovered. Mehdi is a very honest man and had no idea that he was not the original creator of the circuit.

3. Koke Company, trying to capitalize on the reputation of the Coca-Cola® Company, begins marketing its beverages as "Koke."

## Copyright

Copyright law provides for the protection of original works, in multiple fields, including art, literature, music, and drama, to name a few. Ideas or processes from these works of art, however, are not copyrightable. It is the particular expression that is copyrightable, not a particular idea. Let's look at 17 U.S.C. §102 (1992), which covers what may or may not be copyrighted.

§102. Subject matter of copyright: In general

(a) Copyright protection subsists, in accordance with this title, in original works of authorship fixed in any tangible medium of expression, now known or later developed, from which they can be perceived, reproduced, or otherwise communicated, either directly or with the aid of a machine or device. Works of authorship include the following categories:

(1) literary works;

(2) musical works, including any accompanying words;

(3) dramatic works, including any accompanying music;

(4) pantomimes and choreographic works;

(5) pictorial, graphic, and sculptural works;

(6) motion pictures and other audiovisual works;

(7) sound recordings; and

(8) architectural works.

(b) In no case does copyright protection for an original work of authorship extend to any idea, procedure, process, system, method of operation, concept, principle, or discovery, regardless of the form in which it is described, explained, illustrated, or embodied in such work.

Something copied verbatim from another source is not original work within the meaning of the copyright statute, nor is a work that currently exists in the public domain, so no one is entitled to a copyright on that type of material. Merely authoring a work does not satisfy the originality requirement—it must also possess a degree of creativity. However, the U.S. Supreme Court has held that "the requisite level of creativity is extremely low; even a slight amount will suffice" [*Feist Publications v. Rural Telephone Service Company, Inc.,* 499 U.S. 340, 111 S. Ct. 1282, 113 L.Ed.2d 358 (1991)].

The statute also requires that the expression be "fixed in a tangible medium of expression." Clearly, then, live performances are not copyrightable unless they are simultaneously recorded. For example, the Olympics, which are broadcast live and simultaneously videotaped (a "fixed medium"), are protected by the copyright laws. If they were not simultaneously videotaped, however, the actual performances of the athletes would not be copyrightable.

The author of a work owns the copyright in the work and has access to the court system to protect his or her rights, which include reproduction, adaptation, distribution, performance, and display. Sometimes, however, all of these rights are not retained by the owner of a work. Consider the case of an artist who creates a one-of-a-kind painting, which he or she sells. The owner (purchaser) of the work does not own the copyright. The artist retains the right to make prints or posters even though he or she has sold the original; the individual who bought the painting is barred from doing so.

When a person other than the owner of the copyright uses the material without prior permission of the author, that person has committed a **copyright infringement.** It is often impossible to prove that someone actually copied a work, so the courts now use a two-prong test to determine whether there has been an infringement. The original author must show:

1. that the **alleged infringer** [copier] had access to the material and
2. that the copied material is substantially similar to the original work. Whether a copy is substantially similar to the original is a question of fact using an objective standard of an ordinary person.

## FAIR USE

An exception to the infringement rule is called **fair use.** This means that a party can use part of a work of an author as long as the use is "fair." In other words, there must be a balancing of social, economic, and constitutional interests of both parties. Section 107 of Title 17 (17 U.S.C. §107) of the United States Code defines fair use and its applicability.

> 17 U.S.C. §107. Limitations on exclusive rights: Fair use
> Notwithstanding the provisions of sections 106 and 106A, the fair
> use of a copyrighted work, including such use by reproduction in

copies or phonorecords or by any other means specified by that section, for purposes such as criticism, comment, news reporting, teaching (including multiple copies for classroom use), scholarship, or research, is not an infringement of copyright. In determining whether the use made of a work in any particular case is a fair use the factors to be considered shall include—

(1) the purpose and character of the use, including whether such use is of a commercial nature or is for nonprofit educational purposes;

(2) the nature of the copyrighted work;

(3) the amount and substantiality of the portion used in relation to the copyrighted work as a whole; and

(4) the effect of the use upon the potential market for or value of the copyrighted work.

The fact that a work is unpublished shall not itself bar a finding of fair use if such finding is made upon consideration of all the above factors.

## Exercise G. Statutory Interpretation

1. In groups, prepare an explanation of the statute for a client. In pairs, present your explanation to your partner as though he or she were your client. Then reverse roles.

Until recently if the work was for a commercial use, courts generally disregarded the remaining elements of the statute. Now, however, courts consider all four factors when making fair use determinations and, in fact, have begun to add a fifth, nonstatutory element to their determination of what constitutes fair use: **transformative use.** This is a term coined by Pierre Leval in *Toward a Fair Use Standard,* 103 Harv. L. Rev. 1105 (1990), and adopted by the U.S. Supreme Court in its decision on fair use in *Campbell v. Acuff-Rose Music, Inc.,* 510 U.S. 569, 114 S. Ct. 1164, 127 L.Ed.2d 500 (1994). Transformative use requires the transformation of the quoted material: the purpose and the manner of use in the copied work must be different from those of the original work.

## Exercise H. Analysis and Role Play

1. Review the five elements courts now use to make a determination of fair use. Then read the court's recitation of the facts from *Leibovitz v. Paramount Pictures Corporation*, 948 F.Supp. 1214 (S.D.N.Y. 1996) below.

This action examines the extent to which a parody that appears in the form of an advertisement can constitute a fair use of a copyrighted work. Plaintiff is a well-known photographer who shot a photograph of the actress Demi Moore that appeared on the August 1991 cover of *Vanity Fair*. Ms. Moore was eight months pregnant and nude in the photo, the publication of which aroused a great deal of controversy. It is undisputed that plaintiff is the sole owner of the copyright in this photograph. In 1993, the defendant was developing advertising in connection with the release of its film, *Naked Gun: The Final Insult 33 1/3* [sic]. The defendant eventually selected a "teaser" ad which it contends was a parody of the *Vanity Fair* cover. In the advertisement, a model who was also eight months pregnant was photographed against a backdrop similar to that used in the Demi Moore photograph; the lighting and pose were also similar to the Moore photograph. Further, the photograph was subjected to some computer manipulation in order to duplicate the skin tone and body configuration that appeared in the Moore photo. On top of the second model's body, however, appeared a photograph of the face of Leslie Nielsen, the star of the *Naked Gun* series of films. In contrast to Ms. Moore's expression of fulfillment, serenity, and pride, Mr. Nielsen's face wore a guilty smirk. Underneath the photo ran the legend "Due This March."

Plaintiff brought suit, charging that the advertisement infringed her copyright in the Moore photograph. Defendant conceded that plaintiff owns the copyright in the photograph and that its advertisement targeted the Moore photograph, but contended that the ad was a parody and a fair use of plaintiff's copyrighted work. The parties made cross-motions for summary judgment.

2. Divide into teams, one for Paramount and one for Leibovitz. Develop arguments for each side on the basis of the statute and transformational use. Review the language of agreement and disagreement in Part 2, Debate (page 216) before beginning the debate.

3. Use the following information to develop more sophisticated arguments.

   a. Paramount did not request permission to use the photograph.

   b. Parody means to copy the way someone or something looks or behaves in order to make fun of it.

   c. Leslie Nielsen's character in the movie did not want to have children, although his wife did, so motherhood and childbearing were also elements in the movie.

   d. Once you have developed your argument, have one group member present it to the class. The plaintiff's team (Leibovitz) should present the argument first; the defendant's team second.

   e. Class members who are not presenting the case should act as the jury and decide, impartially, on the team who presented the best argument. Once the jury has rendered its verdict, listen to the court's decision on the audio.

2 Live Crew, a rap music group, parodied Ray Orbison's song "Oh, Pretty Woman" in a rap song titled "Pretty Woman." Acuff-Rose Music, Inc., the holders of the copyright on "Oh, Pretty Woman," sued 2 Live Crew and their record company alleging copyright infringement. 2 Live Crew responded claiming that their rap song, as a parody, fell under the fair use doctrine. The case, *Campbell v. Acuff-Rose Music, Inc.*, 510 U.S. 569, 114 S. Ct.. 1164, 127 L.Ed.2d 500 (1994), terminated at the U.S. Supreme Court, whose opinion, in part, states:

> The threshold question when fair use is raised in defense of parody is whether a parodic character may be reasonably perceived. Whether, going beyond that, parody is in good taste or bad does not and should not matter to fair use. . . .

The U.S. Supreme Court then criticized the court of appeals for applying too much weight to the commercial nature of the parody. The court of appeals erred when it held that since the nature of 2 Live Crew's song was commercial, there was a presumption against the applicability of the fair use doctrine.

The central purpose of this investigation is to see, in Justice Story's words, whether the new work merely "supersede[s] the objects" of the original creation, [citations omitted] ("supplanting" the original), or instead adds something new, with a further purpose or different character, altering the first with new expression, meaning, or message; it asks, in other words, whether and to what extent the new work is "transformative." Leval 1111. Although such transformative use is not absolutely necessary for a finding of fair use, [citation omitted] the goal of copyright, to promote science and the arts, is generally furthered by the creation of transformative works. Such works thus lie at the heart of the fair use doctrine's guarantee of breathing space within the confines of copyright, [citation omitted] and the more transformative the new work, the less will be the significance of other factors, like commercialism, that may weigh against a finding of fair use.

## Exercise I: Appellate Argument: Oral Communication

One team is to represent Dr. Seuss Enterprises, the plaintiff, and the other Penguin Books, the defendant.

1. Divide into teams.

2. Decide what law you think is applicable.

3. Debate the issues with the opposing team.

> *Fact Situation*
> Dr. Seuss Enterprises, copyright holders of the popular U.S. children's book *The Cat in the Hat,* written by Dr. Seuss, a pseudonym for Theodor Geisel, are suing Penguin Books for copyright infringement because Penguin has published an illustrated book entitled *The Cat NOT in the Hat! A Parody by Dr. Juice,* inspired by the original *The Cat in the Hat.* The subject matter of *The Cat NOT in the Hat* is the O. J. Simpson murder trial, written in rhyme, as in the original work. Neither the authors of *The Cat NOT in the Hat* nor the publishers obtained permission from the plaintiff prior to publication.

# Products Liability

## Discovering Connections

Who should be liable if a defective product causes injury or damage? Should it be the seller, the manufacturer, or even the consumer? At what level is a product unreasonably dangerous? When do dangers outweigh benefits? Can warnings about dangers relieve manufacturers and sellers from responsibility? These are basic questions that have become more important in recent years. This area of law is still evolving and often involves huge cases worth millions of dollars and thousands of participants.

### ACTIVITY

*Who's to blame? Who's to pay?*

1. Read this story.

> One day Matti invited his classmate, Jennifer, to his house so that they could finish their appellate argument in their "Intro to Advocacy" course. They had spent many hours putting together pictures and documents, and collecting tape recordings, and videotapes. Matti left to buy sodas and chips. A minute or two later, Jennifer picked up the box containing all the materials for their project, turned around quickly, and hit Matti's large aquarium filled with expensive salt-water fish.
>
> She barely touched the side of the aquarium, but it broke. The rush of salt water knocked the box from her hands, and all the materials were ruined. She didn't know what to do with the fish that had been gifts from Matti's rich uncle and just watched them as they lay on the floor dying.

By the time Matti returned, the fish were dead, his carpet was ruined, the materials for the project destroyed, and Jennifer was in shock. Who's to blame, and more important, who's to pay?

Divide into pairs and use the chart to answer questions about who you think should pay for the damages. You each have slightly different bits of information that will help you make MORAL judgments, not legal ones.

Partner A will find his or her information as Part 3, Text 2 (page 279), and Partner B will find his or hers as Part 3, Text 8 (page 286). You will need to ask the following questions of each other to determine who has the information necessary to fill in the chart. Your opinions may be Yes, No, or Don't know. Do not think of specific laws; just use moral logic with the information you're given.

2. What do you think Matti should pay for?

3. What do you think Jennifer should pay for?

4. Does he have insurance for the fish? SHOULD that insurance pay for the loss?

5. How about the carpet company? Should it at least pay to replace the carpet?

6. What about the aquarium company? Should it pay for any loss?

| Who's to Pay? | | | | |
|---|---|---|---|---|
| | Jennifer | Matti | Aquarium Company | Carpet Company |
| the fish | | | | |
| the carpet | | | | |
| the aquarium | | | | |
| the lost work | | | | |

## Legal Listening

## Essential Terms

**products liability:** broad area of the law of torts; manufacturer or seller of a product can be held liable for injuries or damages caused by defects in that product

**damages:** monetary compensation for injuries

**compensatory:** damages that replace money lost by plaintiff due to the injury (lost wages, medical bills, etc.)

**punitive (exemplary):** damages awarded to punish ($1,000,000 for coffee burns at restaurant) someone for wrongdoing (in products liability cases, generally a product seller or manufacturer)

**pretrial discovery:** the process of obtaining information from opposing parties prior to trial

## Putting the Terms to Use

Your instructor will play a mini-lecture about a famous products liability case in the United States. He or she will tell you if you will listen to the lecture once or twice. If the lecture will be played twice, the first time, you should just listen. The second time, you should take notes that will enable you to answer the questions.

1. Why was Ms. Lieback's case the first to reach the public's eye?
2. In which state did the accident occur?
3. In what way did the coffee injure Ms. Lieback?
4. How serious were Ms. Lieback's injuries?
5. To what extent did the jury decide Ms. Lieback was responsible for the accident?
6. How much did Ms. Lieback receive in compensatory damages? Why?
7. What was McDonald's® attitude to the general problem of injury from their hot coffee?
8. What caused the jury to agree to award Ms. Lieback punitive damages?
9. Do we know the terms of the settlement agreement?
10. How did this case alter McDonald's® behavior at least in that city?

## Legal Thumbnail

**Products liability** law **purports** to hold manufacturers and sellers of goods liable for faulty goods that cause personal injury or property damage. Products liability, as it exists now, is a relatively recent legal development that was created and expanded in part to protect consumers in an age of increasing technological complexity. In other words, there has been a policy decision by lawmakers and the courts that the responsibility for an injury caused by faulty consumer products should lie with the maker or seller of the goods and not the consumer.

### Exercise A. Case Hypotheticals and Discussion

Don't worry about the actual law in this exercise. In each of the scenarios you should determine who is "morally" responsible for the damage or injury caused. Your instructor may ask you to defend or explain your choices in either written or oral form.

*Fact Situations*

1. After drinking alcohol all day, an obviously drunk man buys a shotgun from a department store. He takes the gun home and shoots his girlfriend, who now will never be able to walk again. Who's responsible: the clerk, the drunk man, or the manufacturer of the shotgun?

2. An eighteen-year-old woman rents a waverunner [a motorized wind surfer]; she injures her face severely as she hits the unpadded steering wheel when a large wave swamps [sinks] her. Who's responsible: the woman, the rental agent, the manufacturer?

3. A pharmaceutical company hides and falsifies data about very serious mental side effects of a drug. A man taking the drug commits murder. Who's responsible: the murderer or the drug company?

4. A man who is killed in a minor car accident is clearly **at fault** [responsible]. However, it can be demonstrated that he would not have been killed if the car had been designed correctly. Who's responsible: the dead man or the car manufacturer?

5. A supermarket allows a cake manufacturer to set up an unattended table with samples of cakes for customers to try. A customer slips and falls on a piece of the cake on the floor in front of the table and breaks his hip. Who's responsible: the customer, the store, or the cake manufacturer?

# Building a Case

The causes of action in products liability cases are generally not exclusive. For example, you can file an action based on breach of implied warranty and negligence: a claimant is not required to choose one or the other doctrine.

However, no matter what the underlying theory of a products liability case, certain elements are common to all cases. There may be no **recovery** [award— usually monetary—from the court] unless

1. the product is shown to be defective or harmful: something about the product is capable of causing injury;
2. the seller's act or omission with regard to the product is **causally related** [the act or omission is proven to be directly connected to or caused by the defect in the product] to the injury; and
3. the seller is actually connected somehow to the product (i.e., shown to be the seller or manufacturer).

Because of the increasing complexity of the issues involved, the most important of the current causes of action in products liability is **strict liability in tort,** followed closely by **warranty protection** in contract law or, more specifically, the law of sales.

## *Strict Liability in Tort*

Strict liability means liability without fault. Even if a manufacturer has worked hard to develop a safe product, he or she is still responsible for damages if the product later turns out to have been sold in an unreasonably dangerous condition.

Prior to the development of strict liability in tort, a claimant was required to prove **privity of contract** [that he or she had some form of legal relationship with a person or entity] in order to succeed in a lawsuit against that person or entity. For example, if Jiri Cee bought a Minitaur car from Golden's dealership in Minneapolis, Minnesota, and the car later exploded due to a faulty gas line and Jiri was injured, Jiri could only sue Golden and not Minitaur even though it was Minitaur who unwittingly manufactured the faulty product. Jiri's legal relationship—the sales contract—was with Golden and not Minitaur. In other words, there was no privity of contract between Jiri Cee and Minitaur.

Cases such as *MacPherson v. Buick Motor Co.,* 217 N.Y. 382, 111 N.E. 1050 (1916) circumvented the difficult requirement of privity of contract. Prior to *MacPherson,* privity was required in almost all products liability lawsuits. Now, however, privity is required for none of the causes of action: Jiri can sue both Golden and Minitaur.

Although almost 40 years old, Restatement (Second) of Torts §402A is commonly cited by courts or has been codified in various states as the rule governing strict liability in products cases. It states:

> (1) One who sells any product in a defective condition unreasonably dangerous to the user or consumer or to his property is subject to liability for physical harm thereby caused to the ultimate user or consumer, or to his property, if
>
> (a) the seller is engaged in the business of selling such a product, and
>
> (b) it is expected to and does reach the user or consumer without substantial change in the condition in which it is sold.
>
> (2) The rule stated in Subsection (1) applies although
>
> (a) the seller has exercised all possible care in the preparation and sale of his product, and
>
> (b) the user or consumer has not bought the product from or entered into any contractual relation with the seller. [Restatement (Second) of Torts §402A (1965)]

## Exercise B. Reading for Details

1. Which subsection eliminates the need for privity of contract?
2. Does the seller have to be a professional seller for this section to be applicable?
3. Four of the five essential elements for proving a case under strict liability can be found in §402A. What are they?
4. Do you have a similar theory of liability in your country?
5. Manufacturers have been held liable under the doctrine of strict liability even though no negligence on their part could be found. What social goals are met by holding them responsible for injuries caused by their products?

Many strict liability in tort cases involve a failure of **duty to warn** [advise consumers of possible dangers]. For example, if you buy spray paint to paint your factory storage room and a worker has to be hospitalized due to inhalation of paint fumes in an unventilated area, the worker can sue the manufacturer in strict liability in tort if there was no warning about a need to ventilate on the spray paint packaging.

## Express Warranty

Now let's see how warranties enter into products liability cases. The underlying basis for all products liability actions is that the seller of a product owes a duty beyond that of the simple contract to the buyer of the product.

In almost all transactions, there is an **express warranty** [a promise stated by the manufacturer] that does not need to be labeled "warranty." For example, if there is a description of a product on the packaging, that description becomes part of the express warranty. If a salesclerk shows you a sample of a dish, that action becomes an express warranty that all of the dishes you buy will be identical within a range accepted within the industry. On the other hand, in many states there must be a specific nature to the warranty. If a store simply posts a satisfaction guaranteed sign, there isn't necessarily an express warranty.

## Implied Warranties

### WARRANTY OF MERCHANTABILITY

Of course, the product bought must not only meet the terms of the contract or express warranty (it must look like the sample), it must also not harm the buyer. In legal terms, the seller is obligated to warrant **merchantability** [the product is salable and fit for general purposes]. Merchantability means that the product does what it should; for example, a pen writes. It doesn't have to be the best pen in the world to meet the merchantability standard; it simply must write. Failure to provide a merchantable product is a breach of an **implied warranty** [a warranty that is implicit in the sale of the goods and does not have to be expressly stated by the product seller]. Thus, a pen that does not write on normal paper in a normal environment does not meet the implied warranty of merchantability.

Since the Uniform Commercial Code has been adopted in part or in whole by most states, we can look to it for a definition of this implied warranty. Uniform Commercial Code §2-314 defines the implied warranty of merchantability as follows.

> (1) Unless excluded or modified (Section 2-316), a warranty that the goods shall be merchantable is implied in a contract for their sale if the seller is a merchant with respect to goods of that kind. Under this section the serving for value of food or drink to be consumed either on the premises or elsewhere is a sale.
>
> (2) Goods to be merchantable must be at least such as
>
> (a) pass without objection in the trade under the contract description; and
>
> (b) in the case of fungible goods, are of fair average quality within the description; and

(c) are fit for the ordinary purposes for which such goods are used; and

(d) run, within the variations permitted by the agreement, of even kind, quality and quantity within each unit and among all units involved; and

(e) are adequately contained, packaged, and labeled as the agreement may require; and

(f) conform to the promise or affirmations of fact made on the container or label if any.

(3) . . .

The concept of being fit for ordinary purposes has been held by courts to include actions that are reasonably foreseeable. For example, it is common for a person to stand on a chair to reach something on the top shelf of a kitchen cabinet and not just use the chair for sitting. So, standing on a kitchen chair can also be considered ordinary use.

In addition to the requirements in U.C.C. §2-314, the plaintiff must be foreseeable. U.C.C. §2-318 offers three options regarding foreseeability. States, when enacting warranty statutes, choose the option that best suits the needs of the citizens of that particular state. The options are: (a) members and guests of the purchaser's household; (b) all natural persons whose contact with the product is foreseeable and who are injured by the product; and (c) all persons whose contact is foreseeable and who are injured by the product. Note that option (c) includes corporations. There is no requirement of a "natural" or "live" person.

### Exercise C. Writing and Pair Work

1. In pairs, review the statute on the warranty of merchantability given to you on pages 138–39. Using whatever form of statutory interpretation you find easier, analyze the statute. Review Part 2, Statutory Interpretation (page 207) before you begin.

2. Now, write a letter to a client listing the essential elements required to prove a breach of warranty of merchantability under the U.C.C. Don't forget to add in one of the elements of foreseeability from U.C.C. §2-318. See Part 2, Client Letters (page 191), before writing the letter.

WARRANTY OF FITNESS FOR A PARTICULAR PURPOSE

Additionally, the seller is obligated to warrant **fitness for a particular purpose** [the product is appropriate for the special purpose for which it was bought] of a product. If you tell the salesclerk before you buy a pen that you are going to use the pen underwater, his or her selling you the pen creates an implied fitness for a particular purpose: writing underwater. U.C.C. §2-315 provides:

> Where the seller at the time of contracting has reason to know any particular purpose for which the goods are required and that the buyer is relying on the seller's skill or judgment to select or furnish suitable goods, there is unless excluded or modified under the next section an implied warranty that the goods shall be fit for such purpose.

## Exercise D. Case Hypotheticals and Pair Work

1. In pairs, decide if a warranty has been violated in the scenarios. If so, what kind of warranty?

2. What elements are you required to prove? Present your answers orally to the class.

*Scenarios*

a. You buy a loaf of bread that turns out to be moldy when you open the package at home.

b. The new can opener you bought cuts your finger every time you try to open a can.

c. In a dive shop, you talk to the salesperson about your next diving trip to Greenland. You tell the salesperson that you have to be able to dive in very cold water with the equipment he or she wants to sell you. The salesperson sells you a dive suit that is not suitable for the extremely cold water off the coast of Greenland. You develop hypothermia [lowered body temperature] and almost die as a result of using the inappropriate dive suit.

d. "Guaranteed to rid your house of roaches in 30 days." On day 31 you find several roaches picnicking in your kitchen.

e. Serge can't find his screwdriver and uses a knife manufactured by Messing, Inc., to screw a dining room table together. The knife snaps, and a piece flies into his left eye, blinding him in that eye.

## Disclaimers

In many states it is possible to disclaim certain types of warranties. Here is a typical universal disclaimer for an instruction manual that may or may not actually be valid depending on the state in which it is to be used.

---

### Disclaimer of Liability

Neither Dragonflyer, Inc., nor any of its employees make any warranty, express or implied, including the warranties of merchantability or fitness for a particular purpose, or assume any legal liability or responsibility for the accuracy or completeness of any information contained in this manual or represent that its use would not infringe privately owned rights. Information provided in this manual by Dragonflyer, Inc., is provided "AS IS," and any express or implied warranties of merchantability and fitness for a particular purpose are disclaimed. In no event shall Dragonflyer, Inc., or its employees be liable for any direct, indirect, incidental, special, exemplary, or consequential damages (including but not limited to, procurement of substitute goods or services; loss of use, data, or profits; or business interruption) however caused and on any theory of liability, whether in contract, strict liability, or tort (including negligence or otherwise) arising in the use of this information.

---

### Exercise E. Writing and Pair Work

1. The disclaimer above is obviously not written in plain English. Taking into account that courts have accepted the use of the terms *as is* and *with all faults* to put the consumer on notice that there is no warranty, what can you eliminate to make this disclaimer easy for a consumer to read? List your deletions in writing.

2. After you have decided what you would eliminate, compare your answer to your partner's. In pairs, rewrite the disclaimer to make it easier for a consumer to understand. Limit your disclaimer to approximately 50 words (the example contains 150 words).

### Reckless Misconduct

In addition to the warranties of merchantability and fitness for a particular purpose, the seller/manufacturer is also obligated not to include any hidden dangers in the products. Failure to meet this obligation is **reckless misconduct.** In a well-publicized U.S. auto case [*Grimshaw v. Ford Motor Company,* 119 Cal.App.3d 757, 174 Cal.Rptr. 348 (1981)], Ford Motor Company was held liable for serious injuries to a passenger in a Ford Pinto automobile caused by the explosion of the gas tank after the Pinto was rear-ended. Although Ford was aware that the danger existed, the claimant was unaware that there were defects in the gasoline tank; thus that defect constituted a hidden danger in the Pinto. Ford was aware of the defect before the accident, but it found it more economical to leave the car on the market as it was rather than issue a recall [notice by manufacturer to consumers to return a faulty product]. In response to the perceived misconduct of the defendant, the plaintiff was awarded $125 million in punitive damages, which was later reduced to $3.5 million on appeal.

### Negligence

From the claimant's perspective, it is better to file suit on the basis of breach of implied or express warranty or strict liability in tort rather than negligence because the elements of proof are not so burdensome. In negligence, the claimant is required to prove: (1) a duty of reasonable care on the part of the seller, who doesn't have to be a professional seller; (2) a breach of that duty; (3) an injury to a person to whom a duty was owed; and (4) causal connection between the injury and the breach of duty.

### Burden of Proof

In summary, in a products liability action, a claimant must always prove that he or she was injured or suffered loss due to a faulty/defective product and that this product was causally connected with the injury or loss. To simply show an injury or a loss is not generally sufficient to sustain an action. Additionally, the claimant must show that the product was defective at the time it left the control of the seller. It is not enough to show that the product was defective at the time of the injury, particularly if there has been a substantial lapse of time between the sale of the product and the time of injury. This places a substantial burden of proof on the claimant in a products liability case even if the claimant is filing suit under the theories of strict liability in tort or breach of warranty, where he or she is not required to prove negligence on the part of the defendant.

## Exercise F. Reading Comprehension

1. Which cause of action is more difficult to prove, negligence or breach of warranty?

2. Is proving that an injury happened sufficient to prove negligence?

3. What four elements is a claimant required to prove in a breach of warranty action?

4. Define duty to warn, which is often used in strict liability in tort cases.

5. Who has the burden of proof in a products liability case?

# Damages

The monetary damage awards in products liability cases are a cause of great concern both to U.S. businesses and to international businesses doing business in the United States. There are two primary awards.

1. **Compensatory damages** are designed to provide the claimant with a monetary award to compensate for the injury or loss (such as hospitalization/replacement costs).

2. **Punitive damages** are designed to punish the seller of the product for wrongdoing.

The Ford Motor Company case [*Grimshaw v. Ford Motor Co.*, supra] involving the explosion of the Pinto's gas tank when struck from the rear gained notoriety because the jury initially awarded the claimant $125,000,000 in punitive damages, which was reduced by the trial court to $3,500,000. This was the beginning of what some people feel to be extravagant punitive damage awards that have become commonplace in products liability cases.

From a U.S. Supreme Court decision [*BMW of North America, Inc. v. Gore*, 517 U.S. 559, 116 S. Ct. 1589, 134 L.Ed.2d 809 (1996)] it would appear that the Court is in favor of limiting "excessive" punitive damages. Gore, after buying a new BMW, later discovered that the car had been damaged by acid rain during transport to the United States. He sued BMW for, *inter alia*, **fraud** [intentional deception] and in a jury trial was awarded $4,000 in compensatory damages, the amount by which the value of the car had been reduced. The jury also awarded Gore $4,000,000 in punitive damages. The jury's decision was based in part on a BMW policy that was to repair vehicles that had been damaged and sell them as new if the damages were less than 3 percent of the value of the car. The Alabama Supreme Court reduced the punitive damages award to $2,000,000; the size of the award prompted BMW to petition the U.S. Supreme Court for a writ of certiorari, which was granted. The

U.S. Supreme Court found the punitive damages award grossly excessive and in violation of the Due Process Clause of the U.S. Constitution.

In a more recent decision [*State Farm Mutual Insurance v. Campbell*, 538 U.S. 408, 123 S. Ct. 1513, 155 L. Ed.2d 585 (2003)], the Supreme Court again addressed the ratio between punitive and compensatory awards and found that "few awards exceeding a single-digit ratio between punitive and compensatory damages, to a significant degree, will satisfy due process."

In this case, the court overturned the original award that had been reinstated by the Utah Supreme Court of a $145,000,000 punitive award in addition to the compensatory award of $1,000,000. In other words, the Supreme Court thought that a 145:1 ratio was so excessive that it offended constitutional due process. Although the single-digit ratio does provide some guidance, the decision also restated the warning in *Gore* that there could not be "mathematical certainty" in awarding punitive damages. It might be interesting to note that two of the more conservative judges and one of the more liberal disagreed with the majority, but for different reasons; the conservative justices (Scalia and Thomas) did not believe that the Due Process Clause provides protection against excessive punitive damages, while Ginsburg thought this area should be part of the individual state's legal territory. Obviously, more cases will help refine this point.

It appears that the U.S. Supreme Court would require lower courts to look at three issues in determining the issue of excessiveness of punitive damages:

1. the reprehensibility [deservingness of criticism] of the conduct,
2. the ratio between compensatory damages and punitive damages, and
3. the difference between the award and civil/criminal punishments for the same action.

## Exercise G. Analysis

1. Review the fact situation and decide, in light of *BMW v. Gore* and *State Farm v. Campbell*, if the punitive damage award is excessive. You must support your decision based on U.S. law, and under U.S. law the award of punitive damages to a plaintiff in an action is acceptable.

    Angela Harper sued Montana Bottling Company for physical and mental distress she allegedly suffered when she drank part of an iced tea bottled by their company that contained the remains of a partially decomposed mouse. At the trial a toxicologist [expert on poisons] testified that his examination of the bottle showed mouse feces on the bottom of the bottle, which indicated that the mouse must have been in the bottle before the

liquid was added. The jury awarded Ms. Harper $5,000 in com-
pensatory damages, based on lost wages and medical expenses,
and $500,000 in punitive damages. No criminal charges were
brought against the bottling company.

2. Would the plaintiff be entitled to recover either compensatory or punitive damages in your country? On what grounds?

## Litigation Costs

Businesses have often been placed in the position of settling a products liability
case out of court to avoid the costs of litigating the action. Taking into account
attorneys' fees, expert witness charges, filing fees, court costs, possible punitive
damage awards or even bad publicity for the firm, as well as the time involved in
preparing to defend against an action, many businesses have decided that it is in
their best interest to settle even though the claimant might not have a supportable
cause of action against the manufacturer. This is especially true in cases where the
claimant, in attempting to reach the **deep pocket** [the seller with substantial
resources], brings in parties who are so far removed from the action as to be free
from fault.

One example of a settlement that was "forced" for these reasons involved a
European corporation that was sued in strict liability and negligence even though
the product, cable cars, had been sold more than twenty years before and several
other companies, such as wholesalers, refurbishers, and concessionaires, had had
access to and control of the cable cars in that twenty-year period.

The manufacturer of the cable cars chose to settle out of court after a cable car
fell at an amusement park, killing a man and paralyzing a young woman, even
though **intervening parties** [companies or people who had access to and were
involved with the product between the time claimant was injured by the product
and the time it was placed into commerce] and circumstances existed.

The cable car was originally sold by the manufacturer to a company in California, which resold it to a second company, which refurbished and upgraded the
cable cars and then leased the cable car to a third company, a concessionaire at
the amusement park. This third company did not perform the maintenance as
required in the manufacturer's instructions and disengaged safety switches
designed to prevent operation in windy conditions. On the day of the accident, the
cars were swinging violently in heavy winds; however, the operator did not reen-
gage the safety switch and shut down operations. Finally, the cable snapped, causing a car to fall, killing a man standing below and paralyzing the claimant, who
was riding in one of the cars that fell, from the neck down.

The claimant, a young woman, included the manufacturer in the suit because none of the other parties had sufficient insurance or capital to pay a multimillion-dollar award. The non-U.S. manufacturer was concerned about two things:

1. the possibility of punitive damages because of the sympathy that the young (twenty-two years old) woman's plight would have aroused among jury members, and
2. the high cost of attorney's fees in the United States.

If the case had gone to trial, the manufacturer would most probably not have been held liable, but since nothing in law is certain, they chose to settle. The corporation decided that it was simpler to settle for $3,000,000 rather than risk having to pay the requested award of $100,000,000.

## Exercise H. Anaylsis

1. The cable car accident happened in the early 1980s. Do you think the company might have reconsidered its decision to settle out of court after *BMW v. Gore* and *State Farm v. Campbell*? In writing, list the reasons for your stance.
2. The U.S. attorneys for the cable car company recommended taking the case to trial. The European attorneys were against this. In writing list possible reasons for the difference of opinion.

## Exercise I. Reading for Details

Using the information from the legal thumbnail, determine what is wrong with each statement.

1. The plaintiff and defendant must always have privity of contract in products liability actions.
2. A plaintiff may not file an action in both negligence and breach of warranty.
3. The manufacturer's only duty to the buyer is contractual.
4. Products liability law is a totally new innovation in the field of consumer protection law.
5. Punitive damages are awarded to compensate a claimant for monetary loss.

6. A claimant can win a products liability suit if the seller's act or omission with regard to a product is not causally related to his or her injury.

7. The burden of proof on the claimant is easier in negligence actions than in breach of implied warranty actions.

8. If you injure yourself while using a manufacturer's or seller's product, you are entitled to recover if you file a products liability lawsuit.

9. In actions for breach of implied warranty of merchantability, the buyer is not entitled to recovery if he or she is using the product for other than the purpose intended by the manufacturer.

10. When businesses settle out of court, it is solely due to fear of punitive damage awards.

# Contracts

---

## Discovering Connections

### ACTIVITY

Many attorneys like to begin writing new contracts by following a model contract. This means, of course, that many model contracts can be found online or in forms books. Common examples of model contracts are rental contracts that can be bought in stationery shops in Europe or on a CD in the United States.

A typical rental contract in the United States might start with this information.

---

### Rental Contract

In consideration of the agreement of the Resident(s), known as:

_____,

The owner hereby rents them the dwelling located at _____, for
the period commencing on the ___ day of _____, 20____, and monthly thereafter
until the last day of _____, 20____, at which time this Agreement is terminated.

Resident(s), in consideration of Owners permitting them to occupy the above property,
hereby agrees to the following terms:

- RENT: To pay as rental the sum of $_____ per month, due and payable in
  advance from the first day of every month. Failure to pay rent when due will result in
  the Owner taking immediate legal action to evict the Resident from the premises and
  seize the security deposit.
- LATE FEE: Rent received after the first of the month will be subject to a late fee of
  10% plus (3.00) dollars per day.

---

Other typical clauses might include:

- CLEANING: Resident accepts premises in its current state of cleanliness and agrees to return it in a like condition.
- LEAD-BASED PAINT: Houses built before 1978 may contain lead-based paint. Lead from paint, paint chips, and dust can pose health hazards if not taken care of properly. Lead exposure is especially harmful to young children and pregnant women. Before renting pre-1978 housing, landlords must disclose the presence of known lead-based paint and lead-based paint hazards in the dwelling. Tenants must also receive a federally approved pamphlet of lead poisoning prevention.
- SMOKE DETECTORS: Smoke detectors have been installed in this residence. It's the tenant's responsibility to maintain these appliances including testing periodically and replacing batteries as recommended by the manufacturer. In the event a detector is missing or inoperative, the tenant has an affirmative duty to notify the landlord immediately.

### Part A

Work in pairs to decide what the answers are for your country/countries for the following.

- Do you have similar clauses in rental contracts in your country?
- Are warnings about possible lead exposure problems required?
- Do all apartments have smoke detectors?
- What rental clauses do you think exist in your country that might not be included in a U.S. rental contract?

### Part B

If you have time and adequate Internet access, search for "rental contracts" in English or in your own language to compare the different provisions of a common contract.

## Legal Listening

A. Read this contract form, a bill of sale for automobiles. Since you will use this contract in the next activity, don't worry if you don't understand every word right now.

---

### BILL OF SALE

Dated:

_____, referred to as "SELLER," sells, bargains and conveys all of SELLER'S rights, title and interest in:

Make: _____

Model: _____

Style of the vehicle: _____

Year of vehicle: _____

Vehicle Identification Number (VIN): _____

to _____, referred to as "BUYER," his heirs and assigns.

_____ acknowledges receipt of a total of $_____ (_____ & no/100 Dollars) from _____, BUYER, in partial payment of the agreed total sales price of $_____, (_____ & no/100 Dollars).

_____, SELLER, shall remain fully liable for any undisclosed liens or encumbrances. SELLER, _____, warrants that there are no liens or encumbrances on the goods sold, and that _____'s title to the goods is clear and merchantable. _____, SELLER, shall defend _____ from any adverse claims to SELLER's title to the goods sold.

The goods sold herein are not sold by a merchant in the field. THESE GOODS ARE SOLD WITHOUT U.C.C. WARRANTY OF ANY KIND, including MERCHANTABILITY AND FITNESS FOR A PARTICULAR PURPOSE. The BUYER, _____, acknowledges examining the goods sold herein. This provision may not be applicable, and legal rights may vary between states.

The parties agree to the terms and conditions stated herein:

_____, SELLER (signature)

_____ (typed name)

_____, BUYER (signature)

_____ (typed name)

B. Listen carefully. Pretend you are the lawyer interviewing the client regarding the sale of an antique car. As you listen, fill in the blanks on the Client Worksheet for Sale of Goods.

## Client Worksheet for Sale of Goods

Client's Full Name: _____

Address: _____

Telephone Number: _____

Description of property to be conveyed: _____

_____

Buyer: _____

Seller: _____

Consideration: _____

Date for execution that should appear on contract: _____

_____

C. After you have completed the worksheet, use it to fill in the blanks in the Bill of Sale contract on pages 150–51. You may need to "invent" some of the information.

D. In pairs, compare your contract with a classmate's. Do you disagree on any of the information?

---

## Legal Thumbnail

---

## Basis of a Contract

A contract is not merely a promise. It is a promise that one gives voluntarily and with the intent that the contract be enforceable at law. The contract creates legal obligations for both parties. Thus, there is a relationship between the **rights** [what one is entitled to] and the **duties** [what one must do] of the contracting parties. A contract gives each individual a legal duty to the other parties, but each individual also has a right to seek a **remedy** [solution] for **breach of contract** [failure of the other party to fulfill his or her legal duty]. Very generally speaking, to be enforceable a contract must have

1. competent parties,
2. legal subject matter,
3. legal consideration,
4. mutuality of agreement, and
5. mutuality of obligation.

The absence of any of these elements may **render** [make] a contract unenforceable. Now let's discuss them one by one.

### *Competent Parties*

In order to demonstrate the competence necessary to render a contract enforceable, all parties to a contract must have the ability to understand and agree to the terms of the contract. Understanding the contract refers only to the person's innate ability to understand that a contract has been formed, not to his or her misunderstanding, foolishness, or lack of care. Clearly, mental incompetents fall under the protection of this requirement; however, defining just who is mentally incompetent can be challenging. In a similar manner, **minors** [individuals under a legal age limit that can vary from state to state] are often not considered "competent." For example, in a well-known case [*Kiefer v. Fred Howe Motors, Inc.,* 39 Wis.2d 20, 158 N.W.2d 288 (1968)], a young man, technically a minor, bought a car. However, he then decided that he didn't like the car and tried to take it back to the dealer. The dealer wouldn't take the car back and refund the young man's money so the young man sued for **rescission** [annulment of the contract]. The young man won, and the dealer had to give him back his money because a contract with a minor isn't (usually) valid. Additionally, in some cases, one of the parties' inability to read or write the language of the contract may be important in determining if the party is competent or not.

## Subject Matter

The subject matter of a contract must be legal. Thus, one cannot form a legal contract in the United States to have a third party killed; in other words, hit men (and hit women)—professional killers—cannot be sued if they miss their targets.

## Legal Consideration

Consideration is the inducement to enter a contract. Although the consideration for entering a contract is often reduced to an amount of money, it can also be a right, **tangible property** [real or personal property], benefit, or some other interest. Consideration must, however, be legal; those things that are considered "illegal" or "immoral" are not legal consideration.

## Mutuality of Agreement

Mutuality of agreement is a meeting of the minds of all parties to a contract. The phrase "meeting of the minds" as it is used here means that the parties understand and share the common purpose that certain property, rights, or benefits will be transferred and a mutual obligation incurred.

## Mutuality of Obligation

Mutuality of obligation is especially important when it comes to a question of action for breach of contract since unless both parties to a contract are bound, neither is bound. The parties must both incur legal duties before a contract is enforceable.

## Exercise A. Listening

1. Listen to the conversations, and decide if all, some, or none of the essential elements of a contract are present. Play each conversation twice. The first time, just listen; the second time, write the required information in the blanks.

   ### A. In the park

   1. competent parties _____

   2. legal subject matter _____

   3. legal consideration _____

   4. mutuality of agreement _____

   5. mutuality of obligation _____

### B. On the beach

1. competent parties      _____
2. legal subject matter     _____
3. legal consideration      _____
4. mutuality of agreement _____
5. mutuality of obligation _____

2. Prepare an oral explanation of your decision on the contractual elements.

# Forming a Contract

Before a contract can be formed, there must be both an offer and an acceptance of that offer. Sound simple? It's not; lawyers everywhere have earned millions of dollars in fees arguing just whether or not a valid contract existed.

In common law, contracts are formed in this manner:

1. An offer is made by a person or corporation normally referred to as an **offeror.**
2. The offer is then accepted [**acceptance**] by a person or corporation normally referred to as an **offeree.**

Let's reduce what we've learned about contracts to a formula:

offer + acceptance = **bona fide** [valid] contract

if the parties are (a) competent, (b) mutually agree and obligate themselves regarding a specific subject, and (c) there is legal consideration.

## Exercise B. Reading for Detail

In the contract you drafted earlier (the bill of sale):

1. Who was the offeree?
2. Who was the offeror?
3. What was the consideration?
4. Would the contract most likely have been bona fide at common law?

In order to understand contracts more fully, we must add to and clarify our original equation by considering what constitutes a valid offer and acceptance and by discussing what constitutes legal consideration:

enforceable contract = offer + acceptance + legal consideration

## Offer

The elements of an offer at common law are set forth in this formula.

offer = intent + identified offeree + clear and definite terms + specified duration

Though it seems complicated in this formula, an offer itself is merely a **pledge** [a promise] to act or to refrain from acting. A sale of a car is a pledge to transfer the auto's **title** [a legal document of ownership] from a seller to a buyer. An example of a pledge to refrain from acting would be a noncompetition agreement, such as those found in many employment contracts. Let's look at an example.

---

### EMPLOYEE NON-COMPETITION AGREEMENT

For good consideration and as an inducement for _____ (Company) to employ _____ (Employee), the undersigned Employee hereby agrees not directly or indirectly to compete with the business of the Company and its successors and assigns during the Employee's period of employment and for a period of _____ years following termination of the Employee's employment and notwithstanding the cause or reason for termination of the Employee's employment.

The term "not compete" as used in this document shall mean that the Employee shall not own, manage, operate, consult or be employed in a business substantially similar to or competitive with the present business of the Company or such other business activity in which the Company may substantially engage during the term of the Employee's employment.

The Employee acknowledges that the Company shall or may in reliance on this agreement provide Employee access to trade secrets, customers, and other confidential data and goodwill. Employee agrees to retain said information as confidential and not to use said information on his or her own behalf or disclose same information to any third party.

This agreement shall be binding upon and **inure** [have an effect on] to the benefit of the parties, their successors, assigns, and personal representatives.


Signed this _____ day of _____ _____ (year).

_____
Company

_____
Employee

---

We'll come back to this short contract several times. In order to arrive at a fuller understanding of an offer, let's look more closely at the components of an offer.

**INTENT**

Intent, in the legal sense, is not to be confused with motivation. Motive prompts a person to act or results in his or her failure to act. Intent, on the other hand, refers only to the state of mind with which the act is done or omitted. In the context of contracts, legal intent must be a statement that the offeree can reasonably rely on and respond to. In formal legal English, intent is present when one exhibits willingness to enter into a bargain in such a manner that the other party is justified in relying on the fact that his or her assent to that bargain not only is invited but also, if given, will seal the bargain.

Intent is more than a simple statement made in jest. For example, if you are very hungry, you might say in English: "I would give a million dollars for a pizza!" This statement does not show legal intent since no reasonable person would be justified in relying on the fact that the person uttering that statement would actually give a million dollars for a pizza no matter how hungry the person was. However, sometimes it is hard to determine intent.

Consider the facts of *Lucy v. Zehmer*, 196 Va. 493, 84 S.E.2d 516 (1954).

Defendant's Story:

> Mr. Zehmer and his wife (the defendants) are being sued by Mr. Lucy and his brother. Mr. Lucy and his brother **allege** [state without evidence] that Mr. and Mrs. Zehmer entered into a contract with them to sell the Zehmers' 471-acre farm to Mr. Lucy for $50,000. Mr. Zehmer claims that the offer was made in jest while the three of them [Mr. and Mrs. Zehmer and Mr. Lucy] were drinking and that he only wished to **bluff** [trick] Lucy into admitting that he did not have $50,000.

Plaintiff's Story:

> Mr. Lucy (the plaintiff) says he took the offer seriously and that he had no reason to suspect that Mr. Zehmer did not; after all, they discussed the terms together and made sure the agreement (written on the back of a bill from Ye Olde Virginnie Restaurant) had a space for Mrs. Zehmer to sign, and then Mr. Lucy gave Mr. Zehmer $5 to seal the bargain. After the evening of "negotiations," Mr. Lucy arranged for **title examination** [a search of real property records for ownership information]. Mr. Lucy even sold half interest in the contract to his brother (who then became part of this legal action) to raise the $49,995 he needed to complete the deal.

## Exercise C. Review, Summarizing, and Analysis

Answer these questions in writing.

1. Do you think there was a valid contract? Why? Why not?

2. Is Mr. Zehmer's claim that the offer was in jest important?

3. Should Mr. Zehmer be required to sell his farm to the Lucy brothers?

4. Read this legal definition of intent.

> Design, resolve, or determination with which a person acts. . . . [citations omitted] A mental attitude which can seldom be proved by direct evidence, but must ordinarily be proved by circumstances from which it may be inferred [citations omitted]. [*Black's Law Dictionary* 727 (5th ed., 1979)]

5. Summarize the legal definition of intent in everyday English. Does the definition change your perception of the outcome in *Lucy v. Zehmer*? If so, how? See Student Resource Text 6.

6. Would the fact that Mr. Zehmer was acting in jest negate the contract?

## Exercise D. Role Play

Now use the facts of the case, and follow the directions to prepare a role play.

### The Trial

1. Choose a student to be the lawyer for the defendant and one for the plaintiff's lawyer.

2. For each of the "lawyers," select one or more students to serve on his or her legal team.

3. Select students to play each of the witnesses you plan to question.

4. Choose one student to be the judge; the others will serve as the jury.

5. Since the facts are already known, each of the legal teams must prepare questions to ask the witnesses in order to show its case in the best light.

6. After each team has asked all of its questions, the jury will **render** [give] a verdict. Remember that the jury can only base its decision on what it hears in "court."

Consider the following arguments in preparing your case.

Plaintiff:

- The existence of an offer depends on the reasonable meaning of the offeror's acts and words.
- Undisclosed intention is immaterial.
- The memorandum was signed by both defendants.
- The terms discussed and agreed to by all parties were clear and definite.

Defendant:

- The offer was made in jest.
- There was no intention on the part of either defendant to sell the farm.
- All parties were intoxicated at the time of the "contract" negotiations and execution.
- The "contract" does not contain clear and definite terms.

**IDENTIFIED OFFEREE**

Normally, an offeree must be specifically identified; he or she cannot be vague or ambiguous. For example, in the contract in *Lucy v. Zehmer* you know exactly who the offeree (buyer) is. However, the offeree is not always so clear. For example, in many cases, advertisements (often including catalogs from department stores) are not offers but are simply devices to begin negotiations because there is no definite offeree.

In an advertisement (called *ad* in American English), most people would think of the ad's audience [the readers] as the offeree. In legal terms, however, the people who read the ad often become the offerors when they "offer" to buy whatever the ad is selling. Thus, when the buyer contacts the seller, both parties (the advertiser/offeree and the buyer/offeror) are finally clearly identified.

**CLEAR AND DEFINITE TERMS**

The terms of an offer must be clear and definite. For example, Mr. Saidulla (the seller) promises to sell 50 bales of cotton to Mr. Bobur (the buyer), whom he has just met. Mr. Bobur agrees to the sale and promises to pay Mr. Saidulla cost plus "a good profit." There is no contract because Mr. Saidulla and Mr. Bobur could each have a different idea of what a good profit is: the terms are not clear and definite. All parties must be certain what is intended and what action is to be taken once they **execute** [sign] the contract. In general, the more specific the terms of any document are, the more likely one could claim that an offer was made.

## Exercise E. Analysis

1. Review the employee non-competition agreement. What steps are taken to ensure that the terms of the contract are clear and definite?

2. What if we just wrote:

   > The undersigned Employee hereby agrees not directly or indirectly to compete with the business of the Company and its successors and assigns.

   Would that very broad statement probably be acceptable as clear and definite? Why? Why not?


For sale of goods, **reasonable market practices** (sometimes known as **standard business practices**) may be acceptable in lieu of [in place of] specificity. Let's change the facts of the case with Mr. Saidulla (the seller) and Mr. Bobur (the buyer). Let's assume that they have been doing business together for several years. Each year Mr. Bobur has paid Mr. Saidulla cost plus 10 percent. Their business history establishes a reasonable market practice between Mr. Bobur and Mr. Saidulla. Now in their sixth year of doing business, they could state "cost plus a good profit" and each could probably make a good case in court regarding the meaning. However, it would still be much safer for them to state explicitly the definition of "good profit," in this case, 10 percent.

Reasonable market practices do not always require a course of dealing between the parties to be considered binding on them. In the Bobur/Saidulla case, if the standard practice in the cotton industry were to pay a 10 percent profit after cost, then, just as in the situation above, a strong argument could be made that the parties were aware of what "good profit" meant and could be held to a 10 percent profit.

SPECIFIED DURATION FOR ACCEPTANCE OF THE OFFER
An offer is not valid forever but only for a specified period of time. Normally, an offeror should state the specific time frame for acceptance by the offeree. If no time period for acceptance is specified in the offer, there will be an assumption of a reasonable time. What constitutes a "reasonable time" is a question of fact that depends on the circumstances of each case. For example, advertisements for **sales** [a temporary discount on a product] tell the reader how long the sale will continue. Thus, if Ted Vision tries to buy a television from Mark's TV Emporium for the **sale** [discounted] price two days after the sale ends (the time specified in the advertisement), the offer has expired and Mark may choose not to honor the terms of the ad. Of course, Mark may also choose to honor the ad's price just to make a sale if he wishes to.

If an offer is not accepted within the specified or reasonable time period, the offer expires. The next attempt to accept the now-expired offer becomes a **counter-offer.** A counter-offer is also a termination of the original offer and not an acceptance of it.

Offers can be **terminated** or **revoked** prior to acceptance by the offeree. A **termination** is caused by factors normally outside the control of the offeror. A **revocation,** on the other hand, is a statement by the offeror that he or she is withdrawing the offer.

Remember that termination is caused by factors outside the control of the offeror while revocation is within his or her control. Ivan offers to sell his car to Maija. She wants a few days to think it over. In the meantime, a fire destroys Ivan's car before Maija has accepted or declined the offer. In this case, the offer terminates. Other factors that may cause termination are death of the offeror, rejection by the offeree, or a counter-offer by the offeree.

On the other hand, if Ivan simply changes his mind and decides not to sell his car, his notice to Maija serves as a revocation of his offer.

## Acceptance

Before a contract can exist, there must be an acceptance of the offer by the offeree. Acceptance is a communication of agreement to the terms of the offer by words or conduct. Joseph sees a copy machine in a catalog that he would like to buy. Joseph, a clever law student, realizes that the catalog is just an invitation for offers. Joseph "offers" to buy the copy machine; in other words, he completes and sends in the catalog order form. In this case when the copy machine is delivered the following week, the delivery of the copy machine is seen as the acceptance of Joseph's offer.

On the other hand, many states have laws that make ads more like offers. Stores often advertise sale items without noting the quantity they have to sell. Then if people want to buy more of the item than the store has, the store must issue a rain check that allows the customer to buy the item at the sale price when the item is back in stock even though the sale period has ended.

### Exercise F. Case Hypotheticals and Discussion

1. Georgette's Goldfish and Guppies advertises "two regular goldfish for the price of one. This offer good for seven days." They sell out of goldfish on the first day of the sale. Is it probable that they will have to issue rain checks under American law? How about in your legal system?

2. Six months later, Georgette's Goldfish and Guppies advertises "two regular goldfish for the price of one" and changes the second line to "offer limited to stock on hand." Will they have to issue rain checks after they sell the six fish they had on the first day? How do the two cases differ?

Acceptance must mirror the terms of the most recent offer. A response that looks like an acceptance but alters significant terms is not acceptance but a counter-offer. Joseph orders a Lee 6XY model copy machine. However, the Lee 6XY is out of stock, and the company's telephone sales representative suggests that he take a Lee 7XY instead. The sales representative has not accepted Joseph's offer but has made a counter-offer that Joseph can accept or decline. Joseph, of course, can make a counter-offer to the counter-offer and offer to buy the Lee 7XY, a newer, more expensive model, for the price of the older Lee 6XY.

In many countries, this informal **bargaining**, [rapid oral give-and-take of offers] is common for most transactions. However, in the United States, few commonplace transactions permit bargaining. Instead, a price is clearly posted and is never debated orally. On the other hand, stores often have written "offers" such as "buy three for the price of two" or "thirteenth pair of shoes free" posted throughout the store.

## STANDARDIZED FORMS

Many businesses use standardized forms for repetitive transactions. These forms are called **boilerplate forms.** In the past, the use of these often preprinted documents presented problems with both offer and acceptance since they frequently did not mirror every single term and detail. However, for the sale of goods, this issue has been addressed in Section 2-207 of the Uniform Commercial Code (U.C.C.).

> **U.C.C. §2-207. Additional Terms in Acceptance or Confirmation**
>
> (1) A definite and seasonable expression of acceptance or a written confirmation which is sent within a reasonable time operates as an acceptance even though it states terms additional to or different from those offered or agreed upon, unless acceptance is expressly made conditional on assent to the additional or different terms.
>
> (2) The additional terms are to be construed as proposals for addition to the contract. Between merchants such terms become part of the contract unless:
>
>> (a) the offer expressly limits acceptance to the terms of the offer;
>>
>> (b) they materially alter it; or
>>
>> (c) notification of objection to them has already been given or is given within a reasonable time after notice of them is received.

(3) Conduct by both parties which recognizes the existence of a contract is sufficient to establish a contract for sale although the writings of the parties do not otherwise establish a contract. In such case the terms of the particular contract consist of those terms on which the writings of the parties agree, together with any supplementary terms incorporated under any other provisions of this Act.

## Exercise G. Role Play

Work in pairs. One of you is a lawyer; the other is an unhappy client. The client has received an acceptance to his or her sales contract with changes in the mediation and choice of law clauses. He or she wants you to explain if this acceptance has created a binding contract. You will need to simplify the language in U.C.C. §2-207 since the client is upset because he or she has received an acceptance that contains terms that do not exactly mirror the original terms agreed upon.

## *Consideration*

Consideration is a bargained-for exchange of legal value given in return for a performance or promise of performance so that a contract can be formed. Consideration is most often monetary in nature, but it does not have to be. Consideration can also be a promise to act or not to act. In a famous case from 1891 [*Hamer v. Sidway*, 124 N.Y. 538, 27 N.E. 256 (1891)], a man offered to pay his nephew $5,000 if the nephew would not drink, smoke, swear, or play cards or billiards for money until he was 21. The courts held that the nephew's not doing something he had the right to do was sufficient consideration and awarded him the $5,000.

## Exercise H. Analysis

In writing, answer the following.

1. What was the consideration in *Hamer v. Sidway*?

2. In the United States of 2007, it is illegal in almost all cases for anyone under 21 to drink alcohol and in many states illegal to play cards or billiards for money. Do you think the nephew would win his case today based on the same facts? Why or why not?

## Detrimental Reliance

Often promises are broken. Usually, the results of a broken promise are not that important. If, however, you rely on a promise and do something or don't do something and then that promise is not fulfilled and you are injured as a result, you may be able to claim relief under the doctrine of **detrimental reliance** (sometimes referred to as **promissory estoppel**). For example, if your brother-in-law invites you for a visit in May and then has to cancel the invitation, that is generally not a problem. What if he knows, however, that you plan on buying non-refundable plane tickets for your family and doesn't let you know that he is likely to cancel the invitation because that is the busy time of year in the alterations business? Even though it is unlikely that you would sue your brother-in-law, it is possible that the court would find detrimental reliance. In other words, there is no contractual basis for a suit, but under the equitable doctrine of detrimental reliance, your brother-in-law might be responsible for your "losses."

## Exercise I. Listening and Writing

1. Look at the chart (page 164) that demonstrates the events leading to a case based on detrimental reliance. The chart follows and dates the course of business arrangements and negotiations among D & G Stout, Inc., operating as General Liquors, Inc., Bacardi Imports, Inc., and National Wine & Spirits Company [*D & G Stout, Inc. v. Bacardi Imports, Inc.* 923 F.2d 566 (7th Cir. 1991)]. General and National were both wholesale liquor distributors in Indiana. In our sad story, General detrimentally relies on Bacardi.

2. Note that the chart includes several blanks signaled by an asterisk*. Listen to the conversation, and write the important facts.

3. After completing the chart, in twenty words or less, write the basic problem in this case.

4. General sues Bacardi for its loss. What do you think the judgment will be? Why?

5. Now listen to the decision. Do you agree or not? Would it be the same in your legal system?

| Date | D & G Stout (General) | Bacardi | National |
|---|---|---|---|
| April | wholesale distributor of liquor in Indiana | liquor manufacturer using General as distributor | another wholesale liquor distributor in Indiana |
| July 8 | enters negotiations with National for sale of General to National | | |
| July 9 | | * | |
| July 22 | | | negotiations finalized with General |
| July 22 | tells Bacardi that they intend to reject National's offer | Bacardi again assures General that the product line will remain with General. | |
| July 23 AM | rejects National's offer | | |
| July 23 PM | | Bacardi decides to withdraw line from General. | |
| July 30 | * | | |
| August 3 | loses another product line, in part due to Bacardi's withdrawal of its products | | |
| August 6 | | | enters into negotiations to buy General |
| August 14 | * | | |
| November | files suit against Bacardi | | |

# Breach of Contract

If one of the parties does not fulfill his or her promise in the contract, that failure of performance is called a **breach of contract.** The legal actions an injured party can take depend on both the specific clauses of each contract and the facts. For example, in *Stambovsky v. Ackley,* 169 A.D.2d 254, 572 N.Y.S.2d 672 (1991), the plaintiff, Mr. Stambovsky, sued for breach of contract because the house he bought was not vacant when he moved in although the contract had specified the house would be. Although Mr. Stambovsky did eventually win his case, the first court dismissed the case when the plaintiff maintained that the unwanted inhabitants of the house were poltergeists, a kind of ghost. What is the plaintiff who wins her or his action for breach of contract entitled to receive from the defendant?

## Damages

The most common remedy for nonfulfillment of the contract is **expectation or "benefit of the bargain" damages** based on how much the injured person might have gained if the other person had fulfilled his or her promise. Monetary damages compensate an injured party for the loss of any benefits that he or she would have received if the contract had been performed. Of course, it is time consuming and expensive to go through the court process to determine damages. Instead, contracting parties often write contracts that contain **liquidated or stipulated damages** clauses specifying a monetary amount or a formula for computing damages in the event of a breach of contract by either party. The amount of liquidated damages specified in the provision must be based on a reasonable estimate of what the loss would be in the event of a breach of contract. If the amount specified in the contract is not based on a reasonable estimate, it is possible that the court will find the clause to be invalid.

## Specific Performance

Unlike other remedies, **specific performance** is a remedy that does not rely on monetary damages for compensation. Instead, the **breaching party** [the party who breaks the contract] is required by the courts to fulfill his or her part of the bargain to avoid **irremediable damages** [damages that no monetary award can repair] to the non-breaching party. This remedy, which was originally only heard in **courts of equity** [an older form of courts now rarely found as separate courts in the United States], is available only if these criteria are met.

1. Monetary damages will not sufficiently reimburse the non-breaching party.
2. The contract was for personal services unobtainable elsewhere (you cannot force someone to perform but can obtain an injunction to keep him or her from performing similar services elsewhere—common in sports contracts).
3. The property/service is rare or unique.
4. The balance of the hardships to both parties has been considered.

Since specific performance has its roots in equity, a court will always attempt to balance the hardship of performance for the breaching party against the benefit of performance to the non-breaching party.

Albert and Mae Madariaga, manufacturers of Albert's Famous Mexican Hot Sauce, leased their business to James Morris and his partner. Both parties agreed that after a payment of $54,000 over a period of ten years, plus **royalties** [a share of the profits given because one party allows another to use his property] for sale of the hot sauce, Morris would own the business if he exercised the option for **conveyance** [transfer] of the business at a cost of $1,000.00. However, at the end of the ten years, the Madariagas refused to transfer the business to Morris unless

Morris promised to pay royalties to them on each bottle of their secret hot sauce in perpetuity. When Morris sued the Madariagas for breach of contract, the courts forced them to convey their business to Morris in specific performance since no amount of money could resolve the issue fairly [*Madariaga v. Morris*, 639 S.W.2d 709 (Tex. Ct. App., 1982)].

### Exercise J. Case Hypotheticals and Discussion

Answer the questions in writing. Compare your answers with a partner.

1. In *Klein v. Pepsico,* 845 F.2d.76 (4th Cir. 1988), Pepsico "agreed" to sell a Gulfstream G-II (a vintage airplane) through a broker to Mr. Klein. A little while later, Pepsico refused to go through with the sale. Mr. Klein sued. The first court decided that the G-II was unique. Would specific performance (in other words, making Pepsico sell the plane to Mr. Klein) be appropriate in this case? Why or why not?

2. Pepsico appealed and noted in the appeal that later Mr. Klein made offers on two other G-IIs. Do you think the appeals court would now agree with Pepsico that the first plane was not unique? Why or why not?

3. What if Pepsico's G-II had been the former property of a very famous person such as Madonna or Brad Pitt? Would that alter the appellate court's reasoning?

## Parts of a Contract

Most attorneys begin **drafting** [writing] contracts by referring to contract forms or samples that have proved legally binding. Attorneys and students reading older sample contracts should know that a movement is under way in law schools in the United States to simplify legal language and to make contracts and other documents more readable. Deleting a few *hereafters* or *hereinaboves* will not diminish the validity or effectiveness of a contract; the deletions will simply make the contract more understandable.

Although no particular form is required when drafting a contract, many contracts consist of seven parts:

1. The **heading** is a title for the agreement.
2. The **exordium** names the parties and the action. Although this information is not necessary, you will often find items such as business address, country of incorporation, and principal place of business in the exordium.
3. The **recitals** are designed to give additional information about the parties involved. This can include background information about prior contracts or the **premises** [important points upon which the contract is based].

4. The **transition** contains the words of agreement.
5. The **definitions** are given of any terms that the parties feel should be explained in detail. Some contracts don't include a definitions section but simply define terms if necessary in the body of the contract.
6. The body of the contract, better known as the **operative provisions,** is the section containing the language of the parties' agreement.
7. The **testimonium** or closing indicates agreement to the terms of the contract by the parties who sign the contract.

| Parts | |
|---|---|
| **HEADING** | <div align="center">**TRANSACTION AGREEMENT**</div> |
| **EXORDIUM** | TRANSACTION AGREEMENT, dated as of September 1, 2007, is between CoffeeClub, a New York general partnership ("CC"), Tea Time, L.P., a Delaware limited partnership and general partner of CC ("TT"). |
| **RECITAL** | WHEREAS, in accordance with the Letter Agreement, except as otherwise contemplated herein, the parties desire to set forth definitive agreements providing for the transactions contemplated in the Letter Agreement. |
| **TRANSITION** | The parties agree as follows: |
| **DEFINITIONS** | <div align="center">ARTICLE I</div><div align="center">DEFINITIONS</div>For the purpose of this Agreement the following terms shall have the following meanings:<br>1.1. CoffeeClub has the meaning set forth in the Preamble.<br>1.2. Affiliate has the meaning ascribed thereto in the Partnership Agreement. |
| **OPERATIVE PROVISIONS** | <div align="center">ARTICLE II</div><div align="center">THE DEBT CLOSING</div>2.1. Refinancing. Concurrently with the execution of the agreement, CC is obtaining stand-alone financing under one or more credit arrangements secured by the Selected Subsidiary and CC's rights under the "Refinancing Arrangements."<br><br>2.2. ...... |

**TESTIMONIUM**

IN WITNESS WHEREOF, the parties have caused this Transaction Agreement to be executed by their duly authorized representatives.

By:  CoffeeClub,
     a general partner

     By:

     _____

     Name: Susan Varone
     Title: Senior Vice President

By:  Tea Time, L.P.,
     a general partner

     By:

     _____

     Name: Carl Fleet
     Title: Senior Vice President

Although looking at reliable forms is an excellent way to begin writing, you must always be careful to review the facts of your particular case and review the contractual language. Specific terms and conditions will vary from contract to contract and should be drafted to reflect what the parties have agreed to.

## Exercise K. Legal Drafting

1. Review the following contract, not an agency agreement between two firms (names, products, and countries have been changed). The native language of the drafters of the contract was not English.

2. As you read, try to determine exactly what the parties intended. Some of the provisions are confusing, due in part to improper language use.

3. Divide into groups and rewrite the contract as if you are attorneys from the law firm representing the principal. Hints to aid in your revision are provided in bold.

> In the real world, when confusion about the terms of an agreement arises, the attorney can ask management what was intended and write the provision to fit the law and management's expectations. In this contract, you don't have that option. So make equitable choices, but don't forget that you represent the principal in this case.

# AGENCY AGREEMENT

THIS AGREEMENT, made and entered into as of 15 June, 1998 by and between Dominican Manufacturing, Inc., (hereinafter referred to as "Principal"), a company incorporated under the laws of France and with its principal place of business at Toulouse, France; and Singh Engineering, Inc., (hereinafter referred to as "Agent"), a company incorporated under the laws of India and with its principal place of business at Mumbai, India; **[Is all this information necessary? Check the punctuation.]**

WITNESSETH:

WHEREAS, the Principal produces and exports mineral drilling equipment and other products as set forth and specified in Appendix 1 (hereinafter referred to as "Products"); and WHEREAS, the Agent desires and possesses the capacity, knowledge and capability to market and sell the Products in India and Sri Lanka (hereinafter referred to as the "Territory").

NOW, THEREFORE, the Parties have agreed as follows: **[Review the information in the Legal Thumbnail. Some of the language above is unnecessary.]**

1.      APPOINTMENT

1.1      The Principal appoints the Agent as the exclusive sales agent in the Territory to promote the sales of the Products.
**[Is a duty or a right being created here? Use "shall" when creating a duty; "is entitled to" when creating a right.]**

1.2      The Agent shall have no right to **[Can you shorten this?]** solicit or negotiate contracts for sale of the Products with customers situated outside the Territory or to customers who are likely, directly or indirectly, to reexport the Products outside the Territory.
**[What happens if the products are reexported?]**

1.3      Should the Agent receive an inquiry for the Products destined for use outside the Agent's Territory, the Agent shall forward such inquiries for the Principal's handling through **its** [emphasis added] regular marketing channels in the country of use. **[Does "its" refer to the Agent or the Principal? Would the Agent have regular marketing channels in a country outside its Territory?]** However, in particular cases, where there is no legal or business reason to the contrary, the Principal may extend to the Agent its written approval to handle such business. In this connection, the Agent undertakes, in respect of such inquiries, to ascertain the ultimate destination of the Products, and agrees that it will neither quote nor furnish any information received under this Agreement to its prospective client without prior receipt of the Principal's approval.
**[Is a second approval necessary? Is a telephonic approval acceptable? Is a duty created?]**

1.4      The Principal reserves to itself at its sole discretion the right to anytime revise its list of Products **[word order]** by adding items thereto or subtracting items therefrom said revisions to be effective in each case upon receipt of the Principal's notice thereof by the Agent. Exception to the above is when the Principal stops production totally or the production of a product or production line. **[unnecessary, old-fashioned language]**

1.5     While the Principal reserves the right not to accept an order at its sole discretion **[word order]**, the Principal shall assist the Agent in the performance of its duties by informing **[object missing]** on a continuous basis of current delivery terms and of changes in expected delivery dates.

1.6     The Principal will furnish the Agent with price lists and catalogues and shall promptly notify the Agent of any changes thereto. **["Will" is future tense, not a duty.]**

1.7     The Principal shall without delay inform the Agent whether it accepts orders forwarded by the Agent. **[What does "without delay" mean?]**

1.8     The Principal shall promptly pay to the Agent the commission having accrued to him as provided in Article 5.2 hereunder. **[Do you need this here?]**

5.      COMMISSIONS

5.1     The Agent is entitled to the commission provided for in Appendix 2, on all sales of the Products which are made during the term of this contract to customers established in the Territory and to which the Agent has contributed or which are the permanent customers of the Agent in the Territory. The Agent is not entitled to the commission for other sales of the Products to the Territory included but not being limited to such sales. **[Are you creating a duty or a right here? What does the last line mean? The phrase is most often seen as "including but not limited to."]**

5.2     The Agent's right to commission shall become due and the commission shall be calculated quarterly (based on the calendar year) for the Products delivered to and paid in full by the customer during the period in question pursuant to this Agreement. Payment of the commission shall be made by the Principal within thirty (30) days following the full payment of the invoice of the products or services subject to commission. **[When is the Agent to be paid?]**

Appendix 2
COMMISSIONS

In cases where sales of the Products dealt with in this Agreement are effected by the Agent alone, or as a result of the combined efforts of the Principal and the Agent, the Agent shall be paid commissions varying with the type of sales involved and determined in accordance with the following schedules. **[Can you simplify this language?]**

With respect of sales of the Products listed in Appendix 1 following commissions of the ex works price shall be paid: 10%. **[Check prepositions and articles.]**

In cases where sales into the Agent's Territory of the Products dealt with in this Agreement are effected by the Principal, its Affiliate Companies, or its regularly appointed agents or representatives, the Agent's commission will amount to 50% of the compensation payable to the Principal by its Affiliate Companies or its Appointees on such transactions. **[Is this consistent with Section 5?]**

In cases where the Principal obtains orders from third parties outside the Agent's Territory for the delivery of the Products into the Agent's Territory, the Agent's commission will be reduced to 1/3 of the normal rates. **[Is this consistent with Section 5?]**

# The Negotiation

## Discovering Connections

All attorneys eventually take part in a negotiation. Some are simple: What time is our next meeting? Should we hire ABC Consulting firm to improve our image? Others are more complex: Should our client sign an employment contract with a non-compete clause? Still others involve millions of dollars: Should we include a mediation clause between the municipal government and the automotive client in the factory construction contract?

### ACTIVITY

1. Make notes about any negotiations you have conducted (i.e., rental contracts, mobile phone contracts, arranging times to meet).

   _____

   _____

   _____

2. Now think about the role you played in the negotiation. Did you get what you wanted? Did the other party get what he or she wanted? Think about what did and did not work. Then with a partner, list the five characteristics that you think make the best

negotiator and why each one is important. One of you will explain your list to the entire class.

a. _____

b. _____

c. _____

d. _____

e. _____

## Legal Listening

Listen to an attorney discuss a recent negotiation with a colleague. Then answer the questions.

1. What is this negotiation about?
2. Is Mr. Cochran still a big television star?
3. Who is Margaret's client?
4. What title did Margaret offer Mr. Cochran to get him to agree to her proposition?
5. What does Margaret believe to be the real problem that is causing them not to reach agreement?

## The Negotiation

Avalon Resorts, Inc., a U.S.-based corporation, and the Ministry of Tourism for Eritrea are in negotiations for the establishment of an eco-tourism resort on the island of Dahlak Kebir in the Red Sea. The current population is 1,500 people, and there is one hotel, the Luul Resort. The Ministry, working with the local government, is concerned about the influx of tourists to the small island and both the environmental and cultural effect they will have on the island and islanders. Of course, the influx of cash from tourism would be a welcome boon to the economy.

The parties have agreed in principle to the building of the resort. It is now up to the attorneys for each side to reach final agreement on the details of the eco-tourism resort. Because both parties want the resort to be built; you have no option but to reach agreement on the details. Your only concern is what the details will be.

Each negotiating team should have one team member keep track of the points awarded or deducted depending on the outcome of the negotiation. Each team member must also take an active part in the negotiations. Your instructor has the final word, but for each team member who does not take an active part in the negotiation, five points will be deducted from the total. It is in your best interests to keep everyone involved.

The information for the Ministry of Tourism of Eritrea is Part 3, Text 9 (page 280). The information for Avalon Resorts, Inc., is Part 3, Text 1 (page 275).

Before working out your negotiation strategy, review the information on agreeing and disagreeing in Part 2, Debate (page 216), and modals and semi-modals in Part 2, Modals and Semi-Modals (page 229).

## Conducting Negotiations

Hundreds of books have been written on conducting successful negotiations. We are not going to replicate that wisdom here but instead will give you five practical tips for conducting your negotiation. As you spend more time negotiating, refine this list to suit your style and needs.

1. Know what your final offer will be and then have a "fall-back" plan. Negotiations go better if you are fully aware of your clients' needs and wants. You need to work with the client to agree on a final offer and then what will happen if that offer is not accepted. Know what is and is not negotiable for your client.
2. Aim for a "win-win" situation. If you view a negotiation as confrontational, you will have trouble reaching an agreement that is comfortable for both sides. If you are entering into business with someone, it is important to have a collegial, professional working relationship built on fair dealing and trust.
3. Listen and try to understand the needs and wants of the other side. If you understand or can discover what is important for them, then it may be easier for you to reach agreement. What one side considers important may not be important for the other. There is also the possibility of compromise.
4. In U.S.-style negotiation, try to focus on the issues and not the personalities. Culturally, this may not be true in all countries. In many countries and with some U.S.-based businesses, the people you deal with are as important as the issues.
5. State your needs. If the other side has to guess what is important to you, then you may not get what you want.

### PART 2

# Further Language Development

# *Writing Activities*

## Language Activity 1: Audience, Purpose, and Tone

Before we can begin to write, we need to answer two basic questions: for whom are we writing, and what is our purpose for writing? The answers to these questions will actually help you determine the strategies, type of communication, and level of formality you will use.

## Audience

Let's look first at audience. We always need to remember that our audience's interests, goals, and motivations are not the same as our own. We are more likely to accomplish our purpose if we appeal to the audience's interests than by trying to convince them that our interests should be theirs, too.

We begin then by asking who the primary and secondary audiences for each document are. The primary audience is the person/group that is the recipient. Think of it as the to: in an email. The secondary audiences are those who overtly or covertly receive the communication (cc: and bcc: in email format). Additionally, the secondary audiences are those who might only hear about the communication from the primary or secondary audiences. Never assume your message will only go to the person listed after Dear… in a letter. For example, how would your reaction be different if you learned that one of your colleagues had been fired by email or by their supervisor in person?

## Exercise A

Look at the pairs of sentences, and decide which is best suited for the specified audience to whom you are speaking or writing. The first one has been done for you.

*Example:*

   _A_  To your spouse

A. You need a raise because we need a new car and a new roof on the house.

B. You need a raise because you have done such a great job with the clients.

1. _____ To your boss

A. You deserve a raise because you need a new car and a new roof on the house.

B. You deserve a raise because you have done such a great job with the clients.

2. _____ To your instructor

A. You deserve an A in the class because you will lose your scholarship if you don't get one.

B. You deserve an A in the class because you wrote the best research paper even if it did contain a few spelling errors.

3. _____ To the judge in traffic court

A. You shouldn't have to pay the traffic ticket because a branch of a tree was hiding the NO PARKING SIGN.

B. You shouldn't have to pay the traffic ticket because you didn't see the NO PARKING SIGN.

4. _____ To your boss

A. He should pay for your English lessons since it will increase your usefulness to the firm.

B. He should pay for your English lessons since he paid for your colleague's last year.

5. _____ To your instructor

A. You should be allowed to take another class because the instructor you have doesn't like international students.

B. You should be allowed to take another class because you had one very similar in your home country.

# Purpose

Next we need to consider our purpose, such as reporting on an event, persuading, informing, giving opinions, or describing a purpose. When we combine each of these purposes with what we know about different primary and secondary audiences, we can begin to write or even to realize that written communication may not be the best choice.

## Exercise B

Give one example for each of the common purposes in legal writing.

1. To relate an incident: _____

2. To describe a person or thing: _____

3. To explain a process: _____

4. To request information: _____

5. To give an opinion: _____

# Tone

You also need to consider tone or how you address your audience. Do you want to write a formal or an informal letter or email? Are you going to be polite or impolite? In spoken English our tone is often heard—friendly or angry, polite or impolite; however, in writing our word choice is what people "hear" for tone. For example, a polite way to phrase a request would be, *Would you please send the brief to us by Friday?* An impolite request would be, *Send the brief by Friday* or even *Please send the brief by Friday.* Both impolite requests are phrased as commands without the softening of a modal. With friends, we often use what would be considered impolite with strangers to make requests, as in *Pass me the brief.* For more information, see Modals and Semi-Modals, page 229.

**Exercise C**

For each example, decide if the tone is formal or informal, and then decide if it is polite or impolite.

*Example:*

___informal___    1. Martin, can you please mail me the file on the Brown
                          case?
___polite___

_____    2. Mr. James, please report to the court no later than
                          7 AM on Friday.
_____

_____    3. I would like to have the report by Monday if at all
                          possible.
_____

_____    4. Do not forget to forward the brief to the court.
_____

_____    5. Would you mind forwarding a copy of the brief?
_____

---

# Language Activity 2: Paraphrasing

Paraphrasing is restating a text written by someone else. The first step to a good paraphrase is always making sure that you actually understand the original. You can't paraphrase what you don't understand. In fact, a good paraphrase is an explanation of the original text.

Attorneys are often called on to paraphrase statutes, decisions, parts of cases, or legal terms of art. The level of simplification used in a paraphrase will depend on the audience for whom the paraphrase is intended. A paraphrase for a colleague will be much more complex than a paraphrase written for a client with no legal training.

There are four steps to paraphrasing a passage:

1. Once you think you have fully understood a text, write a version of the paraphrase without looking at the original.
2. Compare your paraphrase to the original to make sure that you have included all the essential information. Add anything that is missing.
3. Is your version simpler than the original? If not, simplify it.
4. Make sure that you have not accidentally copied any unique phrase of three words or more exactly from the original. For example, if you are paraphrasing a passage about the U.S. Declaration of Independence, you don't have to try to find a synonym for the Declaration of Independence. However, you would have to put quotes around the phrase "we hold these truths to be self-evident that . . . " to show that it was copied or use your own paraphrase such as *we believe it obviously true that* . . . to explain that quoted phrase.

Here are two sections from a bill introduced in 2002 in the Missouri Senate to change the **dram shop statute** [a law that imposed liability of a provider of alcohol to minors or intoxicated persons for injuries to a third party] that we can use an example of different ways to paraphrase the same passage.

> 7. No employer may discharge his or her employee for refusing service to a visibly intoxicated person.
> 8. All servers of intoxicating liquor by the drink shall receive training to recognize visibly intoxicated persons.
> (Missouri Senate Bills Nos. 817, 978 & 700, 2002)

Once we've read and understand sections 7 and 8, we could quickly write a paraphrase according to the first step. Let's assume that our audience is a bar owner who wants a very simple paraphrase:

> You can't fire one of your employees who refuses to serve drinks to a customer who is clearly drunk. All of your employees who serve drinks have to have training to learn how to recognize drunk people.

If we then follow the second and third steps, we see that this paraphrase is fine. We've changed the structure and the vocabulary completely. However, it would be too simple to put in a letter to a superior who asked for that information. The following would be a more formal paraphrase of the same sections:

> No employee may be discharged for refusing to serve drinks to someone who is clearly intoxicated. All employees who serve alcohol by the drink must be trained to recognize intoxicated customers.

In this more formal paraphrase, we changed the active sentence to the passive and substituted synonyms for unique terms such as "visibly intoxicated persons." In other words, there are many possible ways to paraphrase a passage based on the desired audience and purpose.

## Exercise A

Use the four steps to paraphrase this section of the American Declaration of Independence (July 4, 1776) for two different audiences.

> "That to secure these rights, Governments are instituted among Men, deriving their just powers from the consent of the governed."

*Note:* Be careful with the word *men* since it did in the original quite literally mean only men in 1776. Would you continue to paraphrase *men* to mean that today, or would you change it present the current view that it refers to all people regardless of gender?

1. Paraphrase the sentence in a very informal way as though you were just talking about it with a friend in a normal conversation.

2. Paraphrase the sentence for an educated adult in a style that would be appropriate for a formal letter to the editor of a newspaper.

## Exercise B

Use the four steps to paraphrase this section of the dram shop bill that was introduced in 2002 in Missouri for two different audiences.

> 2. Notwithstanding subsection 1 of this section, a cause of action may be brought by or on behalf of any person who has suffered personal injury or death against any person licensed to sell intoxicating liquor by the drink for consumption on the premises when it is proven by clear and convincing evidence that the seller knew or should have known that intoxicating liquor was served to a person under the age of twenty-one years or knowingly served intoxicating liquor to a visibly intoxicated person.
>
> (Missouri Senate Bills Nos. 817, 978 & 700, 2002)

1. Paraphrase it for a colleague.

2. Paraphrase it for a bar owner who has been charged with selling beer to a 17 year old.

## Exercise C

Here is the federal "knock and announce" statute written in formal legal English. Using English that would be appropriate for an educated audience, rewrite the statute.

> **18 U.S.C. §3109. Breaking doors or windows for entry or exit**
>
> The officer may break open any outer or inner door or window of a house, or any part of a house, or anything therein, to execute a search warrant, if, after notice of his authority and purpose, he is refused admittance or when necessary to liberate himself or a person aiding him in the execution of the warrant.

# Language Activity 3: Summarizing

The scope and length of the summary is determined by the purpose and context for writing it. In legal writing you may be asked to summarize an article/case or to synthesize several articles/cases into a summary. A summary is a shorter version of the original text that clearly conveys the overall meaning of the original text.

We will focus on writing short summaries of a sentence to several sentences in length. In writing such short summaries, obviously brevity is critical. In order to write in such a concise manner, you will need to be sure you completely understand the meaning of the main text. From there, you need to be able to formulate in your own words the main idea(s) and purpose of the original text. It is also important to remember to reference the original source.

Let's take a look at writing the summary step by step.

1. Read the original text carefully to fully understand the author's meaning.
2. Highlight text and/or take notes on the main ideas. Hint: Main ideas are often found in the thesis statement and topic sentences.
3. Rewrite these notes in your own words.
4. Based on the required length of the summary assignment, synthesize the ideas and write your summary.

## Exercise A

Look at the text in the Legal Thumbnail of Chapter 5 under **False Imprisonment**. Highlight the main ideas in the text. Now rewrite them in your own words in a brief summary. You can find an example of a summary in Part 3, Text 4 (page 282).

## Language Activity 4: Email

# Ten Suggestions for Better Email

1. Choose an identifiable email address.
2. Label each email with a clear subject line.
3. Use a signature block.
4. Use attachments only if necessary.
5. Assume that your email is public information.
6. Don't write something in an email that you would not say in person.
7. Make sure you use the right register.
8. Answer or at least acknowledge emails within 24 hours.
9. Read all of the emails from one person before responding to the first.
10. Check, proofread, attach, check.

1. **Choose an identifiable email address.**

   If possible, use your name in your email address, especially for professional emails. It is hard to be taken seriously if your email address is *Legal_Eagle@sue_them.com*. If your email does not identify you, your message may be seen as spam [trash mail] and not even opened.

2. **Label each email with a clear subject line.**

   a. When you send the first email in a series, you should try to make the subject line as clear as possible. Do not use general words that give no real information such as "deposition." Use an identifying subject line such as "Deposition for Ralf Theron case" instead.

   b. If you are not sure that the person you are emailing knows you or will remember you, make sure you give some specific identifying statement as the subject line, such as *Enjoyed meeting you at the Salzburg Festival* rather than a vague *the book we talked about*, which sounds like spam and most likely would never be opened.

### 3. Use a signature block.

Most email programs give you the option of creating a signature block to add automatically or manually to the end of each email. Think of the signature block as a business card and as a chance to remind the recipient who you are and about your connections.

Although your closing may be informal *(Best wishes, Karl)*, your signature block should always be formal and as complete as you can make it. Give telephone or fax numbers, your webpage if you have one, your job title, and the organization for whom you work. In other words, use everything you would put on a business card.

Remember, your email may be printed and shown to others. If there is no signature block, your name and email address may not be sufficient to later identify you as the writer.

### 4. Use attachments only if necessary.

It takes time to download and open attachments. Do not use an attachment unless it is crucial that the recipient see the exact formatting or if the message must be long; the actual email message must be short and concise.

In law offices, email often contains attachments, but attachments should not be used in place of short, concise emails.

### 5. Assume that your email is public information.

a. Even if you put a *This communication is confidential and may not be shown, forwarded, or given* . . . statement at the end of each email, you actually cannot control who sees your email. As a result, never put anything in an email that might be truly damaging if it were made public. Be careful what you say.

b. It is easy for your emails to be edited and only parts of your original messages to be resent, perhaps even to the person you were complaining about. If you are not sure that your complete message will be shown to its intended audience, you may want to send a follow-up hard copy directly.

### 6. Don't write something in an email you would not say in person.

If you would not say something directly to the person you are writing, you should not write it in an email. An email is not an opportunity to be mean and cruel to people to whom you must be nice in public. Many email wars have been started because one person wrote an angry email too quickly. Never email when you are angry. Compose the email, go away for a couple of hours, then reread the email and make it objective and rational, not emotional.

7. **Make sure you use the right register (level of formality).**

   a. Register is another way to say *level of formality*. Just as you would do an audience analysis before you write a letter, you should think about the recipient of your email. Do you have a formal or informal relationship?

   b. Unless you are writing informally to your friends, you should never use SMS (called *text messaging* in the United States) forms such as *b4* or *btw* for "before" or "by the way."

   c. Just as you would in a formal letter, keep your paragraphs short and double space between paragraphs to make it easier to read.

   d. Any correspondence that must be extremely formal should most likely not be sent in the form of an email. A very formal letter can be sent as an attachment to a short email that describes the content of the attachment very briefly.

8. **Answer or at least acknowledge emails within 24 hours.**

   Most emails are delivered quickly and accurately; however, it is important to let senders know that you received their email since some emails are lost. If you cannot answer an email within 24 hours during the workweek, you should at least let the sender know that you received the email and are working on a reply.

9. **Read all emails from one person or series before responding to the first one.**

   Sometimes you will have two or more emails from one person or persons in a series. Always read all of the emails in a series before you respond since a question asked in the first email you read might have been answered or found before you began to read the series.

10. **Check, proofread, attach, check.**

    a. Before you begin to write an email or a reply, check to make sure that only the right recipients are listed. Make sure, especially in a reply or forward, that all the others have been removed unless they need to see your response, too.

       In most email programs, there are three levels of recipients: *to, cc,* and *bcc.* The first is the main recipient of the email; the second, *cc,* means "courtesy copy" and is used to provide others with a copy of what you sent the main recipient, who can see those on the cc list. If possible, you should explain to the main recipient why you are cc-ing others: *Fred, I'm cc-ing Samir and Dominick on this since they might be asked about it by the client too.*

Be careful with *bcc,* which means "blind courtesy copy." When you bcc something, the main recipient does **not** know that someone else received a copy of the email, too. Some organizations or companies officially prohibit the use of bcc's since it can be dangerous not to know who else is receiving information.

b. Many emails have been sent just as the writer sees a missing "not," the wrong year, or a grammar mistake. Always compose important email messages in a word processing program and then paste the completed, spell-checked, proofed, reread message into your email program. Make that your standard, normal practice.

c. When you reply to a message, copy the original message into your word processing program, write your reply, and then cut out the parts of the original that aren't important to your reply before you paste it back into your email.

d. Spell-check programs cannot find mistakes such as *tow* for *two*, *fro* for *for*, or *form* for *from* or the opposite that often happens in legal writing *(Please fill out the attached* from [sic]). These typing errors can only be found by careful proofing.

Also check that you have not confused words that sound exactly alike but are spelled differently, such as *two/too/to* or *there/they're/their*. Even more dangerous are the words that are very close in sound but different in meaning such as *accept/except/expect*. You may know the difference, but if you let your spell-check program choose the wrong one for you, your recipient will think you are either careless or uneducated. One missed *we are willing to except [sic] your offer* can destroy a great deal of credibility. Remember that native writers of English expect 100 percent accuracy in spelling and word usage. They are more forgiving in grammatical matters, fortunately.

e. If an email is extremely important, you should have it proofed by another person who writes English even better than you do before you send it.

f. If you promised attachments, make sure you have attached them.

g. Check the recipients again, proof once more. Now hit send.

## Exercise A

There are many mistakes in this email. Carl Mote wrote to his client Ronaldo Vento about the case he is working on against Jan Drummer for Vento. Correct at least ten mistakes in the email. Refer to Ten Suggestions on pages 184–87 for assistance.

---

from: Craftylawyer@rentalawyer.com

to: Jan Drummer

cc:

bcc:

date: Nov. 17, 2007

subj: RE:

Ronaldo, Sorry it's taken me two weeks to answer your mail. I've attached a couple of short comments for you to read. Also sorry I didn't understand that you had already settled out court. I should have read your other emails before I called Drummer's lawyer and yelled at him. Well, Drummer will get over it. You really were stupid to give him that information; his lawyer would have never found it the way we had hidden it. Make sure you don't give those other emails to anyone, okay? They could really get us in trouble. Now I need you to fill out these froms so that I can get paid by your company. Call me if you need anything else,

Carl

---

# Writing Emails

Remember that you need to consider audience, purpose, and tone every time you write an email.

Even when writing friends, email is basically public information. In many companies you have either implicitly or explicitly given permission for your company to read all of the emails that come through your work computer or your company's email program. People have been fired for writing what they thought were private emails to their friends.

Emails should be brief but clear. In the following model, one friend is trying to invite the other friend to lunch to discuss a project they are both working on. Remember that they are more than colleagues, they are friends. Here is an example of a friendly email.

| Line | Message |
| --- | --- |
| A. | from: Jan.Drummer@black&green.com |
| B | to: Thom.Daum@Hallsaccounting.com |
| C. | cc: Thom.Daum@myname.net.xx |
| D. | bcc: |
| E. | date: Wednesday,15 Aug 07 |
| F. | subj: lunch on Tuesday, 21.8.07 at Sam's to discuss Carpet merger? |
| G. | Sorry I missed your call this morning. I was in court. |
| H. | Do you have time to meet Tuesday for about an hour at noon at Sam's? |
| I. | I want to go over the merger papers for the Carpet deal again. |
| J. | I know you explained the percentages to me before, but I could use another go to make sure I've really got it. Okay? |
| K. | My treat of course. Say hello to Jenny for me. Great seeing her last week. |
| L. | Jan |
| M. | Jan Drummer, J.D. |
|  | Attorney at Law |
|  | Black & Green |
|  | 151 High Road |
|  | Halls TN USA 38000 |

Let's look at the informal nature of this email.

Line C: Just to make sure Mr. Daum has gotten the mail, Mr. Drummer has added Mr. Daum's private email address. That would be inappropriate in a formal email.

Line F: Although this subject line is very effective in giving the basic meaning of the email, it is too informal for a formal letter. We would need to write, *Possible meeting next Tuesday to discuss Carpet merger.*

Line G: There is no need for a salutation when writing friends. Just begin writing.

Line J: The use of *okay* and *another go* are both colloquial forms only to be used in informal language.

Line K: *My treat of course.* isn't even a full sentence. Also the informal *my treat* which means that Jan will pay for both lunches, would need to be *I'd like to invite you to lunch as my guest…* in a formal email.

Line K: We assume that Jenny is someone that Mr. Daum knows, but since they are friends, Mr. Drummer doesn't need to specify the relationship. In a formal letter, he might have written, Please give my best to your wife. It was such a pleasure talking with her last week at the reception at your office.

Line L: Again, since they are friends, there is no need for a closing, just sign off.

Line M: Even though they are friends, the signature block should be used.

## Exercise B

Write an email in response to the one from Mr. Drummer as though you were Mr. Daum. You do have time to meet him for lunch. Remember to keep the tone informal but not too informal since they are both using company email systems.

Email should never be extremely formal; but when writing to clients, superiors, or in the first stages of a new intercultural exchange, it is best to be moderately formal. Young people who have grown up in the age of instant messaging and text messaging (sms) often forget to make the switch from informal to semi-formal language in emails.

### Exercise C

Change the text of this very informal message between friends to a semi-formal one between business colleagues who have just begun to work together via email.

> Fred! Wake up! We gotta meet tomorrow to get something together to show the boss at the weekly meeting. Got any ideas? And don't go looking for help from that guy in Advertising again, he got fired last week. So it's just us, buddy boy. See ya.

## Language Activity 5: Client Letters

Writing a client letter begins like all good writing—with consideration of your audience, purpose, and tone.

- **Audience.** Think about your client. Are you writing to a client who does not have a legal background? If so, then you will have to use fewer legal terms and explain those you do use. Are you writing to a client with an understanding of the law? If so, then legal terms of art may be expected.
- **Purpose.** Why are you writing the client? To explain the law or offer a solution to a legal problem? Think about what you want the client to understand from your letter before you begin to write.
- **Tone.** The next issue to consider is tone. Your choice of words and sentence structure set the tone for the letter. You should be polite and formal, but not incomprehensible.

## Client Letter Organization

A client letter often has five main sections: the introduction, a fact summary, the legal analysis, recommendations, and a final paragraph that includes information on the next step the client should take.

1. The **introduction** sets the tone for the letter, provides an overview (roadmap) of the letter, and summarizes the client's options. This way, as the client reads the letter, he or she better understands the attorney's legal analysis.
2. The **fact summary** is included to make certain that both the client and attorney agree on the facts and that important points haven't been left out or misstated.

3. The **legal analysis** is the attorney's review of the law. If your client has no legal experience, the letter should not be full of legal terminology unless there is also an explanation.

4. The client is paying for **recommendations**. He or she wants to know what the attorney feels is the best thing to do. Provide options for the client based on the legal analysis. Without recommendations, you have an incomplete and, for the client, worthless letter.

5. In the **closing** paragraph, the attorney needs to let the client know what to do next, whether that is setting up a meeting or providing a medical report. The client also needs to know when to provide the information or meet with the attorney.

<u>Note</u>: Honorifics or titles such as Mr., Mrs., Ms., and Miss are not used if the gender of the recipient is unknown. In that situation, no salutation is used or the complete name of the recipient (i.e., Jasmine Smith) is used. However, if you know the gender of the recipient, use an honorific.

## Sample Client Letter

You are the attorney for Mrs. Anna Pointer who is suing her neighbors for the wrongful death of her son, Jason, who drowned in the neighbors' pool.

Read the *Statement of Facts* from Part 2, Legal Memoranda (page 194), for an understanding of the facts of the case before reading the letter.

Argylle & Argylle, LLC
1020 Main Street
Shreveport, LA 10000

May 20, 2007

Mrs. Anna Pointer
238 Pine Avenue
Shreveport, LA 10002

Dear Mrs. Pointer:

Thank you for your phone call. We understand your concern about the response
to the suit alleging your contributory negligence for the death of your son,
Jason. We want to quickly reassure you that in legal terms, contributory
negligence does not mean that you are responsible for the death of your child.
If the Cantrells can prove contributory negligence, part of the damages you are
seeking will be deducted from any possible award by the court.

Because we reviewed this unfortunate situation in an earlier letter, there is no
need to review the facts again. Let us just briefly explain the law in Louisiana
on contributory negligence. In Louisiana, the law is fairly clear that an eight-
year-old child should be aware of the potential danger of a swimming pool
without being reminded of that by an adult. This is especially true in Jason's
case since you have told us that he was mature for his age and on the honor
roll in school.

Before our meeting with the Cantrell's attorney, we would like to meet with
you once again to go over the legal issues and discuss the contributory
negligence claim. We know this will be difficult for you, but we hope that you
will be able to meet with us one day next week. I will call you on Monday to
schedule a time that is best for you.

I hope that this answers your question about the Cantrells' response to your
complaint. If you have further questions, please call or we can discuss them in
detail at our meeting.
Sincerely,

*Maya Garcia*

Maya Garcia
Attorney-at-Law

## Exercise A

Write a letter to your client, Ms. Rosewood, explaining that you need to schedule a meeting with her next week to discuss the property settlement agreement for her divorce. Her husband has agreed to all the terms but one (the ownership of their champion racehorse). Your client must decide if she is willing to forgo ownership of the horse in order to get a $1,000,000 lump sum settlement for the divorce. Based on your understanding of her husband's finances, you think the offer is an excellent one, but the final decision rests with your client. Your client, though educated, does not have a legal background.

# Language Activity 6: Legal Memoranda

A legal memorandum is a structured form of writing. However, in the real world, no two memoranda are ever the same. The sample that follows is simply that: a sample to modify and adapt for each individual situation.

In the United States, the most important part of a legal memorandum is the discussion section, which is where the author explains his or her conclusions about a legal issue. The typical parts of a legal memorandum include:

- **Statement of the Facts**: A brief statement of the facts of the case. Include only the facts that are legally significant. For example, in a defamation case, it is usually not important to provide a physical description of the person who defamed your client (providing, of course, that you know the person's name).
- **Issue or Question Presented**: What legal issue are you trying to answer? This question goes to the heart of the legal matter. This question generally includes the important facts that the legal question hinges on (material facts).
- **Brief Answer:** Beginning with a "yes," "no," "probably," or "probably not," this is the short answer to the issue statement. It is much shorter than the discussion section and only includes a statement of the law on the issue and not the explanation of the law.
- **Discussion:** This is the heart of the memorandum and where the expansive discussion of the law and its application to your case is found. In terms of organization, one of the most popular organizational patterns in the U.S. is CRuPAC organization.

<u>C</u>onclusion
<u>Ru</u>le
<u>P</u>roof
<u>A</u>pplication
<u>C</u>onclusion

The **conclusion** is your legal opinion about your client's problem. Should she sue? Is she liable for trespassing?

The **rule** is the rule of law, either statutory or case law, that is applicable to the facts of your case.

The **proof** is an explanation of the law with details including statutory and case citations. You cannot just cite a statutory provision; you must explain how prior courts have interpreted the statute or case law through cases.

The **application** is the section where you compare and contrast the law you explained in the rule proof to the facts of your client's case. This is the section that most international law students have the most trouble with. Normally, in a first draft, there is no application at all, but simply a conclusion. For a U.S.-style legal memo, this is simply not enough.

The final **conclusion** is again your legal opinion stated in different words to remind the reader of the possible outcome of his or her case.

This pattern should be used for each disputed legal element. Shortened forms of the organization pattern should be used for non-disputed elements.

• **Conclusion:** This section is the conclusion for the entire memo including all legal elements. This explains to the client or other attorneys what to expect and what decisions he or she must make in light of the information provided in the memo. In short memoranda, a conclusion may be omitted.

# SAMPLE MEMORANDUM

TO:  Jackson Argylle, Senior Partner

FROM:  Maya Garcia, Associate Attorney

DATE:  September 24, 2——

SUBJECT:  Contributory Negligence of Anna Pointer for Death of her Child

## STATEMENT OF THE FACTS

Jason Pointer, eight years old, drowned in a neighbor's swimming pool on April 16, 2007. At the time of his death, his mother, Anna Pointer, was cooking dinner while her son played in the backyard. The Pointers had moved into the neighborhood three weeks before, and Mrs. Pointer states that she did not know that the neighbor two houses down had a swimming pool. She had taken her son on a walk through the neighborhood soon after their arrival to point at landmarks and familiarize him with their new neighborhood.

Mrs. Pointer states that she checked on Jason at 5:00 PM and told him that dinner would be ready in 30 minutes. When she called him in for dinner, he did not come and she couldn't find him in the yard. She then walked through the neighborhood looking for him and found him floating in the pool at 221 Jackson Street at around 5:45 PM. The pool gate was open and the owners were not at home. The ambulance arrived at 5:55 PM, but the paramedics could do nothing to save the boy. An autopsy showed that he died of drowning.

Mrs. Pointer has sued the owners, the Cantrells, of the pool for wrongful death, and they answered the complaint claiming contributory negligence of Mrs. Pointer.

## QUESTION PRESENTED

Under Louisiana law, is Mrs. Pointer contributorily negligent for the death of her eight-year-old child when he drowned in a neighbor's pool while she was cooking dinner and he had gone alone outside in an unfamiliar neighborhood?

## BRIEF ANSWER

Probably not. In Louisiana, the courts tend to look at the age of the child to determine contributory negligence of a guardian. Mrs. Pointer had taken reasonable precautions to care for her eight-year-old son in an unfamiliar neighborhood by walking through the neighborhood with him after their move and reminding him to stay in their yard.

**DISCUSSION (of one element for the sample)**

Jason Pointer was old enough to be left alone outside to play in an unfamiliar neighborhood. In Louisiana, the courts look to the age of the child to determine whether a parent can be held contributorily negligent for the wrongful death of a child *Simmons v. Whittington*, 444 So.2d 1357 (La. 1984). The courts in Louisiana have found parents contributorily negligent when children under the age of six have been killed while under the supervision of the parent or their appointed babysitters *Humphries v. T.L. James & Co.*, 468 So.2d 819 (La. 1985); *Anderson v. New Orleans Public Service, Inc.*, 572 So.2d 775 (La. 1990). When the children have been over the age of nine, courts have not found the parents contributorily negligent *Simmons* at 1359; *Argus v. Scheppegrell*, 472 So.2d 573 (La. 1985). In *Simmons*, the mother and grandfather were in the house while the nine-year-old son played outside. The boy drowned in a neighbor's pool. Neither the mother nor the grandfather knew that the neighbor had a swimming pool. Neither was found contributorily negligent. *Id.* at 1358.

The Pointer case is factually similar to *Simmons*. Mrs. Pointer, as Mrs. Simmons, did not know of the existence of a swimming pool in the neighborhood even though she had toured the neighborhood with her son. The child in *Simmons* was nine, and Jason was eight. In terms of cognitive development and recognition of dangers, an eight-year-old is much more similar to a nine-year-old than to the six-year-old boy in *Humphries* or the three-year-old in *Anderson*. A court should find that Jason was old enough to recognize the danger of the swimming pool without the guidance of his mother.

## Exercise A

Using the case synopses on contributory negligence found on page 49 of your text, rewrite the discussion section of the memo with one significant fact change: For this memo, Jason is five years old.

# Reading Activities

## Language Activity 7: Skimming and Scanning

An efficient attorney must be able to adapt his or her reading style to match the type of text and the purpose for which it is being read.

## Skimming

To identify the main idea of a text, we run our eyes quickly over the text. This skimming of the text is usually three or four times faster than normal reading and is very useful to decide if you should then spend more time reading that text closely. It may be of interest for you to know that there is evidence that it is harder for many to skim on the computer than on the printed page.

There are several different ways to skim, and you may wish to try several to find the one that works best for you. We'll present one basic approach that works for most when reading legal texts, such as statutes or cases.

Begin by reading the title, the headings, and the subheadings of the text. If you find one or more sections that may be useful, let your eyes race quickly over the text, looking for key words or phrases. Some expert readers read only the first and last sentence of a paragraph, while others skim the entire text.

### Exercise A

Use a watch to time yourself as you skim this short but complex text. You should spend less than ONE minute skimming it. Then turn to Part 3, Text 7 (page 285), and answer the question about the main idea of the text.

The jury's verdict, based on instructions incorporating the mature minor exception and the evidence in this case, implicitly found that Ms. Cardwell did have the judgment, ability, education, and training at her 17 years, 7 months to have the capacity to consent and did in fact consent to the Defendant's treatment. The same capacity to consent entails the ability to appreciate and weigh the risks and benefits of the treatment she sought and thus to give informed consent to it. The jury also found that the Defendant complied with the standard of care of his practice in providing her with sufficient information upon which Ms. Cardwell could give informed consent. The treatment was relatively minor, with a minimum risk of injury, and Ms. Cardwell expressed no concern about the treatment at the time it was to be administered. The jury could reasonably have found that Plaintiffs did not show that Defendant had deviated from the standard of care concerning the information ordinarily supplied to obtain informed consent to Defendant's treatment. Consequently, having the capacity to consent and having given informed consent, no battery occurred because Ms. Cardwell's consent was effective on the facts of this case.

*Cardwell v. Bechtol,* Tenn. 1987, 724 S.W.2d 739, 67 A.L.R.4th 479

## Scanning

If you are looking up a word in dictionary, you scan the page until your eye catches the word or words you need. Usually when you scan, you are looking for an answer to a particular short question, such as, What is the definition of *informed consent*?

### Exercise B

Use a watch to time yourself as you scan the text to find the answers to these short questions from Article 1 of the U.S. Constitution. This exercise should take less than two minutes.

1. How often are members of the House of Representative chosen?

2. How old must a Senator be to be elected?

3. To be a Senator, how long must he or she have been a citizen of the United States?

4. How long must a Representative be a citizen of the United States before he or she can be elected?

5. Who is the President of the Senate?

6. Originally, who chose the Senators?

**Section 2**

**Clause 1:** The House of Representatives shall be composed of Members chosen every second Year by the People of the several States, and the Electors in each State shall have the Qualifications requisite for Electors of the most numerous Branch of the State Legislature.

**Clause 2:** No Person shall be a Representative who shall not have attained to the Age of twenty five Years, and been seven Years a Citizen of the United States, and who shall not, when elected, be an Inhabitant of that State in which he shall be chosen.

**Section 3**

**Clause 1:** The Senate of the United States shall be composed of two Senators from each State, chosen by the Legislature thereof, for six Years; and each Senator shall have one Vote.

**Clause 2: (omitted)**

**Clause 3:** No Person shall be a Senator who shall not have attained to the Age of thirty Years, and been nine Years a Citizen of the United States, and who shall not, when elected, be an Inhabitant of that State for which he shall be chosen.

**Clause 4:** The Vice President of the United States shall be President of the Senate, but shall have no Vote, unless they be equally divided.

# Language Activity 8: Case Reading

The first year of law school is spent learning how to read legal cases. This brief introduction just touches on the parts of a case and what an expert legal reader does when faced with a new case to read. To improve your case reading skills, you need to read as many cases as you can and discuss them with your colleagues and your professors to ensure that you have correctly understood what you have read.

A typical American case has five parts (not necessarily in this order):

• Procedural History
• Facts
• Legal Issue(s)
• Reasoning
• Holding
• Disposition of Case

**Procedural History:** Because most cases that are published are appellate cases, this section traces what has happened in prior courts. Often questions on appeal are procedural, so it is important to understand what happened earlier in the legal process.

**Facts:** Often the court will set out a brief recitation of the facts. Other times, the fact section can be quite long. Whatever the length, this is where you get the "story" of the case. This is where you find out about the legal problem that has led to this court battle.

**Legal Issue(s):** This is what the appellate court has to decide. Many times the issues are procedural (motions for summary judgment) instead of substantive (is "breaking at night" required as an element of burglary?).

**Reasoning:** This is how the court reaches its decision. There is often a lengthy discussion of prior cases or applicable statutes. Think of these as *because* statements: *A nine-year-old boy is aware of the dangers of a swimming pool because....*

**Holding:** This is the court's decision in the case and what is considered binding precedent. It does not mean "defendant wins" or "judgment is reversed." It means the rule of law as applied to the facts of a particular case. What you include in the holding either expands the law or narrows it. If, for example, we include in a holding that only nine-year-old girls are capable of understanding the danger of a swimming pool, that effectively narrows the holding to only nine-year-old girls. However, that would be too narrow a reading of a holding. Most likely a court would mean something like "young children." It would then be up to the attorneys to do further research to find out exactly what "young" means.

Often a holding is indicated by the phrase, *we hold,* but that is not always the case. In other instances, the court may state a holding more than once, or there may be separate holdings on separate issues.

**Disposition of Case:** This is whether the case is reversed, affirmed, or remanded. In other words, the next step or the end of the legal proceedings (unless there is another appeal).

Of course, it would be nice if these parts were labeled, but that is not how cases are written, so you, the reader, have to determine where each part begins and ends. If you have access to Westlaw® or LexisNexis®, you can review the headnotes before the case. Although they are not actually law, they do provide a short summary of the legal points and may help you understand the actual case itself.

A general guideline is that judges should use *find* for facts and *hold* for the holding. Note, however, that this is just a guideline and as such is not always followed. There are many cases where the word *hold* is never used at all or *find* is used for the holding.

## WILNER DIEUDONNE v. METROPOLITAN GOVERNMENT OF NASHVILLE AND DAVIDSON COUNTY

### Appeal from the Circuit Court for Davidson County
### No. 02C-2796    Marietta Shipley, Judge

### No. M2005-00287-COA-R3-CV - Filed March 30, 2006

### OPINION

| | |
|---|---|
| FACTS | The plaintiff, Wilner Dieudonne, was involved in a vehicular accident on February 8, 2000 with Robert Conley, an officer of the Metropolitan Government of Nashville and Davidson County Police Department. Officer Conley was on duty when the accident occurred. The plaintiff made a claim for personal injuries and property damage. The Metropolitan Government settled the plaintiff's claim for property damage, leaving only the issue of Plaintiff's personal injuries. |
| PROCEDURAL HISTORY | Plaintiff commenced this action by timely filing a civil warrant in General Sessions Court of Davidson County on February 6, 2001. Acting pro se, he listed the defendants on the civil warrant as "Metro Legal Department" and "Robert Conley." A deputy sheriff attempted to serve "Metro Legal Department" and Robert Conley with the civil warrant on February 14, 2001; however, both were returned unserved with the notation, "not to be found." Plaintiff took no further action to effect service of process for sixteen months. |
| PROCEDURAL HISTORY | On May 31, 2002 plaintiff filed an alias summons which was promptly issued by the Clerk of the General Sessions Court. A deputy sheriff attempted to serve the alias summons on "Metro Legal Department" and "Robert Conley." Officer Conley was served on June 17, 2002; however, "Metro Legal Department" was not served, and process was again returned with the notation, "not to be found." |
| PROCEDURAL HISTORY | In July of 2002, Plaintiff filed a motion to transfer the case from General Sessions Court to Circuit Court. The General Sessions judge granted the motion and the case was transferred to Circuit Court on September 12, 2002. Shortly thereafter, counsel, acting on behalf of the defendants, filed a motion to dismiss pursuant to Tenn. R. Civ. P. 12.02(5). The Metropolitan Government contended that neither of the defendants had been properly served, the statute of limitations had run, and that "Metro Legal Department" was not a legal entity capable of being sued. While the motion to dismiss was pending, Plaintiff filed an amended complaint in which the defendants were identified as the "Metropolitan Government" and "Robert Conley." |

| PROCEDURAL HISTORY | The motion to dismiss was heard in January of 2003, at which time the trial court ruled that the June 17, 2002 service upon Conley was proper and that the service of process on Conley constituted service upon the Metropolitan Government. The trial court additionally held that Conley was immune from suit because he was acting within the scope of his employment. As a consequence of this ruling, Conley was dismissed; however, the motion to dismiss the action as to the Metropolitan Government was denied. The case proceeded to trial on November 10, 2004, whereupon the plaintiff was awarded a judgment of $3,382 for medical bills and pain and suffering. |
|---|---|
| LEGAL ISSUE | The Metropolitan Government appeals, contending the case should have been dismissed as time barred due to Plaintiff's failure to timely re-issue summons. This action started out in the General Sessions Court, thus Tenn. Code Ann. §16-15-710 applies. The statute provides: |
| REASONING | The suing out of a warrant is the commencement of a civil action, within the meaning of this title, whether it is served or not; but if the process is returned unserved, plaintiff, if plaintiff wishes to rely on the original commencement as a bar to the running of a statute of limitations, must either prosecute and continue the action by applying for and obtaining new process from time to time, each new process to be obtained within nine (9) months from return unserved of the previous one (1), or plaintiff must recommence the action within one (1) year after the return of the initial process not served. |
| REASONING | When the deputy sheriff returned the summons on February 14, 2001 unserved, the plaintiff had nine months from the return of the unserved summons to reissue the summons, or Plaintiff could have recommenced the action within one year, the deadline for which would have been February 14, 2002. He did neither. As a consequence, the case against the Metropolitan Government was barred by the statute of limitations prior to transfer of the case to Circuit Court. Nevertheless, if it still had a pulse when the motion was heard in Circuit Court, the motion to dismiss should have been granted on the basis of Tenn. Code Ann. §16-15-710 discussed above. Moreover, the case was not resuscitated when it was transferred to the Circuit Court because the Tennessee Rules of Civil Procedure provided no relief. |
| REASONING | All civil actions are commenced by filing a complaint with the clerk of the court. An action is commenced within the meaning of any statute of limitations upon such filing of a complaint, whether process be issued or not issued and whether process be returned served or unserved. If process remains unissued for 90 days or is not served within 90 days from issuance, regardless of the reason, the plaintiff cannot rely upon the original commencement to toll the running of a statute of limitations unless the plaintiff continues the action by obtaining issuance of new process within one year from issuance of the previous process or, if no process is issued, within one year of the filing of the complaint. Tenn. R. Civ. P. 3. |

| HOLDING | Plaintiff waited sixteen months to seek the issuance of alias summons in the General Sessions Court. This delay prevented him from relying on the original commencement to toll the statute of limitations. Actions for personal injuries are subject to a one-year limitations period. *See* Tenn. Code Ann. §28-3-104(a)(1). |
|---|---|
| COURT'S DISPOSITION | For these reasons, the judgment of the trial court is reversed, and this matter is remanded with instructions to dismiss. Costs of appeal are assessed against Appellee, Wilner Dieudonne. |

## Exercise A

Identify and label the sections of this case.

---

**MARY ANN BAINES v. GREGORY TODD BAINES**

**Appeal from the Circuit Court for Davidson County**

**No. 01D2253   Carol Soloman, Judge**

---

**No. M2004-02730-COA-R3-CV - Filed March 21, 2006**

---

**OPINION**

---

|   | Mary Ann Baines, the mother of the child, filed this divorce action in the Circuit Court for Davidson County seeking a divorce from Gregory Todd Baines and custody of their only child. Process was served on the father to which he filed responsive pleadings seeking *inter alia* custody of their child. After commencing this action, the mother moved to Wilson County to live with her parents while the divorce was pending. While living with her parents, the mother entered a drug rehabilitation program following which her parents filed a dependency and neglect action in the Juvenile Court of Wilson County, seeking an emergency order for custody. |
|---|---|
|   | For reasons not fully explained, the dependency and neglect petition filed by the grandparents indicated the petitioners did not know where the father could be served. Although the mother and her parents knew the address of and how to contact the father, he was not given notice of the filing of the dependency and neglect petition or the emergency hearing. Moreover, he was never served with process. Following an emergency hearing, the Juvenile Court awarded temporary custody to the maternal grandparents. Shortly thereafter, the mother consented to her parents' petition, and the Juvenile Court awarded custody to her parents, all of which occurred without the father's knowledge or consent. |

Being ignorant of the proceedings in the Wilson County Juvenile Court, the father pursued this action to obtain custody of their child. Prior to the final hearing in this action, the father learned of the dependency and neglect proceeding. He voluntarily intervened in that action and, following a hearing, was awarded custody of the child. At the conclusion of that hearing the Juvenile Court Judge announced he was dismissing the grandparents' petition; however, no order was entered following that hearing.

Subsequent to the Juvenile Court hearing referenced above, the mother and father voluntarily proceeded with the divorce and custody action in the Circuit Court of Davidson County, during which each of them was represented by counsel at all material times. It is significant to note that the mother participated without advising the Circuit Court of her contention that the Juvenile Court had exclusive jurisdiction over the custody issue. Being unmindful of a potential jurisdictional issue, the Circuit Court Judge dutifully presided over this divorce and custody action to a final hearing. Following a full evidentiary hearing, in which the mother and father and their respective counsel participated, the Circuit Court granted the parties a divorce and awarded custody of the child to the father.

Within thirty days of that order being filed, the mother filed a motion to declare the order of the Circuit Court of Davidson County void, contending the Juvenile Court of Wilson County had exclusive jurisdiction pursuant to Tenn. Code Ann. §37-1-103(a) and (c). The father opposed the motion contending the Juvenile Court had dismissed the dependency and neglect petition and awarded custody to him.

To resolve the conflicting representations of the parents, the Circuit Court, Judge Carol Soloman, corresponded with the Juvenile Court, Judge Barry Tatum. Judge Tatum provided a written reply advising that although the order had not been entered, he dismissed the dependency and neglect proceedings. In furtherance of that, Judge Tatum entered an order confirming the dismissal of the dependency and neglect petition and provided a copy of the order to the Circuit Court. In the same correspondence Judge Tatum advised that "jurisdiction over the minor child, . . . has been and shall continue to be with the Eighth Circuit Court of Davidson County, Tennessee." After corresponding with Judge Tatum, the Circuit Court denied the mother's motion to declare the divorce and custody order void, from which post trial order the mother appeals.

|   | The mother's appeal is based upon subject matter jurisdiction, contending once the Juvenile Court attains jurisdiction in a dependent and neglect action, it retains exclusive jurisdiction pursuant to Tenn. Code Ann. §37-1-103(a) and (c) until the child reaches the age of majority or the case is dismissed. She also contends the courts cannot confer subject matter jurisdiction on a court that does not have subject matter jurisdiction, their agreement notwithstanding. We find no merit with this contention because it fails to recognize the authority of the Juvenile Court to dismiss a dependency and neglect petition, which was done in this matter although the requisite paper work to confirm the dismissal was less than timely. Moreover, when the mother voluntarily participated in the final hearing in this matter, the focus of which was the issue of custody, she was fully aware of the fact the Juvenile Court had announced that it was dismissing the dependent and neglect petition. The fact the paper work necessary to memorialize and authenticate the dismissal had not been entered was as much her fault as it was the father's. Finding this is not one of those cases for which we should place form over substance, or to reward a litigant for being less than candid with the Circuit Court prior to and during the final hearing, we therefore affirm the decision of the Circuit Court of Davidson County to deny her post trial motion. |
|---|---|
|   | The father requests that we declare the appeal frivolous. Although this appeal is perilously close to being frivolous, we decline the invitation to declare it as such. |
|   | The judgment of the trial court is affirmed, and this matter is remanded with costs of appeal assessed against appellant, Mary Ann Baines. |

# Language Activity 9: Statutory Interpretation

Statutory language is complicated, and one way to ensure that you are correctly reading a statute is to draw a flowchart of it. The flowchart permits division of the sentences into component parts, thus making the section easier to read. In the example, the main idea of each sentence is italicized. However, this does not mean that only the italicized information is important. In statutory interpretation, you cannot leave out any of the information; you can simply order it so that it is easier to understand.

**Sentence one:**

Notwithstanding the provisions of sections 106 and 106A

*the fair use of a copyrighted work*

including

such use by reproduction in copies

**or**

phonorecords

**or**

by any other means specified by that section

for purposes such as

criticism

comment

news reporting

teaching (including multiple copies for classroom use)

scholarship

**or**

research

*is not an infringement of copyright.*

**Sentence two:**

In determining whether the use made of a work in any particular case is a fair use

*the factors*

to be considered

*shall include*
*(1) the purpose and*
*character of the use*

including

whether such use is of a commercial nature
**or**
is for nonprofit educational purposes

*(2) the nature of the*
*copyrighted work*

*(3) the amount and substantiality*
*of the portion used*

in relation to the copyrighted work as a whole

and

*(4) the effect of the use*

upon the potential market for
**or**
value of the copyrighted work.

**Sentence three:**

The fact that a work is

*unpublished shall not*
*itself bar a finding of*
*fair use*

if

such a finding is made upon consideration of all the above factors.

# *Oral Communication Activities*

## Language Activity 10: Word Stress

Generally, it is much more important to focus on sentence stress than word stress, but in some instances the stress you place on certain words can change the meaning of the word. Some of the words that change meaning depending on the stress and are important when talking about legal issues are shown in the chart. The stressed syllable is bolded. *Note*: Most people will be able to guess your meaning from the context.

| | Word Stress | Meaning | |
|---|---|---|---|
| 1. | af **fect** (v.) | to have an influence | His behavior during the trial can **affect** the outcome. |
| | **af** fect (n.) | feelings or emotions | He has no **affect.** That is why he committed the murder. |
| 2. | **con** duct (n.) | a person's behavior | His **conduct** during the trial was terrible. |
| | con **duct** (v.) | to lead (or conduct a trial) | The judge **conducted** the trial with dignity. |
| 3. | **con** tent (n.) | Something in a container or the subject matter of a text or case | I still don't know the **content** of the files. |
| | con **tent** (adj.) | satisfied | I am **content** to remain with a small law firm. |

| 4. | con **test** (v.) | To argue about an issue; to challenge a will | The son **contested** his father's will. |
| | **con** test (n.) | A game of skill; common law attorneys are sometimes said to enter into contests with each other about who will win the case | I don't think he will win this **contest**. He doesn't have the law on his side. |
| 5. | con **vict** (v.) | To find someone guilty of a crime | John Doe was **convicted** of second degree murder. |
| | **con** vict (n.) | The person who has been found guilty of a crime | Two **convicts** broke out of prison yesterday. |
| 6. | de **li** ber ate (adj.) | To be carefully considered | It was a **deliberate** attempt to confuse the jury. |
| | de **li** ber **ate** (v). | To seriously consider a question (often used for judges and juries in trials) | The jury **deliberated** on the damage award issues for several hours. |
| 7. | **di** gest (n.) | A collection of published materials (often case summaries or statutes in law) | He used the Federal Practice **Digest** to ensure that he was following the proper filing procedure. |
| | di **gest** (v.) | To convert food into absorbable nutrients | Many people do not **digest** milk well. |
| 8. | ob **ject** (v.) | To complain | The defense attorney **objected** to the question asked by the prosecution. |
| | **ob** ject (n.) | A thing | The **object** (a knife) was placed in evidence by the prosecution. |
| 9. | **re** cord (n.) | A list or note of something. In law, the court/police keep criminal and court records. | The court **record** showed that the defense asked for three postponements. |
| | re **cord** (v.) | To make a note of | The court reporter **records** everything said during the trial. |
| 10. | **sub** ject (n.) | The topic or theme | His favorite law **subject** was torts. |
| | sub **ject** (v.) | To force something on someone | He was **subjected** to a lengthy cross-examination. |

**Exercise A**

1. Listen to the words as they are spoken, and circle the part of the word that you think has been stressed.

    a. OB JECT

    b. SUB JECT

    c. RE CORD

    d. CON VICT

    e. DI GEST

    f. AF FECT

    g. DE LI BER ATE

    h. CON DUCT

    i. CON TEST

    j. CON TENT

2. In pairs, listen to the words again, and check your answers. Now, working together and on a separate sheet of paper, write a sentence for each word that shows the correct meaning.

# Language Activity 11: Obtaining Information

## Asking Questions

When asking for information, we use four basic types of questions to achieve different purposes. Let's look first at the structure of the four.

| Type | Example | Structure (Word Order) |
|------|---------|------------------------|
| yes/no | Were you driving above the speed limit? | aux subject verb |
| wh- | Where were you going that morning? | wh- aux subject verb |
| negative | Weren't you driving too fast? | aux -n't subject verb |
| tag | You were driving too fast, weren't you? | subject aux verb, (neg) aux subject |

(aux = auxiliary verb)
(wh- includes *what, where, when, why,* and *how*)

212 • *American Legal English, 2<sup>d</sup> edition*

Why do we have four different structures? Each of the structures reflects what the person asking the question believes about the basic premise (statement) behind the question. Let's look at our examples and examine what the basic premise in each is.

| Type | Example | What the Person Asking the Question Believes |
|------|---------|----------------------------------------------|
| *yes/no* | Were you driving above the speed limit? | You were driving. |
| *wh-* | Where were you going that morning? | You were driving somewhere specific. |
| negative | Weren't you driving too fast? | I believe you were driving too fast, but I'll give you a chance to disagree. |
| tag | You were driving too fast, weren't you? | I believe you were driving too fast, and I expect you to agree with me. |

## Exercise A. Changing Sentences

Change the sentence in brackets to the correct form of a question based on what the person asking the question seems to believe.

*Example:* **Roxanne, the receptionist:** Hello, Ms. Fernandez. Tuesday, 1 PM, like clockwork. _____?

[You're here to see Mr. Cross.]

Answer: You're here to see Mr. Cross, aren't you?

1. **Ms. Fernandez, the client:** Of course, every week the same. _____?

   [He is free.]

   _____

2. **Roxanne:** I'm sorry, he isn't quite ready for you. _____?

   [You would like coffee while you wait.]

   _____

3. **Mr. Cross:** Roxanne, oh, hello, Ms. Fernandez._____? Time is flying today.

   [It is 1 PM already.]

   _____

4. **Ms. Fernandez:** Hello. I'm in no hurry. _____?

[You need more time before you see me.]

_____

5. **Mr. Cross:** No, no. Please come in. You're always so punctual and organized. _____?

[You brought the corrections to the contract I faxed you.]

_____

### Hidden Negatives

There are a few adjectives and adverbs that are strong negatives (such as *hardly* and *scarcely*) but don't look like negatives. When you form tags with them, you must treat them just as you would *not*.

> *not:* He is**n't** going to appeal after all, is he?
> *hardly:* He would **hardly** dare to appeal, would he?

## Answering Questions

Because different languages have different ways of briefly answering *yes/no* questions, it's very important to be sure that you understand the brief answers you get to your questions. *Yes* or *no* with the repeated auxiliary *(Yes, I did* or *No, I haven't)* is always the safest answer to the three types of *yes/no* questions; other answers are possible but may lead to misunderstanding because of linguistic differences.

| Type | Example | Answer |
|---|---|---|
| *yes/no* | Were you (driving above the speed limit)? | No, I wasn't (driving above . . . ). <br> Yes, I was (driving above . . . ). |
| negative | Didn't you (drive too fast)? | No, I didn't (drive too . . . ). <br> Yes, I did (drive too . . . ). |
| tag | You were (driving too fast), weren't you? | No, I wasn't (driving too . . . ). <br> Yes, I was (driving too . . . ). |

## Exercise B. Sentence Formation

Here is a fictional biography of a Chinese-American lawyer that you will use in answering questions as though you were she.

> Xu Naimin (Ms. Xu) is originally from Hong Kong, but she came to the United States with her parents when she was very young. Her friends call her Naomi. She always wanted to be a lawyer and graduated at the top of her class in law school. Now she enjoys practicing trust and estate law in a firm on the 97th floor of the Empire State Building. She loves New York and has one very ugly cat, Chocolate Tort.

1. Isn't Xu your first name?

   *Answer:* <u>No, it isn't. It's my family name.</u>

2. You're not originally from Hong Kong, are you?

   *Answer:* _____

3. Aren't you working in criminal law?

   *Answer:* _____

4. You didn't really name your cat Chocolate Tort, did you?

   *Answer:* _____

5. Are you working on the 87th floor?

   *Answer:* _____

6. Were you ever not going to be a lawyer?

   *Answer:* _____

7. Did you barely graduate from law school?

   *Answer:* _____

8. Don't you wish you could move somewhere else?

   *Answer:* _____

9. Isn't it false that your legal name is Naomi?

   *Answer:* _____

10. Wouldn't you agree that trusts and estates aren't very interesting?

    *Answer:* _____

## Language Activity 12: Register Analysis

In the United States, even business conversations are normally quite informal by standards in many countries. But there are many levels of informality, and attorneys must be able to use different styles of language in different situations. Look at the sentences *a–e*. Basically, they all have the same content and can be used to bring about the same result.

    a. Bring me that book.
    b. Please bring me that book.
    c. Will you bring me that book?
    d. Could you bring me that book?
    e. Would you mind bringing me that book?

From *(a)* through *(e)*, each sentence is a little more polite or formal. Although in many circumstances *a* would be felt as rude, in a normal working relationship in a moderately informal office, peers would not hesitate to use *(a)* "Bring me that book" with one another. On the other hand, if your superior used *(a)* to address you, it would seem a bit harsh, too brusque.

### Exercise A. Sentence Correction

In each of the following mini-dialogues, there is a problem with the command. It may be impolite or even too polite.

1. At the law library:

   *Law librarian:* Can I help you?

   *Law student* (politely): Give me the latest copy of the *Cornell Law Review.*

   correction:

2. In line at the bank:

   *Bank clerk* (politely but business-like): Would you mind giving me your name, address, and account number?

   *Customer:* Joshua Bark, 3456 W. 12th, 907845

   correction:

3. In law school:

    *Law professor* (as a matter of fact): Would you not forget to turn in your briefs.

    *Students:* Oh!

    correction:

4. At the law library:

    *Librarian* (firmly): Keep it down!

    *Law student:* Sure, sorry.

    correction:

5. In the study group:

    *Law student* (quickly): Could you keep talking? I'll be right back.

    *Second law student* (friendly): Please don't hurry.

    correction:

    correction:

# Language Activity 13: Debate

The phrases and statements that follow are commonly used when expressing agreement or disagreement or when building an argument. Please note that some expressions are stronger and/or more direct than others. This is true in the case of the first two sections **Agree** and **Disagree**. For example, *definitely* and *absolutely* are much stronger than *I agree.* You must also consider your tone and stress and intonation as some of the expressions that are less direct or forceful may be used more directly and forcefully by changing your tone.

All of these expressions may be used in a debate.

**Agree**

*I agree.*

*I couldn't agree more.*

*That's true.*

*exactly/definitely/absolutely/of course*

**Disagree**

*I disagree.*

*I don't agree [at all], and here's why* [list reasons. . . . ]

*Yes, that is true in part, but. . . . .*

*Well, you have a point, but. . . .*

*That's an interesting point; however, . . .*

*Yes, but on the other hand, . . .*

**Build an argument**

*There are [two, three, . . .] reasons why we believe/take the position. . . .*

*In the [first, second, . . . .] place, . . . .*

*For example/instance, . . . .*

*To demonstrate/illustrate this point, . . . .*

**Additional information**

*Furthermore, . . . .*

*Moreover, . . . .*

*In addition, . . . .*

**Emphasis**

*Let me highlight/underscore the importance of. . . .*

*This is important because [showing causation]. . . .*

**Conclusion**

*Let me repeat my/our position.*

*In conclusion/summary, . . . .*

# Grammar Activities

## Language Activity 14: Verb Forms, Tense, Time, and Aspect

There are many different ways to analyze English verbs, so the system we use in this book may not be the same as the one you learned. Even though you most likely have studied the verb system of general English, we need to review certain elements since in legal English some English verbs (such as *shall*) have very different meanings and uses than they do in general English.

We will also use some terms that are in common use but that are not linguistically accurate. For example, English does not really have a future tense but only forms that usually refer to future time. Nonetheless, we will use the future tense to label forms with *will* as in "Congress **will** ratify the treaty next year."

Before we look at the main verb forms in English, let's review the names of the principle parts of the different types of English verbs

| Base (also called infinitive) | Present | Past (also called –ed form) | Past Participle (also called –en form) | Present Participle (also called –ing form) |
|---|---|---|---|---|
| | | *Regular* | | |
| walk | walk(s) | walked | walked | walking |
| | | *Irregular (no pattern)* | | |
| go | go(es) | went | gone | going |
| be | am, is, are | was/were | been | being |
| do | do(es) | did | done | doing |
| have | have, has | had | had | having |
| | | *Irregular (with pattern also called "strong" verbs)* | | |
| sing | sing(s) | sang | sung | singing |
| write | write(s) | wrote | written | writing |
| | | *Irregular (with pattern also called "mixed" verbs)* | | |
| bring | bring(s) | brought | brought | bringing |
| teach | teach(es) | taught | taught | teaching |

## Exercise A

Using the terms from the chart, label these principal parts. Some may have two possible answers.

*Example:* _____*past*_____ rang

1. _____ saw
2. _____ reconcile
3. _____ citing
4. _____ held
5. _____ was

As you read the other grammar activities, you will need this simple review chart that outlines the main active verbs forms possible in English. There is a separate activity for the use and forms of the passive.

| Verb Forms | | | | | |
|---|---|---|---|---|---|
| **NAME** | **EXAMPLE** | **FORM** | **TIME** | **ASPECT** | **USE** |
| Present (also called non-past) | It *is* difficult to amend the U.S Constitution. | base + s in 3rd person | timeless/ present | no beginning, no end | habitual activities— states |
| Past | He *was* liable for the damages. | past form [*was/were* are the only singular/plural forms left in modern English] | past | begun and ended in the past | for actions in the past |
| Future with *will* | By the end of the course, you *will be* able to explain *stare decisis*. | base | future | begins in the future, no end | actions in the future, future predictions, future promises |
| Present Continuous | The judge *is* still *writing* her decision. | present form of *be* +/–present participle | present | no specific beginning, no end | actions happening now |
| Past Continuous | The judge *was writing* her decision when the prisoner escaped. | past form of *be* + present participle | past | no specific beginning, no end | interrupted past action |
| Future Continuous with *will* | Look for me later in the law library. *I'll be looking* for a case with binding authority. | *will* + base | future | begins in the future, no specific end | future interrupted action |
| Future with *going to* | This case *is going to be* only persuasive authority | present of *be* + *going* + *to* + base | future | begins in the future, no specific end | future intent or planned action |
| Present Perfect | a.  The firm *has been* in Warsaw for ten years.<br><br>b.  The witness *has* just *repudiated* his earlier testimony. | present form of *have* + past participle | a.  past into future<br><br><br><br><br><br>b.  recent past | a.  can have specific beginning, no end<br><br><br><br>b.  no beginning, ended in the 'recent' past | a.  an action that was begun in the past and continues into the present.<br>b.  a recent action that has a present effect. |

| Past Perfect | She *had* already *argued* the case before the judge declared a mistrial | past form of *have* + past participle | "very" past | began in the past, ended before the second action | an action that happens before another action in the past |
|---|---|---|---|---|---|
| Future Perfect | Let's hope the dissenting judge *will have finished* his criticism of the other judges before we return. | *will* + *have* + past participle | future | begins in the future with a definite end | to express what will have happened or how long something will have happened up to a certain point in the future |
| Present Perfect Continuous | We *have been studying* torts for six weeks now! | present form of *have* + *been* + present participle | past into future | stress beginning with no end in sight | continuous activity begun in the past and continuing into the future |
| Past Perfect Continuous | She *had been lobbying* for its adoption for months when the legislature finally accepted the model code. | past form of *have* + *been* + present participle | "very" past to past | stress beginning and then ending before the second action | continuous activity begun and ended before another activity in the past |
| Future Perfect Continuous | If he is still studying when we arrive, *he will have been studying* for his bar exam for 36 hours with no sleep. | *will* + *have* + *been* + present participle | past into future | gives beginning but no end in sight | continuous activity begun in the past up to a specified point of time in the future |

You may have been taught that there are three tenses in English: past, present, and future. However, **tense** and **time** in English are not the same. For example, in the boldfaced clause in this sentence, the **time** is clearly the future, but the verb *gives* is in the present tense:

> He will tell the whole story **only if the court gives him impunity tomorrow.**

Likewise, in the next example, the time is obviously the future even though both bold-face verbs are in the present tense:

> We simply **remind** them of the importance of checks and balances when **meet** next week.

On the other hand, there are sentences that have "no" time; they are universal truths (even if they aren't really true):

> The United States **is** in North America and **has** 50 states.

Although these facts are true today, they were also true yesterday and will most likely be true for a long time, so this sentence is in effect "timeless" even though the verbs *is* and *has* are in the present tense.

## Exercise B

In each sentence, first give the time of the underlined verb form. Your choices are basically **past, present, future,** and **timeless,** although for one example you could say "the future in the past" if you wanted to. Then you should try to label the form by looking at the chart on pages 220–21.

> *Example:* <u>timeless present tense</u> Chief Justice Marshall outlined the doctrine of judicial review that implicitly grants the Court the power to invalidate any law that <u>violates</u> the Constitution.

1. _____ _____ If he <u>understands</u> all of the landmark cases by tomorrow, he may just pass the exam.

2. _____ _____ The United Nation often <u>adopts</u> regulations to give effect to articles of its Charter.

3. _____ _____ The House <u>will come</u> to order right now! [This is may be a bit tricky.]

4. _____ _____ She will edit the statutes after she <u>has returned</u> from Angola.

5. _____ _____ The Redress Board <u>is going to look</u> at the case as soon as the results of the tests are back.

6. _____ _____ The Redress Board <u>was going to look</u> at the case, but then the petitioner died before they were able to gather the necessary information.

7. _____ _____ The supremacy of law <u>is</u> central to a democracy.

8. _____ _____ Precedent <u>isn't</u> really <u>going to be</u> that difficult to understand.

9. _____ _____ Would you say that in your system the trial <u>functions</u> as a contest?

10. _____ _____ Some say that the President <u>is trying to extend</u> the power of the executive branch.

In English, it is important to use different forms to tell the listener/reader about the importance of the beginning, middle, or end of an action. We group these pieces of information under the term **aspect.** Look at the next example:

The legislative council is meeting in the Green Room.

When did the legislative meeting begin? The beginning of the action (meeting) is not important in this sentence. When is the meeting going to end? The ending of the action (meeting) is not important either in this sentence. To show that we don't care about the beginning or the end of an action, we can use the progressive [*be* + *-ing*].

Now decide when the next action began or ended.

He worked in the legislative branch for four years.

When did he start working in the legislative branch? We don't know. When did he stop working there? We don't know, but we do know that he doesn't work there anymore because the past tense form *worked* tells us the action stopped sometime in the past. Contrast that with the next example:

He has worked in the legislative branch for four years.

When did he start working in the legislative branch? Four years ago. When did he stop working there? He didn't stop! He is still working there, and we have no idea how much longer he will continue to work there.

The action in the last example began in the past and continues into the future. We often use a present perfect form such as *has worked* [*have/has* + *-en*] to show that an action began in the past but hasn't ended yet. Or, if it did end, the action is still important to the present discussion. We'll review the difference between the past and the present perfect more later (see pages 226–29). There we'll also look at some of the differences in the way British and American speakers use the present perfect and the past.

## Exercise C

Select the most accurate description of when the underlined action begins and/or ends.

> *Example:* From the beginning of Anglo-American law, we <u>have seen</u> the trial as an adversarial proceeding.

a. _____ began and ended in the past

b. _____X_____ began in the past but is still going on with no end in sight

c. _____ will begin in the future but we don't know when it will end

d. _____ we know exactly when it begins and ends

e. _____ began and ended in the past but is still relevant to now

1. Until she received the settlement, she was not able to start getting the therapy she <u>needs</u> as a result of the accident.

   a. _____ began and ended in the past

   b. _____ began in the past but is still going on with no end in sight

   c. _____ will begin in the future but we don't know when it will end

   d. _____ we know exactly when it begins and ends

   e. _____ began and ended in the past but is still relevant to now

2. The clock <u>will stop</u> in exactly two minutes.

   a. _____ began and ended in the past

   b. _____ began in the past but is still going on with no end in sight

   c. _____ will begin in the future but we don't know when it will end

   d. _____ we know exactly when it begins and ends

   e. _____ began and ended in the past but is still relevant to now

3. Their attempts to codify the traditional laws of the group <u>have met</u> with failure over and over.

   a. _____ began and ended in the past

   b. _____ began in the past but is still going on with no end in sight

   c. _____ will begin in the future but we don't know when it will end

   d. _____ we know exactly when it begins and ends

   e. _____ began and ended in the past but is still relevant to now

4. The defense attorney successfully <u>refuted</u> the prosecutor's argument.

   a. _____ began and ended in the past

   b. _____ began in the past but is still going on with no end in sight

   c. _____ will begin in the future but we don't know when it will end

   d. _____ we know exactly when it begins and ends

   e. _____ began and ended in the past but is still relevant to now

5. Quick find a new executrix, so we can get this will witnessed. The one he wanted <u>has just died</u> in an accident on the way to the office!

   a. _____ began and ended in the past

   b. _____ began in the past but is still going on with no end in sight

   c. _____ will begin in the future but we don't know when it will end

   d. _____ we know exactly when it begins and ends

   e. _____ began and ended in the past but is still relevant to now

## Language Activity 15: Simple Past and Present Perfect

Most of you have already studied these verb tenses, but in case you need a reminder review this information before moving to the exercises.

| Simple Past | |
| --- | --- |
| Used to talk about actions that were **completed in the past.** | The jury **found** him guilty of murder even though the doctors **said** he **was** severely depressed at the time of the incident. |
| Often the time in the past is specific; most often with time expressions, such as last week, in 2005, or five years ago. | He **was** convicted **in 2005**.<br><br>**Last week** the court **heard** 15 cases.<br><br>Mark **practiced** law **five years ago** (and no longer practices).<br><br>He **started** to practice law **three years ago** (and still practices law).<br><br>**Note:** When using words such as "**start** or **begin**," we can use the simple past even though the action is still ongoing. This is because the **beginning** of the activity is **finished**. |
| **Present Perfect** | |
| Used with time expressions **"for"** and **"since"** meaning that the activity continues and is not yet complete.<br><br>Also used without the time expressions when actions began in the past and continue into the present, generally when it is clear from surrounding sentences that the action began in the past. | He **has practiced** law for five years (and still practices law).<br><br>He **has practiced** law since 2000 (and still practices law).<br><br>He **worked** eighty hours last week and **will** most likely **work** at least eighty hours this week. He **has worked** too much lately. |
| **Simple Past v. Present Perfect** | |
| In **time clauses** with **since**,<br>a. use the simple past when the time clause ends in the past | a. Jason has worked at the same firm **since** he **graduated** from law school.<br>*Meaning:* Jason still works at the firm and **has done** so **since** his graduation.<br><br>**Note:** In the second example, the present perfect is used because the action continues into the present. It is also not part of a time clause. Remember that a clause must have a subject and a verb. |
| b. use the present perfect when the time clause continues to the present. | b. Jason has tried many cases **since** he **has been** with the firm. |

## Exercise A

1. In the passage taken from *Anderson v. New Orleans Public Service, Inc.*, 572 So.2d 775 (La. 1990), underline the simple past tense.

> Kim Anderson testified that on the day of the accident while she was staying at her Aunt Gail Bailey's apartment in the Calliope Project, she experienced stomach pains. She asked Gail Bailey to watch the children because Ms. Anderson felt drowsy after taking medicine. Ms. Anderson then fell asleep. Moses Pettis, the investigating officer, testified that he interviewed the three children who were with Dennis (the boy who was killed) on the day of the accident. Cornell Webb stated to the officer that Kim Anderson gave Dennis permission to go swimming with the other children.

2. Why is the present perfect not used in the recitation of facts from the case?

3. In the passage taken from 80 *AmJur Trials* 535 §21, underline the simple past tense, and circle the present perfect tense.

> The plaintiff, Billy Minor, sustained a severe head injury with underlying concussion and contusions of the brain, causing plaintiff to suffer headaches, dizziness, and a marked change in his personality. Plaintiff further sustained a severe injury to his left wrist and lower arm as a result of which tendons, tissues, blood vessels, muscles, nerves, and ligaments were cut, torn, and bruised, whereby scar tissue has formed, leaving his wrist stiff, weak, deformed, painful, and capable only of limited motion and use. As a result whereof the plaintiff has suffered and will in the future continue to suffer permanent crippling, discomfort, and physical and mental impairment.
>
> By reason of the injuries complained of the plaintiff was forced to expend and to this date has expended the sum of $35,000, for medical attention, hospitalization, and drugs, of which the following is an itemized statement:
> [*Modifications have been made to the original.*]

4. In pairs, using the charts if needed, explain why the simple past tense was used in some instances and the present perfect in others.

## Exercise B

Complete the paragraph, using the correct verb tenses.

**Attractive nuisance** [A dangerous feature on land that may cause children to investigate it. For example, a swimming pool has sometimes been found to be an attractive nuisance.] is a doctrine that _____ (be) around for a long time. However, the courts _____ (not/find) a way to agree on the best way to approach the doctrine. When considering the applicability of the doctrine, some courts _____ (look) to the Restatement of Torts. In the comments to Rest. Torts § 339, when considering the applicability of the doctrine to children, the following is said:

> In the great majority of the cases in which the rule has been applied, the plaintiff _____ (be) a child of not more than twelve years of age. The earliest decisions as to the turntables all _____ (involve) children of the age of mischief between six and twelve. The later cases, however, _____ (include) a substantial number in which recovery has been permitted, under the rule, where the child is of high school age, ranging in a few instances as high as sixteen or seventeen years. [Modifications made to original.]

In the *Simmons* case _____ (discuss) earlier in the chapter, the court _____ (not/find) the mother negligent when her son, aged nine, _____ (drown) in the neighbor's pool.

## Exercise C

We all need to learn to edit our writing, so in this paragraph find and correct the seven mistakes in simple past and present perfect tense.

> Since graduating from law school, Martin worked at Wuttke Associates in New York City. Lately, however, he considered looking for a new position in a family law firm. In law school, he has wanted to work on child custody issues because of his own background. His parents have divorced when he was a child and have had a long, bitter custody battle over him and his sister. He has entered law school because he wanted to help other children in similar situations. However, upon graduation, he was offered a great job in a top law firm and could not resist the offer. Now, after two years at the firm, he decided to seriously reconsider his legal focus. The eighty-hour work weeks leave him no time to even volunteer in a family law clinic. He believes the time has come to make a change in his legal career.

# Language Activity 16: Modals and Semi-Modals

Modals are words such as *must, will, should, can,* or *may* that modify the meaning of the main verb. They add information about ability, possibility, necessity, or probability. Modals form a unique subset of verbs and cannot occur in certain grammatical structures. Instead, they must be replaced with a semi-modal, such as *have to* for *must* or *be able to* for *can.* Let's look at just a few structures and how they interact with modals in normal, nonlegal language.

| Structure (verb form) | Allows modal? | Example | Explanation |
|---|---|---|---|
| **declarative** (present time) | yes | *Modal:* The judge <u>can dismiss</u> the case. *Non-modal:* The judge <u>dismisses</u> the case. | Modals have no -s for third person singular present forms. Modals are followed by the simple form (infinitive without *to* before verb): *dismiss.* |
| **imperative** (simple form) | no | *Be able to* describe the court system by next week! | Modals have no infinitives (*to must* is incorrect) to form imperatives or subjunctives. |
| **continuous** (-*ing* form) | no | She is *having to* study every night. | Modals have no -*ing* form; semi-modal must be used. |
| **following an auxiliary verb or modal** (simple form) | no | She *must be able to* describe the court system. | Since a simple form must follow a modal (*must*), two modals cannot be combined. |

# Using Modals to Express Advice or Suggestions

Modals in declarative sentences can also be used to express different levels of advice or suggestions.

| Modal | Meaning in Declaratives | Example |
|-------|------------------------|---------|
| *must* | most forceful—obligation or necessity; required by law | All lawyers *must* pass the bar exam before they can practice in Kansas. |
| *should* | forceful but not required; speaker expects the advice offered to be taken | Everyone accused of a felony *should* hire an attorney, but it is not required by law. |
| *might* | polite advice; speaker would like but does not expect agreement | Yes, Harry is a good lawyer, but you *might* want to talk with Phyllis; this is her specialty. |
| *can* | polite negative advice | Of course, Harry *can* represent you, but Phyllis would be better. (Don't let Harry represent you.) |
| *can* | very weak advice; speaker has no strong opinion | Whom would I recommend? Well, Harry *can* represent you. |

## Exercise A. Writing

Answer these questions from a prospective law student in an informal email (or letter).

1. Why should I study law?
2. Why should I study law at your university?
3. Would I have to have studied Latin in secondary school?
4. What courses do I have to take?
5. What courses should I take?
6. Can I study law without working too hard?
7. What should I do now to prepare for my first year?
8. If there is an entrance exam, how can I study for it?
9. What can I expect to do with a law degree?
10. What would you suggest other than law to study?

# *May* and *Shall*

In legal English, declarative *may* usually signals a right or privilege to be exercised as one sees fit.

> (c) Restitution.—An order of restitution under section 3663 of this title with respect to a violation of this section **may** also include restitution—
>
> (1) for the reasonable cost of repeating any experimentation that was interrupted or invalidated as a result of the offense; . . . (18 U.S.C. §43).

Under that statute, there is no requirement that restitution include those items listed in (1), but it may at the **discretion** of the judge. *Shall,* on the other hand, is often used in legal English to indicate an obligation or to establish formally a state of being.

> Section 2. The President shall be Commander in Chief of the Army and Navy of the United States, . . . (U.S. Const. art. II, §2)

And, in other uses, *shall* indicates a mandatory action, one that is required to be taken.

> The United States shall guarantee to every State in this Union a Republican Form of Government, . . . (U.S. Const. art. IV)

## Exercise B. Fill in the Blanks

Use *may* or *shall* in the sentences.

1. The government _____ choose one or two non-voting representatives for each committee.

2. Each representative _____ choose at least one of the following and _____ choose all three: torts, securities, and organized crime.

3. Each person convicted under this section _____ be sentenced to at least six months and no more than one year in the country jail.

4. The rights not specifically granted the government _____ be retained by the people.

5. The age of consent _____ be no lower than 18 in any of the several states.

6. In most states, a person _____ apply for a driver's license at 16.

7. Within 30 days of his 18th birthday, each man _____ register with the Selective Service (military service) or face penalties.

8. Whoever uses an aircraft or a motor vehicle to hunt, for the purpose of capturing or killing, any wild unbranded horse, mare, colt, or burro running at large on any of the public land or ranges _____ be fined under this title, or imprisoned not more than six months, or both. [18 U.S.C. §47(a)]

9. The Supreme Court _____ convene on the first Monday in October of each year.

10. The term "official act" means any decision or action on any question, matter, cause, suit, proceeding or controversy, which _____ at any time be pending, or which _____ by law be brought before any public official, in such official's official capacity, or in such official's place of trust or profit. [18 U.S.C. §201(3)]

# Predictions and Inferences

Modals express predictions and inferences. By choosing our modals carefully, we can indicate the strength of our conviction, that our prediction is accurate, or that our inference is believable.

| Prediction: Will the Mayor Run Again? | Level of Predictive Strength |
|---|---|
| The mayor could run again, but I doubt it. | not likely |
| The mayor might run again if no new scandal pops up. | perhaps |
| The mayor may run again. | possible but not certain |
| The mayor should run again. He seems to have lots of support. | more likely |
| The mayor must run again. He is bound to win. | very likely |
| The mayor is running again. He threw his hat into the ring tonight. | certain |

| Inference: Why Is Iva Not at Work? | Inferential Strength |
|---|---|
| She could be sick, but she hasn't called in yet. | little inference, more predictive |
| She might be sick; she called in, but I didn't hear the conversation myself. | weak inference |
| She may be sick. She's sick a lot. | mild inference |
| She must be sick. She said she was going to the doctors. | strong inference |
| She is sick; I saw her at the hospital. | known for a fact |

## Exercise C. Listening

Listen to two neighbors discuss a traffic accident. At the end of the conversation, you will be asked to make several predictions and inferences orally. You must carefully choose the correct modal to indicate the appropriate response to the questions based on what you hear.

Use a modal to answer these questions based on the information you just heard.

*Example:* How did Frank know to go to the hospital?

Possible answers:
He might have seen the accident.
Someone might have called him.

1. Pam is in intensive care and may not make it. Why?

2. What was the noise Zane heard?

3. Why was the truck driver's license revoked?

4. Was the truck driver drinking last night?

5. Was the truck driver seriously hurt?

6. Why is there a police guard outside the truck driver's hospital room?

7. Will the truck driver be charged with a crime?

[*Note:* Since we don't know for certain that the accident was his fault or that he was drinking or using drugs, we can't be certain that he will be charged with any crimes.]

8. Is Dieter German?
   Possible answer: He might be, but we're not certain.

[*Note:* In spite of the circumstantial evidence (his name and the fact that his mother is in Germany), we cannot be certain that he is German; it is still only a possibility.]

9. Why did Pam's mother get the children?

10. When is the best time for Zane to go to the hospital?

## Language Activity 17: Active and Passive Voice

Clarity in legal writing is critical. When dealing with active versus passive voice construction, it is advisable to use active voice in legal documents of any kind. Why is this so? Statements written in the passive voice often lack the clarity of *who* is doing *what*. In the passive voice, the subject is not doing the action. This means it is possible to leave the person doing the action out of the sentence altogether leaving the reader wondering who is doing the action in the sentence.

What makes the active voice more effective? In general, using the active voice is more concise, gives a clear idea of who is doing the action, and uses a more active verb. Also, when considering subject-verb agreement, the active voice uses the expected order of Subject+Verb (S+V). This is not the case in the passive voice, so the reader's expectation of word order may be thrown off course and lead to misunderstanding.

When might it be appropriate to use the passive voice? The passive voice may be the appropriate writing device when emphasizing and de-emphasizing either the person or the action in the sentence. The passive voice emphasizes the thing acted upon and not the person doing the action. Therefore, use the passive voice when you need to de-emphasize the person doing the action for your own purposes. One situation where this may be the case is when you want to emphasize that a document was indeed sent and de-emphasize who sent it. Other situations may be that you do not know who sent the document or it is unimportant to know who sent it. However, legal writing will, in most cases, call for the use of the active voice maintaining a clear distinction of who is doing what.

Let's look at the construction of the active versus passive voice. First, understand that the active or passive voice are constructions, not verb tenses. You will see that the full range of verb tenses may be used with either the active or passive voice constructions.

Active:  The attorney *assists* the client.
Passive: The client *is assisted by* the attorney. [*be* form +
         past participle+ *by*]

| Active | Passive |
|---|---|
| **Simple present** | |
| The attorney *assists* the client. | The client *is assisted by* the attorney. |
| **Present continuous** | |
| The attorney *is assisting* the client. | The client *is being assisted by* the attorney. |
| **Present perfect** | |
| The attorney *has helped* the client. | The client *has been helped by* the attorney. |
| **Simple past** | |
| The attorney *helped* the client. | The client *was helped by* the attorney. |
| **Past continuous** | |
| The attorney *was assisting* the client. | The client *was being assisted by* the attorney. |
| **Past perfect** | |
| The attorney *had assisted* the client. | The client *had been assisted by* the attorney. |

## Simple future (will)

The attorney *will assist* the client. The client *will be assisted by* the attorney.

### *Be going to*

The attorney *will be going to* assist the client.

The client *is going to be assisted by* the attorney.

### Future perfect [rarely used]

The attorney *will have helped* the client.

The client *will have been helped by* the attorney.

## Exercise A

Identify the passive or active voice construction in each sentence, and determine if you should change it to passive or active voice. The first one has been done for you.

1. An objection *was made by* the attorney. Active: <u>The attorney made an objection.</u>

2. A mistrial was declared by the judge. _____

3. The attorney made an error. _____

4. The evidence was removed from the crime scene. _____

5. The motion was filed by the attorney. _____

## Language Activity 18: Conditionals

All of the activities that surround contracts or the law involve many types of conditionals; some you can recognize easily as conditionals because they contain an *if* clause and a result clause. Let's look at examples from the Supreme Court Rules:

1. *If the Court affirms a judgment,* the petitioner or appellant shall pay costs unless the Court otherwise orders. (Sup. Ct. R. 43)
2. *If the Court reverses or vacates a judgment,* the respondent or appellee shall pay costs unless the Court otherwise orders. (Sup. Ct. R. 43)

Although the *if* clause normally is the first clause, it isn't always.

> A document is timely filed *if it is received by the Clerk within the time specified for filing.* (Sup. Ct. R. 29)

The rules for building conditional sentences in English are fairly complicated, but only a few basic types are important to our discussion.

## Future Real

| *future time* | *action* | *result* |
|---|---|---|
| (next Tuesday) | truck isn't here | we don't accept delivery |

Notice that the action, which is in the *if* clause, stays in the present tense even though the action takes place in the future.

> *future action: If* the truck isn't here by Tuesday,

On the other hand, the result clause can use *will* or any other marker of future time.

> *future result:* we *will* not accept delivery
> *future result:* we aren't going to accept delivery

## Exercise A. Sentence Combining

Combine each pair of sentences to make one future time conditional sentence. In each case, make the first sentence the *if* clause.

*Example:* The plane will arrive late. I am going to miss the meeting.
         If the plane arrives late, I am going to miss the meeting.

1. Your father will sign the contract for you. We can sell you the car.

    _____

    _____

2. You don't smoke cigarettes. Your life insurance premiums will be lower.

    _____

    _____

3. The company will hire you. You must agree not to compete with them later.

    _____

    _____

4. The contract can be ready next week. My clients won't object to the extra costs for express mail delivery.

    _____

    _____

5. The Lucy brothers will accept that the Zehmers were joking. The judge hopes to be able to dismiss the case.

    _____

    _____

# Not Real or Contrary-to-Fact (CTF) Events

If the actions and the result are not real (contrary to fact) in the present or future, we basically just use the past forms.

| *not real action, present time* | *not real result, present time* |
|---|---|
| If my lawyer worked here, | we could fill out the forms right now. |
| (She doesn't work here, | so we can't fill out the forms.) |

This chart will help you with the change when shifting from the real forms to the contrary-to-fact (CTF) forms:

| **Future** | | |
|---|---|---|
| real form | If he <u>has</u> a problem, | I <u>will</u> solve it. |
| CTF form | If he *had* a problem, | I *would* solve it. |
| **Present** | | |
| real form | If he <u>has</u> a problem, | I <u>solve</u> it. |
| CTF form | If he *had* a problem, | I *would* solve it. |
| **Past** | | |
| real form | If he <u>had</u> a problem, | I <u>solved</u> it. |
| CTF form | If he *had had* a problem, | I *would have* solved it. |
| **Pres. Cont.** | | |
| real form | If he <u>is having</u> a problem, | I <u>will</u> solve it. |
| CTF form | If he *were having* a problem, | I *would* solve it. |
| **Past Cont.** | | |
| real form | If he <u>was having</u> a problem, | I <u>solved</u> it. |
| CTF form | If he *had been having* a problem, | I *would have* solved it. |

Notice that in formal American English, we must still use *were* for all forms of *be* in *if* clauses that are contrary-to-fact events:

> *not real action, present time*      *not real result, present time*
>
> If the judgment **were** affirmed,      any penalty allowed by law
>                                        would be applied.

## Exercise B. Sentence Combining

Change the pairs of sentences to unreal conditionals. You will need to make the verbs negative.

*Example:* The budget is tight. I won't give you a raise.
    If the budget weren't tight, I would give you a raise.
    The dam broke. My house was destroyed.
    If the dam had not broken, my house would not have been destroyed.

  1. The appeal isn't timely. The panel won't review your case.

     _____

     _____

2. His paper was too long. We weren't able to accept it for publication.

   _____

   _____

3. The land reform laws were passed. The family lost the land.

   _____

   _____

4. I didn't read the journal article. I didn't know about the change in the law.

   _____

   _____

5. The lawyer missed the filing deadline. The case was dismissed.

   _____

   _____

6. The students didn't study. They failed their exams.

   _____

   _____

7. The guard found the burglar. The diamond wasn't stolen.

   _____

   _____

8. The deed was found in his safe. We could prove ownership.

   _____

   _____

9. An important client is coming to see me later. I am working here at the office on Sunday.

   _____

   _____

10. She is very intelligent. She is working for the Ministry of Justice.

    _____

    _____

# *Unless*

Perhaps the most confusing of the conditional forms is *unless* since it is the "negative" of *if*. These two sentences mean just about the same thing.

> **Unless** he **arrives** by 6, we will not be able to honor his request.
>
> **If** he **doesn't** arrive by 6, we will not be able to honor his request.

## Exercise C. Sentence Combining

If the following contain *unless*, rewrite them with *if* and vice versa.

*Example:* Original: If he isn't late, let him take the exam.
Rewritten: Unless he is late, let him take the exam.

1. Unless they have left a credit card as a deposit, they must pay the full amount in advance.

   _____

   _____

2. The contract requires them to complete the work by next week if it doesn't rain.

   _____

   _____

3. If either party is incompetent, the contract is not enforceable. [*Hint:* Replace *either* with *both*.]

   _____

   _____

4. Generally, acceptance must mirror the terms of the offer unless you use boilerplate forms.

   _____

   _____

5. Unless it is market practice, silence doesn't normally constitute acceptance.

   _____

   _____

## Exercise D. Simplification

Break this complex passage into a series of *if* statements. Compare your answers with your classmates' answers.

> Whenever any record to be transmitted to this Court contains material written in a foreign language without a translation made under the authority of the lower court, or admitted to be correct, the clerk of the court transmitting the record shall advise the Clerk of this Court immediately so that this Court may order that a translation be supplied and, if necessary, printed as part of the joint appendix. [Sup. Ct. R. 31]

# Language Activity 19: Gerunds, Infinitives, and *That* Clauses

To make the relationship between two sentences closer, we can use *that* clauses or gerund and infinitive phrases.

| Form | Example | Explanation |
|---|---|---|
| *that* clause | Luc is furious *that* he lost a case. | must have pronoun and verb following *that* |
| gerund | Luc can't stand *losing a case*. | no pronoun needed; *ing* form of verb |
| infinitive | Luc can't stand *to lose a case*. | no pronoun needed; *to* + base form of verb |

There are many structural possibilities when we use *that* clauses, gerunds, and infinitives with verbs. Some verbs only take infinitives; others can only take gerunds.

1. Statutes *tend* to be easier to interpret than cases.
2. Three times I *postponed* taking the bar exam.

Some can even take all three forms. However, we must be careful, or the sentences we produce may be ungrammatical and hard to understand.

Since gerund phrases require an *-ing* form and the infinitive phrases require a *to* plus a simple verb form, we cannot use modals (such as *may, will, can, should,* or *must*) to form a gerund or an infinitive structure.

    3. *Incorrect:* Luc can't stand *musting* study torts.

    4. *Incorrect:* Luc hopes not *to must* address the court tomorrow.

We must replace the modals with their nonmodal equivalents, such as *have to* for *must* or *be able to* for *can.*

    5. *Correct:* Luc can't stand *having to* study torts.

    6. *Correct:* Luc hopes not *to have to* address the court tomorrow.

# Gerund or Infinitive

As we look at the different ways we can use the infinitives and gerunds, we should keep two general guidelines in mind. There are numerous exceptions, but they will help in many cases.

Guideline 1: Infinitives are often used with verbs that talk about events or states that haven't happened yet or haven't been fulfilled.

| Verb | Example | Time Frame of Infinitive Phrase |
|------|---------|--------------------------------|
| *want* | Blane *wants* <u>to get</u> the hearing postponed. | "future"; hearing hasn't been postponed yet: unfulfilled event |
| *hope* | McDonald's® *hoped* <u>to settle</u> out of court. | "future"; they hadn't settled yet: unfulfilled event |

Guideline 2: Gerunds are often (but not always!) used with verbs that talk about states or events that have already happened or are happening. These events or states are fulfilled.

| Verb | Example | Time Frame of Gerund Phrase |
|------|---------|----------------------------|
| *regret* | Blane *regretted* <u>taking</u> the case. | "past"; case was taken before it was "regretted"; fulfilled event |
| *deny* | McDonald's® *denied* <u>serving</u> a defective product. | "past"; serving of allegedly defective product preceded the denial: fulfilled event |

## *Verbs That Use Only Infinitives*

There are two basic types of verbs that take only infinitives. Let's look at an example of a verb from each group first.

| Group 1 with *for* | Example | Explanation: Allows Same Subject Deletion |
|---|---|---|
| *intend* | The judge *intended* <u>to hear</u> the tape before ruling. | subjects of *intend* and <u>hear</u> the same: the judge |
| *intend* | The *judge intended* **for** the jury <u>to hear</u> the tape. | subjects of *intend* and <u>hear</u> not the same; must add **for** |

| Group 2 without *for* | Example | Explanation: Does Not Allow Same Subject Deletion |
|---|---|---|
| *persuade* | I *persuaded* my client <u>to present</u> the tape as evidence. | subjects of *persuade* and <u>present</u> not the same: I, client |
| *persuade* | I *persuaded* **myself** <u>to present</u> the tape as evidence. | although subjects of *persuade* and <u>present</u> the same **cannot** delete the subject; must use reflexive (myself) |

Here is a brief list of the most important verbs in these two groups.

| Group 1 | | Group 2 | |
|---|---|---|---|
| agree | appear | advise | allow |
| care | consent | appoint | authorize |
| decide | desire | believe | cause |
| fail | guarantee | challenge | command |
| happen | hesitate | convince | forbid |
| hope | intend | force | get |
| learn | manage | help | hire |
| mean | offer | instruct | invite |
| plan | promise | name | permit |
| refuse | seems | persuade | remind |
| swear | tend | request | teach |
| vow | | tell | warn |

## Exercise A. Sentence Combining

Using the list of the most important verbs, make sentences from the parts and verbs provided. The first one has been done for you.

1. we challenge / [You will make sentences]

   *We challenge you to make sentences.*

2. Last week / the teacher remind/ [we should study for our products liability exam]

   _____

   _____

3. I ask / [the study group helped me understand strict liability in tort]

   _____

   _____

4. I / force / [I studied every day last week]

   _____

   _____

5. The work and effort / permit / [We all passed those difficult exams]

   _____

   _____

## *Negative Infinitives*

What happens when we try to turn a negative *that* clause into an infinitive phrase?

| Form | Example with Negative | Explanation |
|------|----------------------|-------------|
| *that* clause | The company decided **that *it* wouldn't move** to Ohio. | needs pronoun referring to subject in *that* clause (*it*) |
| Group 1 infinitive | The company decided **not to move** to Ohio. | *decide* is a Group 1 verb; delete pronoun and modal; use infinitive form |
| *that* clause | The company had warned the employees **that *we* shouldn't expect to be transferred.** | needs pronoun referring to subject in *that* clause (*we*) |
| Group 2 infinitive | The company had warned *us* **not to expect to be transferred.** | *warn* is a Group 2 verb, delete modal but must leave "subject" (*us*) of the infinitive *expect*. From **[we expect to be transferred]** |

## Exercise B. Rewriting Sentences

Change each underlined negative *that* clauses to an infinitive phrase. Some of the verbs may come from Group 1 and others from Group 2.

1. All the employees, whom I'm representing in the negotiations, agreed <u>that they wouldn't ask for a raise for one year</u>.

   _____

2. The union members decided <u>that they wouldn't strike while talks continued</u>.

   _____

3. For its part, the company did promise <u>that it wouldn't cut health benefits</u>.

   _____

4. Everyone expects <u>that next year won't be as difficult as last year</u>.

   _____

5. Most employees are simply glad <u>that they aren't being fired from their jobs</u>.

   _____

## *Infinitives and Levels of Formality*

In the chart, the first sentence is grammatical but sounds very formal, while the second sentence is a less formal version of the same sentence. In legal English you often see the more formal version, so understanding its usage is important.

| Level of Formality | Example | Explanation |
|---|---|---|
| very formal | <u>Not to provide free legal counsel to the indigent</u> would be unconstitutional. | begins with infinitive phrase (here in negative form) that is the subject |
| less formal | <u>It</u> would be unconstitutional <u>not to provide free legal counsel to the indigent</u>. | *it* holds the subject place; infinitive phrase at end of sentence after verb |

## Exercise C. Rewriting Sentences

Rewrite each sentence to make it more formal.

1. It is a moral imperative to follow the code of ethics at all times.

   _____

   _____

   _____

2. It is not easy to put aside your personal beliefs when representing a client who you believe might be guilty.

   _____

   _____

   _____

3. It would be unethical not to be as prepared as possible for each case.

   _____

   _____

   _____

4. It would be necessary to prove unethical behavior before an attorney could be disbarred.

   _____

   _____

   _____

5. Even if she were a personal friend, it is improper to address a judge by her given name in court.

   _____

   _____

   _____

# Verbs That Use Only Gerunds

For certain verbs and adjectives, there is a required preposition that must be added when we change a *that* clause to a gerund phrase. Unfortunately, you will need to learn most of those verb/preposition or adjective/preposition combinations [collocations] through memorization. We have listed a few, but there are many others. Although every good dictionary will tell you which preposition is paired with any given verb or adjective, we've provided a short list of important legal combinations.

| Form | Example | Verbs/Adjectives Requiring Prepositions |
|---|---|---|
| *that* clause | They were excited <u>that they would be hearing the Chief Justice speak</u>. | no preposition since there is a *that* clause |
| gerund | They were excited **about** <u>hearing the Chief Justice speak</u>. | The prepositions vary; check a dictionary if you are uncertain. |

| Legal Phrases: Verb or Adjective plus Preposition | | | |
|---|---|---|---|
| absent from | in accordance with | according to | accuse of |
| acquainted with | advise on | in agreement with | answer to |
| approve of | aware of | base on | believe in |
| blame on | collect from | conceal from | conscious of |
| contribute to | critical of | deprive of | difficult for |
| disapprove of | eligible for | engaged in | incapable of |
| independent of | inferior to | intent on | jealous of |
| obtain from | opposed to | persist in | prevent from |
| profit from | prohibit from | tolerant of | wary of |

**Exercise D. Rewriting Sentences**

Change the underlined *that* clauses to gerund phrases. We have done the first one for you.

1. The manufacturer insisted <u>that he could produce a safer product</u>. The manufacturer insisted <u>on his being able</u> to produce a safer product.

2. He intended <u>that his settlement offer would satisfy those filing the class action suit</u>.

   _____

3. Of course, the plaintiffs' attorneys were confident <u>that they would win the case</u>.

   _____

4. As a result, they weren't at all doubtful <u>that their clients would be awarded a large settlement by the court</u>.

   _____

5. The manufacturer wasn't yet aware <u>that the attorneys were able to gather so much clear-cut evidence of negligent behavior</u>.

   _____

# Verbs That Use Both Gerunds and Infinitives

There are even some verbs that can be followed by either a gerund or an infinitive with almost no change in meaning. For other verbs, there is a major difference in the meaning when we choose to use an infinitive or a gerund. However, for most of the verbs that allow either gerunds or infinitives, the difference in meaning is very small.

## No Meaning Changes: Near and Far

Some very common verbs, such as *hate* and *like*, can be followed by either a gerund or an infinitive. The differences in the use of a gerund or an infinitive with these verbs are very, very slight. However, some native speakers do feel that there is a slight difference, which is noted on the chart.

| Type of Speech | Example | Explanation |
|---|---|---|
| gerund | Mr. Sampson hates *trying* products liability cases. | The gerund form is felt by some native speakers to be more concrete |
| infinitive | Mr. Sampson hates *to try* products liability cases. | Native speakers often feel the infinitive form is a little more distant or hypothetical. |

## Meaning Changes

There is a very small class of verbs that can take both gerunds and infinitives with a regular change in meaning based on the concept of fulfilled and unfulfilled events that we discussed at the beginning of this section. You may wish to refer to the two guidelines we gave.

| Type of Speech | Example | Explanation |
|---|---|---|
| gerund | He remembered *postponing* the meeting until Tuesday. | A fulfilled event. He is looking back and might say, "I know that I told them to postpone the meeting. Here's a recording of that conversation." |
| infinitive | He remembered *to postpone* the meeting until Tuesday. | An unfulfilled event. He would say, "Jase, I'm sorry but I just remembered; we'll need to postpone our meeting till next Tuesday." |

### Exercise E. Fill in the Blanks

Do we need an infinitive or a gerund? We have filled in the first blank for you.

1. *Witness:* I'm not sure if he was the one who mugged me or not.
   *Lawyer:* [see] How could you forget <u>seeing</u> him just outside your building?

2. *Lawyer:* [take] Had you forgotten _____ your wallet when you first left your apartment?
   *George:* Yes. I did go back in for my wallet and my cigarettes.

3. *Lawyer:* What did you do when you left for the second time?
   *George:* [smoke] I immediately started _____. I can't smoke inside. My daughter has asthma.

4. *George:* [buy] I'd been up all night working and my head hurt, and my wife wanted me to stop _____ some aspirin while I was taking my morning jog.

5. *George:* [see] Wait, now I remember _____ him. Yes, he's the one.

## *That* Clauses and the Mandative Subjunctive

In formal English, when a *that* clause is used with a small group of verbs and adjectives, the verb in the *that* clause must be in the bare form [infinitive without *to*]. This structure is called the <u>mand</u>ative because it is used with these verbs and adjectives when they are used as de<u>mands</u>, very strong suggestions, or com<u>mands</u>.

| Form | Verb or Adjective | Example | Explanation |
|---|---|---|---|
| present | demand | The courts demand that the pleading **be filed** by Tuesday. | *Be* is the simple form. |
| past | require | The statute required that *mens rea* **be** established. | still *be* even though the main clause is in the past |
| future | imperative | It will be imperative that the jury **be able to believe** the witness. | can't use modals *(will, can, should)*: e.g., there is no infinitive of *must* or *will* or *should* |
| passive | insist | His attorney insisted that he **be released** immediately. | again *be* for all forms |
| negative | request | The company was requesting that we **not discuss** the case with the media. | *not* precedes base form of verb; no *do* |

Some verbs may use both the mandative subjunctive and present and past tense forms depending on the meaning of the verb. If the verb is used as a strong suggestion or a command, it takes the subjunctive, but if it is being used as a synonym for another verb such as *say* or *offer* (as in *offer an explanation*) then the indicative form is used.

| Verb | Example | Explanation |
|---|---|---|
| insist | The detective insists that he **had faxed** the deposition to the courthouse. | In this case, *insist* is being used as a synonym for *say,* so we use the normal indicative form. |
| | The detective insists that the depositions **be faxed** to the courthouse. | Here *insist* has the meaning of *order* or *command,* so we use the subjunctive form: *be.* |
| suggest | The detective suggested that the forms might have already **been faxed.** | Here the verb is a synonym for another nonsubjunctive verb: *suggest = offer an explanation.* |
| | The detective suggested that the pleadings **be faxed** rather than mailed. | *Suggest* is being used as a polite command, so we need the subjunctive form. |

## Exercise F. Sentence Combining

Combine the two parts of the sentence. You may need to make changes in the verb forms. If there is strong suggestion, use the mandative subjunctive; otherwise, use normal forms.

> Example: [It is essential that] [the transcripts must be released by Monday.]
>
> It is essential that the transcripts <u>be</u> released by Monday.

1. [The judge ordered that] [the lawyers don't discuss the case until then.]

_____

_____

2. [He stressed that it was important that] [everyone should have equal access to the information.]

_____

_____

3. [Furthermore, he threatened that] [he would charge anyone who spoke to the press before then with contempt of court.]

_____

_____

4. [My colleague proposed that] [we should hold a joint press conference.]

_____

_____

5. [We think that would meet the requirement that] [no one leaks the news of the settlement.]

_____

_____

## Language Activity 20: Reported Speech

Working in the legal world involves a great deal of reporting what others have said. For example, after every formal meeting, someone must prepare the minutes of the meeting: what happened and who said what or was assigned to do something. At other times, lawyers will be asked to draft depositions, reports, or statements, all of which require reported or indirect speech.

# Changing from Direct to Reported Speech

## *Past Conversations*

In the chart, note the major changes in form that occur when direct speech from past conversations is changed to indirect speech.

| Type of Speech | Example | Explanation of Required Change |
|---|---|---|
| Direct (present) | Simon said, "*I'm* in *my* fourth year of law school." | |
| Reported (from past conversation) | Simon said *he was* in *his* fourth year of law school. | Present tense from direct speech changes to past tense. Pronouns change. |

| Type of Speech | Example | Explanation of Required Change |
|---|---|---|
| Direct (past) | David said, "She *showed me* how to use the Internet." | |
| Reported (from past conversation) | David said she *had shown him* how to use the Internet. | Past statement to past perfect. Pronouns change. |

| Type of Speech | Example | Explanation of Required Change |
|---|---|---|
| Direct (imperative—order) | Evan said to Peter, "*Bring me* the file *right now!*" | |
| Reported (from past conversation) | Evan *told* Peter *to bring him* the file *immediately.* | Imperative goes to infinitive. Verb changes to *tell*. Pronouns and time word change. |

| Type of Speech | Example | Explanation of Required Change |
|---|---|---|
| Direct (negative imperative) | Evan *said* to Peter, "Don't put the evidence *there!*" | |
| Reported (from past conversation) | Evan *told* Peter not to put the evidence *on the table.* | Imperative changes to *not* + infinitive. Verb changes to *tell*. Specific location is named instead of *there*. |

There are many other changes that are possible. Basically, just remember to make the speaker's original meaning clear.

## Exercise A. Reported Speech in the Past

In writing, change this short conversation to indirect speech.

1. Mr. Coke, the district attorney, asked, "Mr. Sammy, where were you December 21, 2006?"

2. Mr. Sammy replied, "I was at home with my wife."

3. Mr. Coke asked, "Did anyone other than your wife see you there?" [*Hint:* Use an *if* or a *whether* clause.]

4. Mr. Sammy whispered, "Well, no, I guess not."

5. The district attorney said, "No further questions. Thank you."

_____

_____

_____

_____

_____

_____

_____

# Modals

Modals such as *will, must, may,* and *can* must also undergo changes in form when direct speech is turned into reported speech.

| Type of Speech | Example | Explanation of Required Change |
|---|---|---|
| Direct (future) | Linda said, "Joan *will* bring *me* the file later today." | |
| Reported (from past conversation) | Linda said Joan *would* bring *her* the file later that day. | *Will* changes to *would.* Pronouns change. Main verb doesn't change. |

Other modal changes would be *can* to *could* and *may* to *might*.
*Must* has two possibilities.

| Type of Speech | Example | Explanation of Required Change |
|---|---|---|
| Direct (present) | The judge said, "Mr. Sammy *must* repay his client." | |
| Reported (from past conversation) | The judge said *that* Mr. Sammy *had to/must* repay his client. | *Must* changes to *had to* or stays *must*. Can use *that* but not necessary. Main verb doesn't change. |

Normally, *could, should,* and *would* don't change.

| Type of Speech | Example | Explanation of Required Change |
|---|---|---|
| Direct (present) | The lawyer asked the judge, "Could *we* have a ten-minute recess?" | |
| Reported (from past conversation) | The lawyer asked the judge *if they* could have a ten-minute recess. | Add *if* or *whether*. Pronouns change. Main verb does not change. |

## Exercise B. Modals in Reported Speech

In writing, change the following conversation to reported speech.

1. The client asked his lawyer, Ms. Anna Janovich, "Do you think I should plead guilty?"

2. Startled, Ms. Janovich asked, "Is there something I should know?"

3. "Perhaps I could be wrong about the amount I asked the accountant to put on the form," he replied.

4. She thought to herself, "Can he really not remember? Or is he just trying to bluff me, too?"

5. "Yes, it could have been closer to a million like Mr. Able says it was," he mumbled.

_____

_____

_____

_____

_____

# Present Time and Universal Truths

Notice what happens if the reported speech takes place in present time.

| Type of Speech | Example | Explanation of Required Change |
|---|---|---|
| Direct (present) | My professor says to me, "*Your* class will be the best ever." | |
| Reported (in present conversation) | My professor says *our* class will be the best ever. | Only the pronouns change. |

If the quote contains information that is "always" true, we don't change the verb tense. It does not matter when the conversation took place.

| "Always True" Information in Past Time | | |
|---|---|---|
| Type of Speech | Example | Explanation of Required Change |
| Direct ("always true") | Yesterday our civics instructor told us, "The United States is not a democracy but a republic." | |
| Reported (in past conversation) | Yesterday our civics instructor told us *that* the United States is not a democracy but a republic. | No change in verb or pronouns. Can use *that* but not necessary. |

## Exercise C. Reporting on a Conversation

One day on the subway you overhear this conversation between a man and a woman. Since the conversation deals with a case your office is working on, you think you should give your supervisor a written report of what you heard. Of course, you'll need to use reported speech.

1. You'll hear the conversation twice.

2. Use the chart on page 258 to help you take notes on the conversation. The first time, just listen.

3. After you listen the second time, record the conversation as accurately as possible in reported speech.

| | **Drafting Date** | **Settlement** | **Injunction** |
|---|---|---|---|
| Chemcorp attorney | | | |
| Colleague on subway | | | |

## Exercise D. Changing Reported Speech to Direct Speech

Let's reverse the process now. In pairs, use this slightly edited section of reported speech from a U.S. Supreme Court case [*Maryland v. Wilson*, 519 U.S. 408, 117 S. Ct. 882, 137 L.Ed.2d 41 (1997)] to create dialogue for a role play. The transcript from the trial court was reviewed by the Supreme Court in making its decision, but the actual questioning of the police officer was conducted at trial court level. The attorney was conducting a direct examination of the police officer who made the original arrest in this case. As you write your questions keep the rules for direct examination in mind.

1. Leading questions are not allowed. (You cannot provide the answer to the witness through the phrasing of the question.)

2. Narrative questions are not allowed. (You cannot have the witness give the information in story form. You probably don't want him or her to do that either.)

3. You cannot ask repetitive questions.

4. Nonexpert witnesses are not generally allowed to offer opinions. A police officer can testify regarding estimated speed of a vehicle and a suspect's behavior.

We've done the first sentence for you as an example.

> *Maryland v. Wilson*
>
> Reported speech: At about 7:30 PM on a June evening, Maryland state trooper David Hughes observed a passenger car driving southbound on I-95 in Baltimore County at a speed of 64 miles per hour.
>
> Dialogue:
>
> *Lawyer:* "Officer Hughes, tell us what you saw at around 7:30 P.M. on the evening of June 14, 2006."
>
> *Hughes:* "Well, I saw a passenger car driving about 64 miles an hour."

1. The posted speed limit was 55 miles per hour, and the car had no regular license tag.

2. Hughes activated his lights and sirens before signaling the car to pull over, but it continued driving for another mile and a half before it finally did so.

3. During the pursuit, Hughes noticed that there were three occupants in the car.

4. As Hughes approached the car on foot, the driver alighted [got out] and met him halfway. The driver was trembling and appeared extremely nervous but nonetheless produced a valid Connecticut driver's license.

5. Hughes instructed him to return to the car, and the driver complied.

6. During this encounter, Hughes noticed that the front seat passenger, respondent Jerry Lee Wilson, was sweating and also appeared extremely nervous.

7. While the driver was sitting in the driver's seat looking for the papers, Hughes ordered Wilson out of the car.

8. When Wilson exited the car, a quantity of crack cocaine fell to the ground. Wilson was then arrested and charged with possession of cocaine with intent to distribute.

**Exercise E. Role Play**

1. Give your written dialogue from Exercise D to another pair for review.

2. Perform a role play with one partner as the police officer and the other as the attorney. Remember that the attorney conducting the direct examination is questioning "his" or "her" witness. Normally that means that the witness is not hostile and is willing to respond to all questions asked without hesitation.

# Language Activity 21: Building Connections between Clauses

Many sentences in legal English consist of two or more clauses connected by a subordinate or coordinate connector. A clause has a subject and a verb; a main (or independent) clause is one that can stand alone while a subordinate (or dependent) clause has a subject and a verb but cannot stand alone:

> *main clause:* She specializes in intentional torts.

> *subordinate clause:* although she enjoys contract law as well

| subordinate connector | **When** vacancies happen in the Representation from any state, *the executive authority thereof shall issue writs of election to fill such vacancies.* U.S. Const. art. I, §2 | combines *main clause* with a subordinate clause |
|---|---|---|
| coordinate connector | *The trial of all crimes, except in cases of impeachment, shall be by jury;* **and** *such trial shall be held in the state where the said crimes shall have been committed.* U.S. Const. art. III, §2 | combines two *main clauses* of equal importance |

These connectors are used extensively in English to act as traffic directors; they guide the reader in the interpretation of the text. The connectors can only be used to combine clauses that are in some way related. For example, the following sentence combines two unrelated clauses and therefore is not correct.

> Tort law excludes contracts, and the octopus has eight tentacles.

Remember that the basic purpose of connectors is to show how clauses are related. Connectors are like traffic signs on a highway. One "road" must lead to another before signs can be used to guide a driver.

To show these relationships, we use three different types of connectors that have different structures but similar functions.

| Type of Connectors | | |
|---|---|---|
| **Group 1** | Clause, **connector** clause. | Connie was elected to the government last week, **but** she won't take office until next month. |
| **Group 2** | **Connector** clause, clause. | **Although** Connie is moving to Ottawa now, her husband may not join her until next year. |
| **Group 3** | Clause; clause, **connector**. | Connie will be living near Ottawa; her husband will stay in Vancouver, **however**. |

Every time you learn a new connector, you should determine to which of these three groups it belongs. You will learn some rules that will help you do this.

# Group 1 Connectors: Coordinate Conjunctions

Notice that the Group 1 connector always goes between two independent clauses.

[clause 1], *connector* [clause 2]

| Group 1: Coordinate Conjunctions | | | |
|---|---|---|---|
| Connector | Function | Example | Level of Formality |
| *and* | addition | We will be filing in Texas, **and** the others will be filing in Florida. | all |
| *but* | contrast | Torts are civil wrongs, **but** they exclude contracts. | all |
| *or* | choice | He must apologize to my neighbor, **or** she will file slander charges against him. | all |
| *so* | cause/effect 1 causes 2 | I wanted to go to law school, **so** I majored in English in college. | informal |
| *for* | effect/cause 2 causes 1 | They were disbarred, **for** they had committed mail fraud. | formal |
| *yet* | contrast | He normally supports the Democrats, **yet** this year he voted for the Republicans. | formal |
| *nor* | and not | She has not yet been charged with trespass, **nor** has her husband.* | formal |

* Notice change in word order: *nor has he.*

## Exercise A. Sentence Combining

Use the conjunctions in brackets [ ] to combine the following sentences. Don't forget to change the punctuation and the capitalization.

1. [and] We bought a new house last year. We moved into it in April.

   _____

   _____

2. [so] The neighbors seemed very nice. We expected to get along well with them.

   _____

   _____

3. [but] We tried to get to know them. They acted cold and unfriendly.

   _____

   _____

4. [so] Their dog barked all night. We didn't get any sleep.

   _____

   _____

5. [yet] We asked them to stop the dog from barking. They didn't pay any attention.

   _____

   _____

6. [for] We couldn't talk or watch television. Their stereo blasted loudly all day and all night.

   _____

   _____

7. [nor] They wouldn't discuss the problems with us. They wouldn't respond to letters we sent them. [Be careful with word order in this one!]

   _____

   _____

8. [or] We decided we could sue them. We could move out.

   _____

   _____

9. [and] We moved out of the house. The neighbors' best friends bought it!

_____

_____

10. [but] We think they made us miserable on purpose. We'll never know for sure.

_____

_____

# Comma Splices and Fused Sentences

In English, we have specific rules about the punctuation of sentences. When we use a coordinate conjunction to combine two clauses, we must use a comma (or in a very complicated sentence, a semicolon) before the conjunction.

> The moot court students will be using the yellow room, **but** they must not move the furniture.

Forgetting to follow that rule causes three main errors. However, they are also very easily corrected.

| Error | Example | Explanation |
|---|---|---|
| Comma splice | The moot court students will be using the yellow room, they must not move the furniture. | combining two independent clauses with no conjunction |
| *Correction* | The moot court students will be using the yellow room, **but** they must not move the furniture. | add appropriate conjunction |
| Fused sentence | The moot court students will be using the yellow room they must not move the furniture. | no punctuation, no conjunction |
| *Correction 1* | The moot court students will be using the yellow room, **but** they must not move the furniture. | add appropriate conjunction and punctuation |
| *Correction 2* | The moot court students will be using the yellow room; they must not move the furniture. | (*a*) add semicolon or (*b*) add period and capitalize first word of new sentence |
| No comma | The moot court students will be using the yellow room **but** they must not move the furniture. | conjunction but no comma |
| *Correction* | The moot court students will be using the yellow room, **but** they must not move the furniture. | add comma |

## Exercise B. Error Identification and Correction

For each sentence, identify the error and then correct it.

a. missing comma    c. fused sentence
b. comma splice    d. correct punctuation

____a____ 1. Normally, trespassing is a property tort but it can also be a crime.

_____

_____

_____ 2. Damages are not required for intentional trespass only for negligent trespass must damages be shown.

_____

_____

_____ 3. Last year I was charged with trespass and the owner took me to court.

_____

_____

_____ 4. I really thought that I was still inside the city park, the land belonged to a Mr. Ubel.

_____

_____

_____ 5. As he jumped out from behind that tree, he frightened me, and I nearly fainted.

_____

_____

_____ 6. Then he pointed his shotgun at me I had to go with him to his house.

_____

_____

_____ 7. He called the local sheriff, we waited for a couple of hours for him to show up.

_____

_____

_____ 8. I was very embarrassed, but the sheriff seemed to think it was funny.

_____

_____

_____ 9. As he drove me into town to fill out the papers, he told me funny stories about others who had trespassed on Ubel's land.

_____

_____

_____ 10. Well, he may have thought it was funny but I didn't when I had to pay over $200 in fines and fees!

_____

_____

## Sentence Fragments

As discussed, a subordinate clause cannot stand by itself.

> *Incomplete:* Because you are presumed innocent until proven guilty.

This sentence is only a part or a *fragment* of a complete, grammatically correct sentence. Fortunately, it is easy to correct this type of fragment once we recognize the subordinate conjunctions.

> *Incorrect:* The burden of proof is on the prosecution. Because you are presumed innocent until proven guilty.

> *Corrected:* The burden of proof is on the prosecution because you are presumed innocent until proven guilty.

How did we correct this sentence? We took out the period and changed the capital *B* to a small *b*.

# Group 2 Connectors: Subordinate Conjunctions

This second group includes important connectors such as *although, because, if,* and *since.* Let's see how its rules differ from those of Group 1.

| | | |
|---|---|---|
| **Rule 1:** Group 2 connectors can come at the beginning of the sentence. Group 1 connectors cannot. | [**If** clause 1], [clause 2]. Note comma between clauses. | **If** he is not sick, he will still address the jury. |
| **Rule 2:** They can also be in the middle of the two clauses. Group 1 connectors cannot. | [Clause 2] [**if** clause 1]. Note <u>no</u> comma. | He will address the jury **if** he is not sick. |
| **Rule 3:** Group 2 clauses cannot be complete sentences by themselves. They must always be combined with a main clause. In some cases, clauses that begin with a Group 1 connector can be complete by themselves, but ESL writers should avoid those forms. | Incorrect: [**Because** clause]. Correct: [**Because** clause], [clause]. | **Because** state of mind is difficult to prove. **Because** state of mind is difficult to prove, most intent is proven through circumstantial evidence. |

This chart provides uses and examples of the most common Group 2 connectors, called subordinators.

| Function: Cause/Effect or Effect/Cause | |
|---|---|
| **Connector** | **Example** |
| *because* | Shane must ride the bus because his license has been suspended. [effect **because** cause] |
| *since* | Shane's license was suspended **since** he was arrested for DUI (driving under the influence—of alcohol or drugs). |
| *as* (slightly formal) | Shane must ride the bus **as** his license has been suspended. |
| *so that* | Shane must complete an alcohol/drug program so **that** he can apply to have his license reinstated. |
| *whereas* (formal) | **Whereas** you have been found guilty of driving under the influence, we hereby revoke your driving privileges for the period of six months. |

| Function: Contrast | |
| --- | --- |
| **Connector** | **Example** |
| although | Shane likes taking the bus **although** his license has been reinstated. |
| even though | Shane will continue to take the bus **even though** his license was reinstated last week. |
| whereas | Shane served no time in jail **whereas** his sister had to spend six months in jail for her second DUI offense. |
| while | Shane cooperated with the arresting officers **while** his sister attempted to flee the scene of the accident. |

| Function: Time/Order | |
| --- | --- |
| **Connector** | **Example** |
| before | Shane always drove **before** he started taking the bus. |
| until | Shane drove his motorcycle **until** his license was suspended. |
| while | Shane slept **while** he was awaiting release from jail. |
| once | Shane will take the bus everywhere **once** he learns the bus routes. |
| when | Shane might ride the bus even **when** his license has been restored. |
| whenever | He will continue to take the bus **whenever** he needs a little extra sleep. |

## Exercise C

Use a Group 2 connector in the pairs of clauses. Make sure that the connector you use performs the cued function.

In law schools, torts is a required course [cause/effect] _____ the methods and concepts are fundamental to functioning as a lawyer [contrast] _____ it is in more advanced courses where students learn jurisdiction-specific information and practice-oriented skills. [contrast] _____ torts focus on the empirical and sociological realities of how the system of civil justice works, students should also consider what is happening in the real world. [cause/effect] _____ this is the case, practicing lawyers often visit these classes [time order] _____ these courses begin.

# Group 3 Connectors: Linking Words

Look at the position of *however* in the examples.

> Aimee has left; **however,** she did leave you the forms to fill in.
> Aimee has gone; she did, **however,** leave you the forms to fill in.
> Aimee has gone; she did leave you the forms to fill in, **however.**
> Aimee has gone. **However,** she did leave you the forms to fill in.

Words such as *however* are called *linking* words or *transitional expressions* because they help make links clear between sentences or independent clauses. Linking words can occur in four positions.

| Position 1 | [Clause 1]; [**however,** clause 2]. |
| Position 2 | [Clause 1]; [part of clause 2, **however,** rest of clause 2]. |
| Position 3 | [Clause 1]; [clause 2, **however**]. |
| Position 4 | [Clause 1]. [**However,** clause 2]. |

| Function: Cause/Effect | |
| --- | --- |
| **Connector** | **Example** |
| *therefore* | Shane rides the bus; **therefore,** he will save money on car insurance. |
| *consequently* (formal) | Shane rides the bus; **consequently,** he won't need a car in the city. |
| *as a result* (slightly formal) | Shane rides the bus; **as a result,** he saves money on gasoline. |
| *accordingly* (slightly formal) | Shane rides the bus every day; **accordingly,** he has bought a bus pass. |
| *thus* (slightly formal) | Shane rides the bus; **thus,** he doesn't have to try to find a parking space. |

| Function: Addition | |
| --- | --- |
| **Connector** | **Example** |
| *furthermore* | Shane rides the bus to school; **furthermore,** he may start riding it to work, too. |
| *moreover* | Shane rides the bus; **moreover,** he is urging all concerned citizens to do the same. |

| Function: Contrast | |
| --- | --- |
| **Connector** | **Example** |
| *however* | Shane rides the bus; **however,** he won't sell his car just yet. |
| *even so* | Shane rides the bus; **even so,** he still owns a car. |
| *nevertheless (slightly formal)* | Shane rides the bus every day; **nevertheless,** his neighbors insist on driving to work in separate cars. |

| Function: Restatement | |
| --- | --- |
| **Connector** | **Example** |
| *in other words* | Shane rides the bus for environmental reasons; **in other words,** he wants to help clean up the pollution in our city. |

| Function: Time/Order | |
| --- | --- |
| **Connector** | **Example** |
| *for a start* | Shane has begun to ride the bus; **for a start,** he will ride it to school during the week. |
| *initially* | Shane has begun to ride the bus; **initially,** he will ride it only on Sundays. |
| *next* | Shane has begun to ride the bus; **next,** he hopes to convince his family to do so also. |

| Function: Summarizing | |
| --- | --- |
| **Connector** | **Example** |
| *in summary* | Shane has begun riding the bus, recycling trash, and conserving energy; **in summary,** he is becoming more responsible about the environment. |
| *in general* | Shane is not the only one riding the bus these days; **in general,** more responsible people are choosing to ride the bus to reduce pollution. |

## Comma Splices and Missing Commas

When we use linking expressions to relate clauses, it is easy to create comma splices by accidentally leaving out required commas.

| Status | Example | Explanation |
|---|---|---|
| Incorrect: Comma splice | Binh Vu was first in his class, as a result, he gave the graduation speech. | a two main clauses joined by a comma |
| Correction 1 | Binh Vu was first in his class. As a result, he gave the graduation speech. | add period, capitalize first word of new sentence |
| Correction 2 | Binh Vu was first in his class; as a result, he gave the graduation speech. | add semicolon |
| Incorrect: Missing commas | People forget *for example* when the linking expression comes in the middle of the clause to use commas. | linking expressions must be "surrounded" by commas |
| Correction | People forget, *for example,* when the linking expression comes in the middle of the clause to use commas. | surround linking expressions with commas |

### Exercise D. Fill in the Blanks

Choose an appropriate connector to fill in the blanks. Make sure your connector performs the cued function.

1. [time/order] _____ I traveled to Paris to consult with an authority in European Union law, an embarrassing thing happened.

2. [cause/effect] Before meeting him to discuss estate planning, I wanted to take a quick walk around the city, _____ I put my money and passport into a "fanny pack"—a purse that fastened around my waist like a belt.

3. [contrast] I was a little hungry; _____, I wanted to see the Eiffel Tower before I stopped to get something to eat.

4. [addition] I wandered along the Champs-Élysées; _____, I did a little window shopping and went into a legal bookstore near the university.

5. [time/order] _____, I finally found the lovely little outdoor café that I knew was frequented by law students and professors.

6. [addition] I ordered coffee, _____ I watched the people walking by.

7. [time/order] _____ I went to pay the bill, I discovered that my money and passport were gone!

8. [contrast] I went to the police station, _____ they said I would have to go to the embassy about my passport.

9. [cause/effect] I had to spend three hours at the embassy explaining the situation and filling out forms; _____, I missed my appointment with the attorney I had intended to see.

10. [time/order] _____ I got back to my hotel room, what do you think I found? My money and passport—in my suitcase where they had been all the time!

## Exercise E. Error Identification and Correction

Correct the errors in the paragraphs on a separate sheet of paper. There may be punctuation problems, misused connectors, or incorrect verb forms.

1. Although, we don't always realize it, but people who commit crimes are not very smart. For example one man in California was arrested, after he tried to steal a stereo from a car. He broke into the car then he climbed into the trunk to disconnect the speakers. While he was in the trunk, the lid closed; so, he was locked in. When neighbors heard him yelling and pounding on the trunk lid, they had called the police. The police officer reported hearing the man yell, "Let me out!"

2. In another case, a man was trying to rob a bank. He asked the teller to give him all the money, when she told him that bank regulations required him to give his name and address. He wrote the information on a piece of paper. And she gave him the money. Because he gave the correct address. The police were able to arrest him an hour later. While some criminals may be the masterminds we see on television shows, in general I think crooks are pretty stupid!

# *Culture Activities*

## Language Activity 22: High-Context and Low-Context Communication

Although every culture is unique, it is convenient to place a given culture along a continuum ranging from low context to high context. A high-context culture is one in which most people share the same background, the same values, the same history. On the other hand, a low-context culture is one in which the participants don't really know or seem to share all of the same values or history that the others do.

For example, Japan is a prototypically high-context culture, while the United States is generally regarded as a low-context culture. "All" Japanese share the same history, and there might be said to be a general consensus of values and beliefs. On the other hand, in the United States there are thousands of different backgrounds and beliefs, from those of the Native Americans to those of the refugees who first arrived in the United States yesterday. Of course, these classifications are just general; there are many exceptions. There are many high-context groups within the United States such as the Amish, Hassidic Jews, and even certain corporations that have very elaborate, unwritten cultures.

Review the following chart for an overview of some of the elements of low- and high-context cultures. As you read, try to determine whether you come from a low- or high-context culture.

| Low-Context Culture | High-Context Culture |
|---|---|
| Direct communication: "Get to the point." | Indirect communication: "beat around the bush" |
| Time moves quickly and in a straight line: "Time is money." | Time moves slowly, and many things can happen at once. Emphasis is on building relationships. |
| In an initial business context, a certain level of formality is expected, such as shaking hands and using titles. However, a more casual approach is rapidly adopted. (First names used: Fred, Paul, Marina.) | More status markers (Mr., Dr., Mrs., Ms.) and used for longer periods of time. Often there are grammatical markers such as different linguistic forms of *you* for different relationships. |
| Low tolerance for silence | High tolerance for silence |
| Interactive: "Hey, John (his Supervisor). You're sure that's the right way to do this?" | Authoritarian—top-down |
| High tolerance for questions | Sense of authority threatened by questioning |
| Adversarial, blunt | Build consensus |
| Self-disclosing | Discussion of intellectual issues |
| Low value placed on "phatic" communication (small talk): "Let's get down to business." | Phatic communication important ("grooming" speech) |
| Precise and technical | Metaphors and allusions |

## Exercise A. Case Hypotheticals and Discussion

1. Use the chart to determine whether the following scenarios are typical of a low-context or a high-context culture.

   a. At a school: A teacher asks a difficult question of a student; the student doesn't answer immediately. The teacher asks, "What? Didn't you do your work last night?"

   b. Two businessmen meeting for the first time don't discuss business for the entire dinner.

   c. Subject for a TV talk show: My husband snores too loudly for me to sleep in the same room.

   d. An oral agreement and a handshake seal a three million dollar deal.

   e. In a restaurant at lunch: "Hello, June, good to see you again. This is Glenn, my supervisor."

2. In terms of high-context and low-context cultures, explain the miscommunications in the following scenarios.

   a. An American instructor is frustrated because no one asks questions in a legal methods class in Japan.

   b. A new American employee at an American corporation is sent home by his American supervisor when he shows up in tennis shoes on "Casual Friday." The supervisor explains, "I thought everybody knew that you can't wear tennis shoes on casual day."

   c. A German lawyer continues to call his American counterpart "Mr. Bodary" although "Mr. Bodary" has asked the German to call him "Mike" many times.

   d. A Japanese firm decides not to award a contract to an American firm whose attorneys made a brilliant presentation but insisted on discussing business during the evening dinner welcoming them to Japan.

   e. A law professor briefly chats with a Korean student on her way to her office and says, "See you later." Several hours later she walks out of her office and sees the student sitting in front of her office. She asks, "What are you doing here?" The student answers, "You told me to see you later."

## Language Activity 23: Silence

Many Americans are afraid of silence in a conversation. Silence makes them nervous. As a result, they jump in to fill what they consider long periods of silence in a conversation. Unfortunately, this attempt to rescue the conversation often seems rude or impatient to speakers of other languages or English speakers from other cultures.

### Exercise A. Listening

1. Listen to the dialogue, and identify what happens because of different perceptions of silence.

2. Write each the problem that was created and how it could have been solved.

3. Compare your answer with a partner. Are the answers the same? Are the solutions the same?

PART 3

# Student Resources

# Student Resources

## Text 1 (page 174)

## Information for Avalon Resorts, Inc.

Avalon has been running a live-aboard dive boat operation near the Dahlak Archipelago for several years, but clients continually ask for land-based facilities. That, combined with the pristine conditions of the reefs around the archipelago, has led them to believe that the resort will be a great success. This will be their first Red Sea land-based resort, and they are willing to take some risks and spend millions of dollars to make this a success. They view this as a long-term investment for the company and as the beginning of an eco-resort structure throughout the Middle East.

The Dahlak Archipelago is relatively safe in terms of terrorist threats, a definite plus for Avalon as its first resort in the Middle East. There is insufficient water for a 150-room hotel, which is what Avalon prefers to build, but they would like to work with the Eritrea government to build a desalination plant, funding half of the costs.

Additional concerns include (1) Eritrean tax-free status during the construction (estimated two years) and first five years of operation, (2) work and residence permits for future employees because the local population is untrained, (3) exchange controls—Avalon needs to be able to freely import and export money to Eritrea, and (4) limitation of live-aboard dive boats at the sites to maintain the pristine condition of the reefs.

**Points Added:**

1. 2 points for each year of tax-free status (14 maximum points)
2. 5 points for work and residence permits for the resort management team
3. 5 points for each year that all hotel personnel can be brought in from outside Eritrea (20 points maximum)
4. 2 points for each dive site that is exclusive to Avalon (Shumma, Madote, Urania, Nokra Channel, Dry Dock, Duur Gaam, Duur Ghela, or the Russian Cargo Ship)
5. 5 points if the Eritrean government agrees to fund half the desalination plant
6. 2 points for each year of unlimited exchange access (10 points maximum)

**Points Deducted:**

1. 5 points if Avalon must fund the entire plant
2. 10 points if Avalon must agree to build a 50-room resort
3. 5 points if Avalon must agree to build a 100-room resort
4. 1 point for each dive site that is not exclusive to Avalon
5. 2 points for each year that exchange is limited (10 points maximum)

## Text 2 (page 133)

## Partner A

1. Matti is a poor student, but his rich uncle had given him a "fish insurance" certificate slightly less than a year ago when he gave the fish to Matti that guarantees the fish will live at least 12 months if cared for as described in the booklet attached to the policy.
2. Matti had been very busy working on the project and didn't have time to remove the fish from the aquarium.
3. The carpet company will not replace the carpet if it has been ruined from use in an industrial setting.
4. The aquarium company is responsible for replacing only the aquarium if a defect in construction occurs.
5. Before he went out, Matti warned Jennifer that she shouldn't go near the aquarium because there might be a problem with it.
6. The water destroyed the videos, tape recordings, pictures, and even the spare computer disks with copies of the work.

# Text 3 (page 89)

## Part B

### SUMMONS

Civil No. _____

IN THE _____ (name of court)

_____Utah_____ (county)

STATE OF _____Utah_____

_Margaret Acorn, CEO, Wholesale Imports, Inc._

Petitioner/Plaintiff

vs.

_____

Respondent/Defendant

THE STATE OF UTAH TO THE RESPONDENT:

_____ (respondent)

You are hereby summoned and required to file an Answer to the attached Complaint

for _____ on file with the Clerk of the above enti-

tled Court at:

_Provo District Court_____

_214 North Main St._____

_____ (court address)

and to serve upon, or mail to Petitioner's/Plaintiff's attorney, at

_____Jacobs & Hall_____

_____

_____Provo, UT 84604_____ (attorney's address)

a copy of said Answer, within 20 days if you are served in the State of Utah or within

30 days if you are served outside the State of Utah, after service of this Summons upon

you. If you fail to do so, judgment by default will be taken against you for the relief demanded in said Complaint, which has been filed with the Clerk of the above entitled Court and a copy of which is hereto annexed and herewith served upon you.

READ THESE PAPERS CAREFULLY. These papers mean that you are being sued for _____ Wholesale Imports, Inc. _____ order tracking software system _____ six months _____. (brief case description).


DATED: _July 23, 2006_____

_____

Attorney for Petitioner/Plaintiff


_____ (street address)
_____ (city) _____ (state) __84601_____ (zip)

## Text 4 (page 119, 184)

What you've done should look something like this:

> In the case of *Big Town Nursing Home, Inc. v. Newman,* 461
> S.W.2d 195, the plaintiff, Newman, was constrained in a nursing
> home without a commitment order for a period of one month as
> arranged by his nephew. Newman made attempts to leave, but
> was apprehended and taped to a chair. After seven weeks in con-
> finement, he successfully escaped and sued the nursing home for
> false imprisonment and won.

## Text 5 (page 50)

One of the most important factors in determining whether a parent has been contributorily negligent in the death of a child is the child's age. [22A Am. Jur. Death §209 (1988)]

## Text 6 (page 156–158)

*Lucy v. Zehmer*

The existence of an offer depends upon the reasonable meaning to be given the offeror's acts and words. For the formation of a contract, the mental assent of the parties is not required. If the words and acts of one of the parties have but one reasonable meaning, his undisclosed intention is immaterial except when an unreasonable meaning which he attaches to his manifestations is known to the other party. Accordingly, one cannot say he was merely jesting when his conduct and words would warrant reasonable belief that a real agreement was intended.

1. Do the Zehmers have to sell their farm to the Lucy brothers?
2. Can you think of any other "evidence" that could have helped Mr. Zehmer prove that he was only jesting?

## Text 7 (page 198)

Which of the statements that follow best describes the main idea of the text from *Cardwell v. Bechtol?*

1. Ms. Cardwell was not able to give consent to the medical treatment because she was still a minor.
2. Ms. Cardwell was able to give consent to the medical treatment even though she was still a minor.
3. The jury found that no battery had occurred because Ms. Cardwell's treatment went well.
4. Informed consent was not given by Ms. Cardwell.

## Text 8 (page 133)

**Partner B**

1. The certificate from the fish store explicitly rules out death by exposure to air under any circumstances.

2. The day before, Matti had called the Aquarium Company to say that he thought there might be a small leak in the aquarium. They told him to watch carefully but that they couldn't send out a technician for two days. They also told him that for safety's sake, he should remove the fish at that time.

3. The warranty from the carpet company that the landlord has says the company will replace the carpet if it is ruined through normal household accidents, including spilled wine or ground-in dirt. Only accidents from fire or flooding are excluded.

4. The landlord had warned Matti that having such a big aquarium on the fifth floor might be dangerous.

5. Jennifer was in the bathroom washing her hands as Matti left and wasn't quite able to hear what he said exactly. She thought he said something about looking at the aquarium. She said, "Okay, fine" in response.

6. Jennifer had paid to have the videos and tape recordings done with the money she had gotten for her last birthday from her relatives. It was her gift to Matti because they are to be married in two months.

# Text 9 (page 174)

### Information for the Municipal Government of the Dahlak Archipelago

The Minister of Tourism has told the Archipelago inhabitants that economic prosperity is not far away now that the conflict with Ethiopia is at an end. However, unless he is able to attract the tourist industry to the island, he will not be able to keep his promise. The Minister is certain that he will be able to provide for work and residence permits for the resort management team; however, he expects Avalon to train local inhabitants in housekeeping and maintenance, as well as hire management trainees from inside Eritrea. Because Eritrea wants to encourage tourism, he will also be able to agree to a limited number of years of unlimited exchange access. As far as he is concerned, three years would be sufficient.

The size of the hotel concerns him. The Archipelago is small, and he would like to see exclusive resorts built there. He prefers a 50-room luxury hotel to a large 150-room hotel. He has been to Costa Brava and does not want to see his beautiful islands turned into a cheap vacation resort.

The Minister is also willing to limit the access to a few dive sites to Avalon, but not all the dive sites in the vicinity. Even though they do not get much money from the live-aboard dive boats, there is still some influx of currency from them. Considering the lack of resources on the archipelago, he cannot afford to alienate the diving community.

## Points Added:

1. 10 points if Avalon agrees to fund the entire desalination plant
2. 10 points if Avalon agrees to a 50-room hotel
3. 2 points if Avalon agrees to a 100-room hotel
4. 2 points if you agree to residence permits for management personnel only
5. 10 points if you get Avalon to agree to train Dahlak inhabitants to work in the hotel as housekeeping and maintenance staff
6. 5 points for each manager trainee from the local inhabitants Avalon agrees to hire (10 points maximum)
7. 2 points for each open dive site (Shumma, Madote, Urania, Nokra Channel, Dry Dock, Duur Gaam, Duur Ghela, or the Russian Cargo Ship)

8. 2 points per year when there are exchange controls in place (10 points maximum)

**Points Deducted:**
1. 4 points if you agree to a 150-room hotel
2. 2 points if you agree to a 100-room hotel
2. 1 point for each dive site that belongs exclusively to Avalon
4. 2 points for each year you agree to tax-free status (14 points maximum)
5. 2 points per year without exchange controls (10 points maximum)

# Index

# Table of Cases

Printed and bound by CPI Group (UK) Ltd, Croydon, CR0 4YY

09/06/2025

14685649-0001